THE RELIGIOUS URGE

THE REVERENTIAL LIFE

THE NOTEBOOKS OF PAUL BRUNTON

(VOLUME 12)

THE RELIGIOUS URGE

THE REVERENTIAL LIFE

PAUL BRUNTON

(1898–1981)

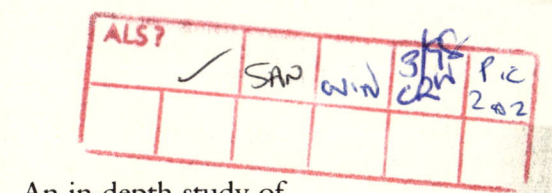
An in-depth study of
categories seventeen and eighteen
from the notebooks

Published for the
PAUL BRUNTON PHILOSOPHIC FOUNDATION
by Larson Publications

International Standard Book Number (cloth) 0-943914-36-1
International Standard Book Number (paper) 0-943914-37-X
International Standard Book Number (series, cloth) 0-943914-17-5
International Standard Book Number (series, paper) 0-943914-23-X
Library of Congress Catalog Card Number: 87-83595

Manufactured in the United States of America

Published for the
Paul Brunton Philosophic Foundation
by
Larson Publications
4936 Route 414
Burdett, New York 14818

2 4 6 8 10 9 7 5 3

The works of Paul Brunton

A Search in Secret India
The Secret Path
A Search in Secret Egypt
A Message from Arunachala
A Hermit in the Himalayas
The Quest of the Overself
The Inner Reality
(*also titled* Discover Yourself)
Indian Philosophy and Modern Culture
The Hidden Teaching Beyond Yoga
The Wisdom of the Overself
The Spiritual Crisis of Man

Published posthumously

Essays on the Quest

The Notebooks of Paul Brunton

volume 1:	Perspectives
volume 2:	The Quest
volume 3:	Practices for the Quest
	Relax and Retreat
volume 4:	Meditation
	The Body
volume 5:	Emotions and Ethics
	The Intellect
volume 6:	The Ego
	From Birth to Rebirth
volume 7:	Healing of the Self
	The Negatives
volume 8:	Reflections on My
	Life and Writings
volume 9:	Human Experience
	The Arts in Culture
volume 10:	The Orient

(continued next page)

CONTENTS

EDITORS' INTRODUCTION

This twelfth volume in *The Notebooks of Paul Brunton* emphasizes the importance of veneration for the source of Life at all levels of human development. It focuses in detail on *The Religious Urge* and *The Reverential Life*, categories seventeen and eighteen (of twenty-eight) in the personal notebooks Dr. Paul Brunton reserved for posthumous publication.

With broad tolerance and critical insight, *The Religious Urge* speaks directly to the individuating modern mentality. It welcomes the diversity in religion and acknowledges, with profound gratitude, the invaluable services of inspired spiritual teachers throughout the world's history and in the contemporary scene; but at the same time it fully sympathizes with those for whom institutional religion has become an oppressive cause of fruitless conflict. It will be useful to those struggling to re-establish reliable religious values, to those struggling for freedom from religious systems that have become stifling, to those who overvalue religion, and to those who undervalue it.

This section distinguishes the heart's ineradicable religious instinct from traditional religious forms, and clarifies the services and disservices of institutional religion. It stresses that fulfilling the religious instinct is an essential step toward the attainment of wholeness, and that this step may or may not involve the rituals and teachings of an established religious organization.

As throughout his writings, P.B. here discusses religion as the most elementary of three levels of spiritual development, succeeded in turn by the practice of mysticism and by the study and practice of mystical philosophy. A key point of this section, however, is that we should not take "most elementary" to mean "least important." Rather, we should see a complete activation and integration of the religious instinct as our *most fundamental* resource when exploring the nature of self and world. A proper integration of this instinct, in its mature form, is essential to the establishing of a correct relationship between the ego and the divine individuality.

A final introductory remark on this section concerns the fifth chapter. Readers for whom this volume is a first contact with P.B.'s writing should not be misled by the fact that most of the paras on specific religions address Christianity. While this chapter does indeed seem to be intended primarily for an audience whose religious experience has been with and through Christianity, material on a variety of other religions runs throughout *The Notebooks.* (See especially volume ten, *The Orient.*)

Part 2, *The Reverential Life,* focuses on the development of our relationship to the divine through the feeling function. It gives an individualized, practical approach to honest communion with the Sacred through intelligent prayer, rational devotion, and informed, mature humility. A wonderful resource of aspirations, devotions, and practical techniques for reducing the ego's obstructive arrogance, it is first a section to be drawn upon for inspiration and only secondarily a text to be studied.

In preparing these paras for publication, we questioned whether an intellectually contrived structure would help or interfere with material intended to evoke the feeling of reverence. At times it seemed that a thoroughly random arrangement—without a breakdown into major themes like surrender, devotion, prayer, or grace—was most desirable. But later, as the material became more familiar, the need to distinguish true reverence from false, the need to focus eventually on understanding certain practices in order to do them more effectively, became clear.

Because this section addresses primarily the feelings, however, we suggest that the reader begin by reading randomly until a para catches the attention; then pause, let the idea or suggestion sink in. Continue reading in this fashion: as moods of reverence, aspiration, humility, and reflection evoke the deeper spiritual feelings within your heart, carry those feelings into your meditation period. Done regularly and over a period of time, this kind of reading will unfold the depth and power of the insight behind these paras—will enrich not only meditations but also daily living.

The feeling function, by its own nature, learns in a cyclic rather than linear fashion. Only through creative repetition are the feelings transformed from the level of unreflective emotions to that of the subtlest sensitivity to Spirit. The way we learn to appreciate music, or a particular piece of music, illustrates this principle. For this reason, frequent small and inspiring doses of the material in this section should prove very helpful to the quester's daily practice. As the material becomes more familiar and certain questions naturally arise, or if there is a desire to concentrate on a specific practice—of prayer or devotion or humility or surrender—then the organization of the paras into specialized groups will be helpful.

One theme that emerges throughout this material is the need to understand the simultaneous presence of two points of view within each human being—the ego's and the higher self's. What role, for example, does self-effort have in evoking Grace? Can the ego really teach itself humility? Can it really surrender without the help of Grace? En route to developing a standpoint that serves both these perspectives, P.B. addresses each of these themes from a mystical viewpoint in the earlier chapters, and then from the viewpoint of philosophy in the final chapter on Grace. The double standpoint is developed further in categories nineteen and twenty and will be discussed more in the introduction to volume thirteen.

Editorial conventions with regard to quantity and structuring of material, spelling, capitalization, and other copy-editing practices for this volume are the same as have been outlined in earlier introductions. As in earlier volumes, (P) at the end of a para indicates that the para also appears in *Perspectives*, volume one of *The Notebooks* series. Once again we have many friends at Wisdom's Goldenrod and the Paul Brunton Philosophic Foundation to thank for this volume's being ready for press. We would also like to thank, on behalf of the foundation, the still growing number of readers throughout the world whose additional financial support is helping to make it possible for these books to be published at their current rate. Further information about publication schedules and related activities can be obtained from the

Paul Brunton Philosophic Foundation
P.O. Box 89
Hector, NY 14841

Part 1:
THE RELIGIOUS URGE

The essence of religion does not consist in dogma and ritual but in faith in a higher power, worship of that higher power, and moral purification to come closer to it.

One of the Commandments warns men not to take the name of God in vain. The simple and obvious and usually accepted meaning of this is not to utter the word "God" without seriousness and reverence. But the truer meaning is not to talk of religion—and especially of attending places of religious worship—while avoiding the effort involved in seeking a truly religious experience.

1

ORIGIN, PURPOSE OF RELIGIONS

Introductory

Religion should provide a passage along the journey to reality and not a prison for the aspiring soul.

2

Although religion is only the beginning of the quest—the first form which a recognition of the existence of a higher power takes—it would be an error to believe that it is only for the simpler types of person, that worship of this power, that the attitude of reverential devotion which it engenders, is not for more developed and also more educated minds. It is for all.

3

It would be a mistake to believe that because his search will lead him beyond religion, therefore religion is to be thrown aside. It would be more than a mistake: it would imperil his whole quest.

4

Men seek for God because they cannot help themselves. They endure tribulations and make sacrifices in this search because they love God. And the source of this driving urge lies in the tremendous contradiction between what they pathetically are and what they intuitively feel they ought to be.

5

The strength of religion does not come from the strength of popular ignorance or popular superstition. It comes from the innate need of every human creature to worship its source. The religious instinct cannot be killed.

6

Whether in the mosques of Islam or the tabernacles of Israel, the instinct which makes man acknowledge that there *is* some Power behind it all is an authentic instinct.

7

The external observances and visible signs of a formal religion are its least valuable features. More important is the living impulse which gave it birth. It must be sought in the heart's most delicate intuitions and the mind's deepest place, not in the symbolic theatrical shows.

8

The quality of religious veneration is needed by all, from the child in school to the philosopher in the world.

9

Just as the human embryo is nourished and kept alive in complete dependence upon the mother inside whose body it is carried, its consciousness being in dreamless slumber like a hibernating animal, so the human adult is in reality just as dependent for his own existence on the Overself. His spiritual yearnings are a kind of nostalgia for the direct, free, unimpeded-by-the-ego consciousness of that dependence, which is blessfully similar to the embryo's. The womb is a great symbol in several ways.

10

A quester necessarily becomes a pilgrim seeking his destination in a Holy City. He may be a metaphysician or mystic, a profound thinker or connoisseur of Orientalisms, but he may not leave out the simple humble reverences of religious feeling.(P)

11

A human being without the feeling of reverence for the higher power is an uncompleted being.

12

Religiosity as a quality is to be practised rather than religion as a creed, dogma, or sect.

13

It is essential that the religious man should believe in the existence of this power beyond himself, that he should seek to establish some kind of communion with it, and that he should practise virtue and abstain from injuring others.

14

The longing for a worthier kind of life, the aspiration for some sort of linkage or communion with Divine Power, is a sign of the transition from a purely animal consciousness to the animal-human phase of today. To be destitute of these urges quite entirely is uncommon. In the rotation of body-mind cycles—Shakespeare's "seven ages of man"—they appear or vanish briefly or durably in most persons. But because suppressions exist, substitutes often replace them.

15

Too many millions stop with their religion as a cult of worship, and do not go on to extend it into being a way of life also.

16

One day the modern world will wake up to the fact that the four fundamental tenets which the inspired religious prophets taught the old world are as literally true as that two times two is four. That there is an indefinable Power—God—which was never born and will never die. That evil-doing brings a punitive result. That man is called to practise regularly the moral duty of self-control and the spiritual duty of prayer or meditation. The prophets may have erred in some of their other teachings; they may have introduced personal opinion or inherited suggestion or imagined heavens: but they generally agreed on these four things. Why? Because these truths have always been present, outside human opinion, suggestion, or imagination, inherent in Life itself.

17

One who gives the first dynamic impulse to a spiritualizing movement inevitably creates a religion if the emotions of the masses are touched, a metaphysic if the intellect of the elite is touched, a mysticism if the intuition of individuals is touched.

18

We are like flowers torn from our natural soil and suffering the misery of separation. Our fervid mystical yearnings represent the recognition of our need to reunite with our Source.

19

If he were not *already* rooted in spiritual being—yes, here and now!— he would not be able to feel the longing to find that being.

20

All things and all creatures are within the World-Mind, draw their current of life and intelligence from this source. This is why, *in the end*, they come to feel nostalgic for it; this is why religions arise and mystics seek.

21

It is this absence of Spiritual consciousness from man which, when his experience of taking on body after body is sufficiently ripe, drives him to seek its presence.

22

Until the heart is deeply touched, religion remains a mere external form with little value to the individual and less to society.

23

Religion's value arises from its function of morally regulating the common people, teaching them elementary spiritual truths, and repeatedly reminding them of the higher purpose of their life on earth.

24

The first purpose of religion is an individual one. It is to inculcate belief in a higher power and an immaterial reality—God. The second purpose is a social one. It is to teach a code of morals to govern human relations.

25

We must face facts as they are, not as they are imagined to be, and the fact remains that the only kind of religion with which millions of its myriad adherents are acquainted is the kind which takes puerile rituals for communions with the Absolute, and degenerate priests for true vessels of It.

26

To know why he is here and what he has to do is the destiny of every man. Religion should keep pace with his mental growth and feed him this knowledge as his capacity for blind faith decreases. Where it does not do so, he either remains religious in name only and not in reality or turns away altogether from it to destructive atheistic and totalitarian movements.

27

The Light of the Overself impinging on the intellect from behind, or from a realized man, impels it to move upward. This creates a response that appears as a restless mental state, an obscure longing to know what is beyond itself, a blind aspiration. It does not know the real origin of this impulse.

28

In its original purity, before men got hold of it and turned it into organizations and institutions, a religion was a faith beyond such things, in spirit born of felt experience, or an experience born of faith.

29

The religious feeling itself is irradicable but it may get covered up by materialistic feelings or thickly overgrown by animalistic ones.

30

The spiritual instinct may appear to be totally dormant in a man but it is never killed. In another birth, and after other experiences, it will return.

31

What is true in the old religions that have vanished and in the existing ones that have survived can never become outdated, outworn. Even when the religion itself passes on, the truth in it stays among us, reincarnated into a new form, perhaps.

32

The need for religion is a need that most men have for holding on to something higher than themselves.

33

Why did the aspiration toward a higher kind of life appear in human beings? Why does the instinct to worship get felt? Why do men seek the truth about their inner being? Because their Source draws them secretly and presses them outwardly.

34

It is an urge which is felt more often than it is understood.

35

The urge to know our deeper being and the aspiration towards the Perfect lead to one and the same result, for God—perfect being—is within ourselves.

36

Religious fervour is needed but it ought not to lapse into religious fanaticism.

37

True religion would not suffer if a little intelligence were mixed with it.

38

Despite the imperfections and impostures which religions have sometimes practised, despite the superstitions which have been mingled sometimes with their official teachings, there still remains a large residue of basic truth.

39

Multitudes believe they can live without religion, which is possible, and without God, which is not. The very mind which makes this assertion and thinks it has turned its back on such a superstition as God is itself a projection from God.

40

All such turning to religion and mysticism is really due to a sense of nostalgia, a yearning for our true Home.

41

A religious revelation is also a carrier of good news, the gospel that there *is* a higher power, that we are all in relation with it, and that because of this relationship we can have access to truth, goodness, beauty, reality, and peace.

42

The reference of religion is to the unknown. Its means of reference is the incomprehensible.

43

We are moving towards a more reasonable presentation of religion and mysticism, not towards the extinction of both. Yet at times the latter possibility has seemed very real. There has been a passage in several lands from decaying religion to dynamic atheism. It is a change that is inevitable. Out of its present evil there will eventually come forth future good. If the guardians of religion have the foresight and courage to handle this transition by self-reform and self-purification they might avoid its horrors and evils. Alas! history does not support such a likelihood.

44

A groping for his godly source is instinctive in man, although it may take camouflaged forms such as absurd superstition or truth-seeking rationalism.

45

Religion includes all religions. It is a feeling rather than a form of ecclesiasticism.

46

We may accept the fact that great contributions to human welfare have been made by traditional religion while denying its claim to represent the highest truth.

47

The race has not evolved out of true religious ideas because it has not even practised them yet.

On evaluating religion

48

Those who try to make a religion out of ethics alone miss the point. They are well-intentioned but are mixing up two things which belong to different levels.

49

Those foolish men who would remove all ecclesiasticism and priesthood, all rite and dogma, do not understand in what danger they put mankind. For along with the abuses and impostures, the untruths and intolerances which have gathered around these things, there have also been precious moral guidance and precepts, valuable spiritual testimonies and reminders, benevolent philanthropies of a personal and corporate kind. This is the legacy handed down by every religion, every Church. Ought this too to be attacked and destroyed? Is it not better to purify the religion, to reform the Church, than totally to throw it to the dogs?

50

We can get a just view of religion only by placing its defects in parallel with its merits. To get at the truth about religion, and by "religion" is meant here not any particular one but the entire cluster of authentic sacred revelations throughout the world, it is quite insufficient to consider it only in decay and corruption. We must also consider its early purity and original concepts. It is quite unfair to examine only the superstitions that degrade it. We must also examine the truths that inspire it. A balanced view would recognize that underneath all its evils which atheists point out, religion holds much that is good and beneficent.

51

What is it that leads humans to seek satisfaction in religion or in mysticism? The materialists may tell us that biological or personal frustration drives many spinster women to do so, that decaying intellect drives many ageing men to do so, that the natural need of consolation drives many widows and widowers to do so. Marxists call the idea of God "the opium of the masses." That there is some basis of truth in all these criticisms must be admitted, but that there is an immeasurably broader basis of truth in the time-old declaration that man is really related to God and must fulfil the responsibilities of such a relation must be more emphatically affirmed.

52

After we have made our worst criticism of religion we have still to recognize the fact that a world left without any religion at all is a world left in grave peril. For the vacuum left by the disappearance of an outworn religion must be filled with something else. If it should be atheistic immorality, then the belief that evil-doing, selfish aggression, and injury to others are justifiable and unpunished will be rampant.

53

The shameful facts in the history of religious organizations should not be allowed to obscure the basic need of religion itself, nor to detract from the greatness of religious ideals.

54

It is only when religion divides people into hostile hating groups—those who belong to a particular denomination and those who do not—or when it keeps them from becoming acquainted with mystical and philosophic truths, that it becomes a failure, in the first case, and a traitor to itself, in the second one.

55

The history of religion is too often a history of bigotry and fanaticism. But it also shines with the record of divinely inspired, reverence-deserving men and women.

56

Without falling into harsh stricture or bitter criticism, without minimizing the unquestioned services of religion to humanity, it is still needful to be guarded against its disservices.

57

He may consider someone else's religious belief to be idiotic, but this does not mean that he should therefore be disrespectful to it. Men come to God eventually through curious ways and through various ways. Their starting points may be completely different, but their lines of movement will necessarily converge upon the same point.

58

For the karma yogi, all his activity takes on something of the nature of a ritual. Even where religions have become empty, hollow, and hypocritical, we need not be too eager to welcome their destruction. For even then they preserve a teaching, a message, a memory, and a tradition of a holier and better time in that religion's history.

59

The right answer to these questions can never be got so long as the origin, nature, place, and purpose of religion remain misunderstood by its leaders no less than by its adherents. It is this misunderstanding which accounts for its contemporary failures and historic deficiencies. The proponents of religion exaggerate its consolations and services, while the opponents exaggerate its persecutions and crimes. In the upper ground above both, we may hope to discover a truer view, for every institution can be properly appraised only by justly noting *both* its merits and demerits. We may meditate on these questions and unfold a profounder analysis not only if we collect and collate the primitive cultures in a spirit of critical pitying superiority, but also if we listen in tentative, intellectual sympathy to what these cultures have to tell us about themselves. Then only may we learn that modern critics who concentrate only on the fabular side of religion are ill-balanced judges: its significance will be found to be much larger than that.

60

It is ironical indeed that although so much of religion is mere superstitious nonsense, the portion that remains is tremendously worthwhile to humanity.

61

It is needful to weigh the services of religion against its disservices. Nor will it be useful to over-emphasize what it once was historically, whether good or evil. We must consider what it is now, in our own time.

62

The absence of such virtues as kindliness, justice, and sincerity in human relations is testimony to the absence of true religion.

63

The ecclesiastical structure and sacerdotal services of a church are useful to those who believe in them. Those who lack this faith should be tolerant, and not seek to destroy things which still help others. They have their place. The error starts when they are given the *only* place, or when the emphasis is so heavy upon the *outer* forms that the greater need of correcting and shaping the character is missed.

64

Perhaps Emerson was premature when he wrote, "The day of formal religion is past."

Prophets and Messengers

65

While the force of inward attraction and the working of evolution through outward experience are the best guarantees of the triumph of ideals, man is not left to these vast impersonal processes alone, without visible help and visible guidance. Prophets, teachers, sages, and saints appear at his side from time to time, like beacons in the darkness.

66

It was not fear of human ghosts which gave birth to early religions, as so many anthropologists believe, but faith in the Holy Ghost. It was not negative emotion that first gave moral guidance and spiritual hope and cosmic meaning to our race, but positive revelation.

67

Buried underneath the contemporary form of every religion there exists the original and authentic gospel, that which was transmitted by its Seer to his living followers, but which is too subtle or too spiritual for his present-day ones. The truths of religion and the intuitions of mysticism have nothing at all to fear from reason, but the superstitions of religion and the simulations of mysticism may well shrink from the cold contact.

68

The religious teachers of mankind are forced to make concessions to the mental aridity and the emotional coarseness of their followers. They have secrets which they are unable to share with those who lack the power to comprehend such secrets. They have touched levels of consciousness unknown to, and unknowable by, the earthly, the gross, and the complacently self-centered.

69

If a man asks himself the question, "How did I first come to think of the soul?" he will probably have to answer, "Its existence was suggested to me by others." From where did they in their turn get the idea? At some point in the line it must have originally come from a prophet, seer, or mystic.

70

Religion has taken sublime forms but it has also taken grotesque ones. The first happens when men let themselves be led aright by inspired far-seeing prophets; the other happens when they let themselves be misled by blind ones.

71

It is the great individual, and not the great institutions which come after him, who most advances mankind's spiritual progress. .

72

Countless men—both laymen and clergymen—have sought to deceive God at some time by their hypocrisy, but God has never yet deceived a single man. The promises given through every inspired prophet have always been fulfilled. If any think otherwise, it is because the prophet's own mind transmitted the message faultily, or because those who sought fulfilment failed themselves to live and think according to that pattern of a higher life which was a prerequisite condition to it.

73

Mystical experience will not be nullified and philosophical truth will not be falsified even if it could be conclusively proved that men like Jesus and Krishna were mythological constructions of the human mind and never had any historical existence. Nevertheless, we insist that they did once live in a fleshly garb, whatever fancies and fairy tales may have been embroidered around their stories by unphilosophical devotees or priestly cunning in later times. Scientific criticism may easily dispose of these fancies and tales, but it cannot so easily dispose of the fact that only a Jesus-like mind or a Krishna-like character could have invented their existence and forged their teachings—which amounts to much the same as the actual existence of Jesus or Krishna themselves. Their wisdom comes from a source that transcends the common reach.

74

If Jesus and Gautama never existed, some other men with the same deep insights must have existed to have voiced such thoughts and conveyed such inspirations. If the traditions concerning them are scanty, uncertain, and mixed with fable, this need not diminish the belief in their actual existence on the part of any just-minded person. And whatever he may think of the Churches which claim to represent them, of their contradictory teachings and all-too-human history, he ought to give his unhesitating admiration and reverence to this pair of Lights, who themselves gave three-quarters of the human race such sorely needed ideals.

75

The Incarnation-myth, which rests on the possibility of a being who is half-God and half-man, covers a partial truth. The real nature of such a being differs from the ordinary in this, that although still human, he has incarnated on this earth from a higher sphere or a more advanced planet. And he has made this great sacrifice—nearly as great indeed as a human entity's voluntary and altruistic incarnation among a group of gorillas would be—to guide, uplift, and spiritualize his less-grown fellows at a grave crisis of their existence.

76

The philosophical teaching is that the return of every prophet is an inward event and not a physical one. The common people, with their more materialist and less subtle apprehension, expect to see his body again. The initiates expect only to find his mental presence in themselves.(P)

77

If Jesus could have met Buddha, the differences in their teaching would not have prevented their delighted recognition of one another for what each was.

78

Jesus called men to life more abundant, Buddha called them to cessation of desire, Krishna to a training of the thoughts and feelings, Confucius to proper courteous and moral behaviour, while Lao Tzu gently reminded them of their higher allegiance.

79

It is quite proper to give homage and show esteem to a great soul. But it is quite another thing to deify him, to worship him, to forget utterly that he is still a human being, with human fallibility and imperfection.

80

The prophets of God are the servants of God. To deify them is to destroy this truth about their relationship. Such a false attitude must lead to false situations, priestly innovations, sectarianism and intolerance.

81

A prophet is primarily one who brings a *revelation* to mankind, who gives out what has been given to him from on high, not reasoned out by him from available facts.

82

By measuring the degree of enlightenment attained by a prophet we are able to measure the extent of reliance to be placed upon his revelation.

83

Whatever there is of abiding truth in these revelations comes from the prophet's Overself, the rest from the man's own opinion.

84

If the inspiration is received from a superhuman source, its expression goes out as a human activity. This puts all statements about God within the limitations and under the colouring of human beings: that is to say, all religions are imperfect, may at some points be at fault, or even in error. The truly educated man can only accept them as such, if he is to continue as a religious person also. Otherwise he must keep to himself and silently adore the godlike in his own heart.

85

There is room for both—a divine revelation from a personal God and a teaching from an inspired man.

86

Most professors cannot light the mystical fire, but a prophet may. For where they are served only by intellect, he is served by intuition.

87

Only after severe investigation or after severe calamity do men awaken to the dismal fact that their spiritual guides are unreliable, their religious beliefs invalid, their clichés of prayer naïve and useless. Whichever way leads them to be confronted by these unpleasant realities, they cannot go on living in doubt and discouragement for the rest of their years. So they either cast the subject of religion out of their minds altogether or, in the efflux of time, search for a more reliable guide, a better set of beliefs, and a more effective form of worship. But because the ignorant masses are incapable of finding this for themselves, someone must arise as a prophet to guide, teach and help them. He may be quite minor and quite local but if he shows them the next step ahead, he is to that extent a messenger of God.

88

Because in the past it was invariably men who appeared as prophets or founded religions while women became their followers, since the nineteenth century we have witnessed the beginnings of a reversal of this situation. That became evident when a number of minor sects arose in England, all started by women, and when Mrs. Eddy, in America, founded Christian Science, a religion to which many men have attached themselves.

89

Christ and Krishna were actualities in their lifetimes and became felt Presences after their deaths. But with time they were only symbols to remember for most people. Today they can still be found by penetrating heart and mind deeply enough. Its reality is then drawn from their own Overself.

90

When the *Koran* was imparted to Muhammed and the *Upanishads* to the

Rishees of those early times, something more than a momentary glimpse was experienced by the recipients. They were destined to play a historic role in the spiritual education of sections of mankind.

91

All religions are the outgrowth of various men's different statements about their glimpse, discovery, realization, or messenger-ship.

92

Buddha swore an oath under the sacred banyan tree, where he came to know himself, that he would not pass from our sphere of evolution until he had been reborn again and again, to help laggard humanity reach what he himself had reached. So Jesus keeps ever in inner contact with those who need him—and that means millions. He is not dead, cannot die. And the love which brought him here from afar keeps him here.

93

There are two kinds of religious founders—the Prophets and the Messengers. Jesus was a Prophet but Muhammed was a Messenger.

94

He who descends into the crowd to serve some amongst it, and to help many more to come in the generations after it, may know in advance that the crowd will persecute or kill him and yet not falter from making his appearance. If he thought only of his body and not of his purpose, or even more of the one than the other, he would surely desist from such a dangerous mission.

95

If he strives to make the public movement his own in the sense that a man strives to make his own career, he is working for the ego rather than mankind, he is serving professional ambition rather than spiritual aspiration.

96

Jesus and Gautama did not speak to mankind from different levels of being. They spoke from different levels of intellect. Their realization of the truth was one and the same. For there is only one truth. But they could only communicate it to others according to the intellectual equipment, degree, and background of its receivers.

97

Men and women were being enlightened before Gautama arose and after Jesus went. And they are being enlightened today as they will still be in ages yet unborn. Inspired teachers may come and go but the Soul in every man is eternal.

98

The mesmerized members of long-established Churches do not know, cannot comprehend, and will not be persuaded that a man can write revelation even in our own times, that the history of human inspiration has not come to an end. It is true to say that men who could report to us some news of celestial import were always rare and that they are just as rare, even rarer, today. But it is not true to assert that they became long ago extinct. If that were so, if life today, this very moment, did not still hold its possibility of delivering its divine message to some listening mind, then it would be worthless and meaningless. God would be absent from this world, the soul eviscerated from man's Being.

99

That one man could pay by his own suffering for the wrong-doing of all men is not only illogical and unfair but also impossible. It would be a claim that guilt is transferable. Such a transfer is morally wrong and karmically impossible. This is the answer to those in the West who put forward the tenet of the vicarious suffering of Jesus as the price of God's forgiveness of man, as well as to those in India who assert that substitutionary suffering of Ramana Maharshi and Ramakrishna is the result of lifting the burden of karma off their disciples' shoulders.

100

When established religions no longer reflect the pure light which their prophet originally received and radiated to his followers, and reflect only its discolourations by men's own mental creations, then the operation of the cyclic law of evolution begins to bring new prophets into incarnation. They will either purify the old corrupted religions or else establish new ones.

101

There is a wide difference in the styles of two men who meant so much to aspirants. Consider the style of Jesus' sayings and contrast it with Gautama's. The first moves directly to the idea in a pithy, if poetic, announcement, and then leaves it almost immediately. The second seeks to persuade, circles round and round it, and leaves only after its meaning is abundantly clear, only after its logic is sufficiently acceptable. That each man puts a value upon style cannot be gainsaid.

102

Had any sage who later became known as the begetter of a great religion been born in another land at another time, we may be sure that his doctrine would have been different, that both the extent and content of his teaching would have been adjusted to the altered circumstances. For he would not have revealed too much, and thus sailed over people's heads, nor spoken metaphysically where they could comprehend only physically at the most.

103

The sage who ventures forth into public with a message to deliver or a work to perform must shape both message and work to suit the circumstances that surround him.

104

Unless the message is couched in terms with which his contemporaries are familiar they cannot understand it. The prophet who is wise will adjust himself to this fact.

105

Fifteenth-century Kabir, who as a young disciple sometimes taught his own guru, said: "The saints and prophets are all dead. Only the Everliving God lives forever"—which is a hint on what to worship.

106

Why was mention of Jesus' name omitted by all contemporary historians, which could not have been the case if he had secured a really wide following? Why did the Buddha, when speaking of the Messianic teacher Metteya who would come in the far-off future, say: "He shall gather round him a following of brethren that numbers many thousands, just as I have gathered round me a following of brethren that numbers many hundreds"? How relatively disproportionate were such hundreds when compared with the millions of his contemporaries!

107

Who that reads these divine proclamations of a Jesus, these inexorably logical analyses of a Gautama, can fail to recognize that he is in the presence of uncompromising sincerity and unbending truth?

108

Old or new religions which have been established and organized soon lose much of their moral force, to the extent that their teachings become stale through excessive repetition and their tenets become meaningless through constant familiarity. This is why they must produce inspired preachers among themselves or, failing to do so, give way to inspired prophets who can restate the Message in fresh terms.

109

No one has been in the past the only recipient of divine illumination, and no one is so today.

110

Buddha knew, Jesus knew, that what was true for himself was true for all other men.

111

Revelation must precede redemption.

112

It is to be expected that primitive people in most parts of the world are more easily impressed by rituals and ceremonials than educated intellectuals are. They will more readily follow a religious preacher if he shows miracles. Whatever he then tells or teaches them receives assent and evokes faith more quickly. Even the masses of the modern industrialized world, fractionally educated as they mostly are, will to a lesser extent show the same psychological reaction. Even if he only promises a miracle but never shows one, a following will still gather around him and linger on for years, sometimes even imagining that something magical has happened: it will not be long before their invention will pass into history for the benefit of later generations! Philosophers, not desiring to impress anyone nor to acquire a following, do not generally attempt to produce a miracle, even if they might have developed some unusual powers.

113

Not a single word was ever written by Jesus. And yet others collected his spoken words and wrote them down for us. The same is true of Gautama the Buddha.

114

He "inquired of the Lord and was given the answer that any man who forbids the use of meat is not ordained of the Lord." This happened when he, the founder of a religion, was asked by a follower to adopt vegetarianism. So is human opinion delivered as God's command and human activity taken for divine working.

115

A contemporary prophet, Antonio di Nunzio, wrote: "We are only advocates of our Father, God."

116

Is it not worth noting that among those who left their spiritual mark on mankind it is the young rebels who are foremost? Both Buddha and Jesus broke with their traditions.

117

He feels sincerely that he has been entrusted with a revelation, that he has a message to deliver which is valuable and important to thousands of people, and that the task of delivering it is an exalted service, a holy privilege that needs no other reward than the moral satisfaction it brings him. Nor will it make any difference if there be only one man to listen to him during his own lifetime. The need to bear witness has become a matter of inexorable conscience. The result of bearing witness, whether it be worldly honour or worldly persecution, is a matter to which his ego has become emotionally indifferent.

118

Jesus and Buddha tried to purify great religions from the selfishness and sinfulness and commercialism which had destroyed so much of their value to humanity.

119

The message which a prophet gives to his own generation will usually hold elements of value to those of all other generations.

120

Wisdom did not stop appearing among men with any particular century for the simple reason that men did not stop appearing. Nor was it confined to any particular land. Despite that, it is correct to say there were certain great periods when it flourished most and widest. These can be found across the world and across time.

121

It might be too much to ask for an angelic or other transcendental contact, but something visible in space and present in time, some human being who is aware of his link with divinity, would—if he were to make himself known, or to be discovered—be one of the rarest of persons.

122

We do right to turn worthy traits of the character or mystical grades of the achievement of such a man into an ideal to follow. But we do wrong to turn his whole personality into an idol to worship.

123

To mistake the bearer of God's message for God is to fall into idolatry.

124

Such a man, although not a God, is still superior to all other men. For he was born to serve the highest purpose and fulfil the divinest mission.

125

It would be a mistake in philosophy or mysticism to glorify men instead of truths, but it would not be so in religion.

Purpose of popular (mass) religion

126

Those whose feeling is moved and whose mind is impressed by the beauty, antiquity, mystery, and dignity of religious ceremonial must find here their proper path.

127

Religion is the earliest, the easiest, the least-demanding response of the masses to the inner call.

128

Where there is no particular yearning for truth, no particular willingness to work on oneself, to practise discipline, and especially to learn to stand aside from the ego—which refers to the multitude of people—religion provides ideas and goals that can more easily be accepted and followed.

129

All popular religions are intended to help the larger number of people who are not ready for the deeper truth of mysticism, let alone the still deeper truths of Philosophy.

130

Those who do violence to their reason by finally accepting the dogmas of a religious authority because they have become intellectually tired, unable to arrive at firm conclusions, do so because they feel the need of some Power to lean against, to depend on, to check the activity of their own brain. This authority provides what they need, if only because it claims to represent the Higher Power.

131

Religions offer a medium for reaching the masses, who might otherwise be left by the wayside—untutored in higher values, unaware of the idea of God, the very basis of their being, unable to draw on it as the associated source of peace, comfort, healing, and hope.

132

The millions who are wrapped up from the first moment of awakening until sleepfall in their small affairs, who do not know any kind of life other than the personal ego's, need help as well as the questers. It is religion's business to give this help.

133

Most people, and certainly most uneducated people, have not developed the capacity for metaphysical thought or psychic exploration. They cannot mentally deal with invisible realities. They need the simplicities and personalizations of religion, its forms which can be seen or touched or pictured rather than abstract principles, its music which can be heard, and its rites which can be shared. They are necessarily concerned with the little matters of domestic and working life, not with the larger issues requiring leisure, interest, patience, and aspiration beyond the personal self.

134

Philosophy agrees that the bulk of mankind must be furnished with a religion and that religious doctrine must be simplified for their benefit into a few comprehensible dogmas. It is consequently a necessity for human nature at its present evolutionary stage that organized religions should take on a dogmatic character and a creedal form.

135

Whereas philosophy can be brought only to the few qualified to receive it, religion can be brought to a whole people—nay, to the whole of mankind.

136

Sacrament and symbol, rite and image belong to forms of worship intended chiefly for the populace, being outward and touchable.

137

Sorrow-laden men and disappointed women are as much entitled to the services of philosophy as those who are happier and more successful. But religion is more suited to afford them emotional solace, just as they are more likely to seek it in religion.

138

They are too much absorbed by the toil for existence and by the few pleasures that enable them to relax from this toil, to trouble themselves about the higher meaning of that existence. Nor do they possess the means—intuitional or intellectual—of solving the problems connected with the search for such a meaning.

139

Those who can give complete faith to childish dogmas, who can thrust all reason aside and throw themselves blindfolded into the arms of the religious organization sponsoring such dogmas, may certainly find a full peace of mind by doing so. They are persons who have either too little intellect or too much.

140

The masses would not listen to the truth because they could not comprehend the truth. It is practical wisdom to let them keep their myth.

141

The subtle metaphysical truths may be unintelligible to untutored minds whereas the simple religious ones may gain quick belief.

142

It is inevitable too that the poorer and unsuccessful classes should need and seek the consolations of religion much more than the wealthy or successful ones. Despite all the truth and nonsense talked about this matter, it is a fact that the latter are more contented than the former. Their spiritual yearnings are less urgent and less strong, whereas the others have to find internal or over-worldly compensations for their external and this-worldly frustrations.

143

The general mass of people cannot help but stop short of the more developed forms which spiritual seeking takes. Their inward receptivity and outward circumstances usually fix limits for them. Orthodox religion operates within these limits.

144

It is better that people should take a few steps along the Quest than none at all, better that they should rise to their higher manhood than remain in its animal phase only. Therefore mass religion—popular religion—was first created. It was better to have churches and priests so as to remind the people periodically of their religion than none at all; it was better that some priests should be allowed to marry, and others should undertake not to marry, so that both kinds could be helped. All these stages are merely provisional, for the time being, and as the lay folk and the priests progress, they can undertake further commitments.

145

Most of the religious lawgivers—but not all—were also social hygienists, like Moses and Manu. For the multitude, born to be followers, such instruction by advanced individuals was necessary.

146

The poor, having little, come to religion for relief from their burdensome lives; the rich, having satiated themselves, come to it out of curiosity about its mystery.

147

Religion must be simple in form and doctrine because it has to appeal to the unthinking masses. Alone, it is not enough to guarantee the advancement of man. It needs psychology also.

148

If men feel the need of formal religion let them have it. Let them have their churches and temples, attend their masses or mutter their creeds. But let them also be told of what is beyond these things.

149

The popular religion is usually an adjustment to the popular mentality. It is not for searchers after absolute truth. The planet is not peopled by the few searchers but by the multitude.

150

The religious viewpoint is excellent for those who cannot rise to a higher one. Like love and art it provides them with one of their supreme emotional experiences. It brings them a faith in God, hope for and love among themselves. The moral restraints which religion provides for the masses are its practical contribution to social and individual welfare, while its provision of ethical standards to limit the baser actions of men would alone justify its existence. So far as any religion succeeds in imposing moral restraint upon millions of ignorant and simple people and prevents wholesale crime among them, it succeeds in justifying its existence. But of course that is not the primary purpose of religion. It is only one-third part of that primary purpose. Therefore, we may accept the fact that great contributions to human welfare have been made by traditional religion while denying its claims to act as sole intermediary with God, as well as its exaggerated promises and apparently profound assertions which turn out to be the wildest guesses. Asseveration is hardly a suitable substitute for proof.

151

The assertion that religion has failed was often heard in World War I and sometimes heard in World War II. But the fact is that real religion has never failed and never could fail. What have failed are the false ideas and foolish dogmas, the caricatures of God that have got mixed up with what is true in religion. And not less than these, the ecclesiastical hierarchies themselves have failed, sacrificing the proper mission of religion for the selfish preservation of their institution, privilege, power, and income.

152

Until about the turn of the previous century, the truth about religion was never published frankly and plainly. This was because those who wrote about it were either one-sidedly biased in its favour and so refused to see the undesirable aspects, or else they were hostile in their personal standpoint which stopped them from mentioning the deeper merits. Those who really knew what religion was in theory and practice, what were its goods and bads, kept silent. This was because they did not wish to disturb the established faith of the simple masses or else because the latter, being uneducated, were unprepared to receive subtleties which required sufficient mental development to comprehend.(P)

153

Is it strange or is it reasonable that among every people on this planet the idea of this higher power has existed in every epoch? Whence did this idea come? To answer that priests implanted it in simple mentalities for their own selfish benefit does not answer the question but only puts it farther back. Who implanted it into the minds of the priests? No—it is one of those concepts which are absolutely necessary to human existence, whether it takes the most superstitious form or the most developed one. Its absences have always been temporary because their causes can only be temporary.

154

Judge the degree of a faith by its power to make men sacrifice their attachments, whether to things or habits—which is the same as its power to make them sacrifice themselves.

155

Behind the cruellest persecutions of misguided religious organizations and the worst impostures of faithless ones, there hides that which transcends all rituals, dogmas, priests, morality, persecution, and impostures. There is something higher than man in this cosmos. Religion is historically the most widespread way in which he marks his relation to this higher Power.

156

Whether it be a religion of impressive ceremonial and organized priesthood, or one of utter simplicity and without intermediaries, it will serve men only to the extent that it helps each individual follower to come closer to the Overself.

157

The following of moral principles is evidence of having reached a higher evolutionary stage than that of worshipping human leaders. Yet neither faith alone nor morality alone can constitute a religion. It is not enough to believe sincerely in the existence of a higher power. It is not enough to practise righteousness. The two must combine and co-operate if man is to live what may truly be called a religious life. For he is here both to exalt his consciousness above material things and to abase the selfishness of his conduct. A religion which does not inspire him to follow this twofold aim is only a half-religion. This is why a merely ethical humanitarianism can never by itself take the place of any divinely inspired religion.

158

Sceptics, whose spiritual intuition lies dormant, whose religious veneration remains inactivated, are sometimes willing to concede that religious ethics may keep mankind's wickedness within certain bounds, preventing it from being worse than it is, and may be useful for social purposes by providing charities, medical service, educational help. In short, they make religion's purpose more concerned with the community than with the individual. But this is quite imperceptive. It misses the central message of every scripture, that man must establish some sort of a connection with his Maker, be it the blindest faith or the most mystical communion. His is the responsibility to do so; it is a personal matter: for even if he attends church, participates in sacraments, listens to sermons, or accepts an imposed dogma, he has unwittingly given his own sanction to the transaction, pronounced his own judgement upon it. The accepted morality or service merely follows from this.

159

Some kind of worthy religious belief is indispensable to the true well-being of a nation. Without it existence is still possible, but it will be an existence morally flawed to an extent that will in the end, through vice, crime, and selfishness, endanger the nation.

160

The rigours of ego-crushing must be mitigated, the truths of mentalism must be diluted, if the multitude is to be reached. This is why popular religions are born.

161

The multitude need to be consoled and comforted: they need celestial messages of hope, the promise of help. The bare truth is too harsh on the ego, too impersonal to be welcome.

162

In days of anguish men turn to something, someone, some belief, or some idea to help endure them.

163

In the moment of his greatest trial, in the hour of his greatest danger, man looks to the Infinite for his last resource as a babe looks to its mother.

164

We have only to read recent or distant history to see how foolish it would be to expect the average person to accept the ethical ideals of philosophy, let alone live up to them. This is why some sort of accommodation must be made towards his moral limitations by giving him a code which he can accept and to some extent try to live up to. Here is the usefulness of popular religions which do contain such codes.

165

If everything was not told to the masses, it was largely because everything would not be acceptable to the masses, or "the simple ones," as Origen, a Church Father himself, called them. Or it was too metaphysical for them, as the history of Alexandria, with its violent riots against the schools of Philosophy, showed. Origen staunchly included reincarnation and meatless diet in his teachings there, but how far has either of these two been taken hold of by the masses then or since?

166

For most people the history of our time has put a strain upon belief— not the belief that a higher power exists, but that it protects man against his own viciousness. It helps a little at weakening moments to turn to the seers, prophets, and illumined poets to regain some strength.

167

There are many people to whom the ceremonies, the Masses, and the symbols of their religion mean life itself. By these things they are sustained to bear the troubles of human existence or are inspired to rise above them.

168

Religious beliefs, metaphysical conclusions, and mystical experiences are good and necessary in themselves; but they are more valuable still as vehicles to instigate, in those who accept them, the practice of noble virtues.

169

The sincere acceptance of any religious or mystical belief is really one response to the human need of security. Such belief offers inner security, however vaguely, as a bank balance offers outer security, for it puts the believer into favourable relation with the all-pervading mind and force behind the Universe's life and consequently behind his personal life too.

170

The first social utility of religion is to curb the passions and instincts, the hatreds and greeds of the multitude.

171

Even the worship of an imagined God is not all waste of energy. The good in it develops the worshipper himself even when no useful result is directly developed in his life outside.

172

It is not a Church's business to meddle in politics. That is the business of other kinds of organizations which desire to make social reforms or economic changes or administrative betterments. A Church has to try to change men because that is where the roots of such troubles lie.

173

If no truth at all is given the masses, they are left defenseless as soon as any great calamity falls upon them and they dare not think about it.

174

Those malefactors who cannot be deterred from evil-doing by awe of the law and its penalties might yet be put in awe of the invisible powers and their post-mortem penalties. This was in the mind of those who in classical Greek and Roman times formulated worship of the gods. This was their pragmatic and practical conclusion whether they themselves personally believed or disbelieved in the gods' existence at all. Their inheritors among statesmen, priests, and leaders supported popular religion as good for the masses, even when their own education made them sceptical of it.

175

Such people could not be at home in philosophy and would soon find that it is not what they want at all. It is better that they should not experience the discomfort of trying to be. The consolations of religion will help them more.

176

Religion carries with it certain commandments and injunctions of a moral nature. Whoever accepts a particular religion theoretically accepts these obligations with it.

177

The moral restraints which religion imposes upon its believers are a social necessity. Religion cannot be injured without injuring those restraints. But when it is no longer able to impose them, it loses much of its social value.

178

After many years of propaganda work in Europe, Miss Lounsberry, Secretary of the "Friends of Buddhism Society" of Paris, had ruefully to confess (in the *Maha Bodhi* Journal in the middle of World War II): "How can we help now, how can we bring the truth forcibly to bear on men's minds? Surely not by just saying there is no God and no Soul? For God in the West means many things, among others an inherent justice, which is to us Buddhists—Karma." This confession based on experience justifies our own attitude that religion is needed in the sense that belief in a higher Being is needed.

179

Much as we may deplore the weaknesses and failures of religion, we have to admit that without it men abolish all ethical standards and begin to act like wild beasts.

180

Without the religious faith in a higher power, without the religious organizations, buildings, and bibles which keep up and channel this faith, the mass of people might have fallen into a dense materialism devoid of any moral content.

181

Let us be perfectly clear on the matter when its critics say that Christianity (or, equally, Buddhism or Hinduism) has failed. This noble teaching has never failed anyone who has tried to live up to it, but the organizations and institutions which have taken advantage of its name too often, only to betray it, have failed.

On diversity in religion

182

Truth needs to be expressed again and again, each time differently, because it must be expressed each time in the idiom of its period.

183

In its present half-developed state, human nature would soon turn universal religion into an instrument of tyrannous repression of all ideas not held by it and into an agency for totalitarian persecution of all exponents of such ideas. The healthy, free competition of sects and creeds tends to prevent this and to compel tolerance.

184

There is a teaching to meet the need of each type of mind. Because there is such a variety of types in the world, there is room for a variety of teachings. But this said, and in practising our tolerance, we need not blind ourselves to the fact that just as there is a progression of levels of quality among these minds, so there is among the teachings.

185

The differences between men will not vanish, although they may alter as time slowly alters the men themselves. Not only are no two individuals alike but they will never become alike. What is true of their bodies is also true of their minds. All attempts to bring about a uniformity of ideas, a sameness in thinking, in character, and in behaviour, are doomed to fail in the end. Such oneness, whether coerced or suggestioned, would be artificial and unnatural, boring and undesirable.

186

The unequal development of human minds and the wide variation in human temperaments render it as undesirable as it is impossible to impose a single universal religion upon all mankind to the exclusion of all others or to unify all these varieties of belief.

187

A contemporary Indian master, Sitaramdas Omkarnath, was invited to become one of the leaders in a movement organized to unify different religions and establish co-operation among them. In his reply he wrote: "I cannot even believe that a co-ordination of the sects may ever be practicable. The sacred texts differ and the views of their writers clash. They all contributed to the good of the world, but each in his own way. I do not understand how these vast and numerous differences may be reconciled. . . . My rules come from God. Will it be possible for me to conform to rules framed by you and your associates in the proposal for unification? This is of secondary value. What is wanted is direct vision of God."

188

There is no single approach which is the only true one, the only true religion. God is waiting at the end of all roads. But some suit us better than others.

189

Each man is strongly influenced by his inborn tendencies and past experiences, including pre-reincarnational ones, to remain in, or attach himself to, some particular form of spiritual approach. It will be one most suited to his moral, intellectual, and intuitive levels *at the time.*

190

So long as there is variety among human minds and feelings, so long will there be variety among human views. Groups, parties, sects, factions, and schisms will continue to appear in religion as in politics. Given enough time this is unavoidable but not reprehensible. If in one sense it hinders a beginner's search for truth and ideals, in another sense it helps by offering more choices.

191

There are no lost souls, no individuals doomed to everlasting perdition. Nor are there saved souls, a favoured group of God's elect. There are only ignorant or well-informed individuals, immature or mature beings, unevolved or evolved persons.

192

Salvation is for all, the atheist and the devotee, the wicked and good, the ignorant and learned, the indifferent and earnest. It is only the time of its realization that is far off or near at hand but realization itself is certain. "Let no one of Thy boundless Grace despair"—thus Abu Said, an eleventh-century Persian mystic of high degree, holds out the prayerful hope to all men of their impending or eventual liberation. The New Testament parallels the *Bhagavad Gita's* promise of ultimate salvation for all, sinners and good alike. It says: "God willeth that all men should be saved and come to the knowledge of the truth."—1 Tim. 2:4.

193

A religion which would gather into itself the common truths of all existing religions would be an artificial one. It might satisfy the academic intellects. It could not satisfy the intuitive hearts. Religion is real only when it is the spontaneous flowering of one man's communion with the Divine. All attempts to invent a synthetic universal religion based on doctrines common to the existing principal ones are merely academic and bound to end in sterile futility, if not failure. For every religion worth the name must issue forth from one man, one inspired prophet, who gives it life, spirit, reality.

194

We do not say that one faith is as good as another. We acknowledge that divisions in doctrine are significant of grades in development.

195

That form of religion which will suit one temperament will not neces-sarily suit another. What would benefit one man might not benefit an-other. There is no universal religion which could profitably be adopted by everyone. The belief that a single religious form will suit all the different peoples throughout the world is naïve and just the kind of mechanical doctrine likely to spring up in the minds of materialistic believers. Each type will have to find the form suited to its own special temperament and special mentality. Each will and ought to continue following the different spiritual path dictated by its particular evolutionary grade. All this said, there exist certain fundamental principles which are common to all the varying forms of religion. There still remains a certain minimum founda-tion upon which all these different forms rest because they have to fit both human needs and divine revelations.

196

Several years ago my much esteemed friend, Sir Francis Younghusband, asked me to join the Council of the World Congress of Faiths. I reluctantly refused to do so, because although I sympathized greatly with his noble motives in forming the Congress I could not help regarding such well-intentioned efforts as being unlikely to lead to any practical result. Toler-ance between the members of different faiths is something greatly needed in the world today as much as it ever has been. However, I believe it is a purely personal matter which can only come with the development of individual character and not by any organized efforts as such. I am disin-clined to give active support to the World Congress of Faiths and the Fellowship of Faiths partly because it will never be more than a drop in the ocean, so far as effectiveness is concerned, and partly because the old religions have had their chance and decayed. A mere mixture of such decaying religions will not renew their vitality or render them more ser-viceable to mankind. It is wiser for me to devote energies to a *new* faith, which will have the vigour of youthfulness and *do* something, than to support a stew of stale faiths.

197

Not only are there intellectual differences between people; there are also emotional and even aesthetic differences. Most are natural, some are devel-oped. The preferences for bare cold services in one group are caused by personality traits as much as the preferences for ritualistic incense-filled services in another group. Why not accept their existence as we accept other divergences, other variations in nature or life? Why use them as reasons for contention and competition instead of friendship and co-oper-ation?

198

Wherever we look in the four kingdoms of Nature, we find that she is perpetually striving to achieve diversity. She rejects and abhors a monotonous uniformity. And if we restrict our gaze to the human kingdom, we find that the differences in thought and the divergencies in feeling are the expressions not only of variations in evolutionary growth, but also of this innate striving of Nature herself.

We live in a world where every entity is formed as an individual one. Each is unique. If people have different ideas about the same thing, this is the inevitable result of the differences in their own capacities and perceptions. Why, then, should they not be themselves and therefore different?

It is useless to regret the unavoidable, to pine for the unattainable, and to strive for the undesirable. We should not waste time seeking for unity of thought or creating unity of outlook. These aims are unfeasible; these endeavours are impracticable. Even amongst the very proponents of unity, unity—whether of association or doctrine—has been non-existent. During the course of their short history, they have periodically separated themselves into factions under rival leaders. The ladder of incarnated life stretches all the way through progressively different levels of intelligence and character. It is to be expected, therefore, that there should be inequality, disagreement, and disunity. Men can arrive at the same views when they arrive at the same standpoint, when they all attain an identical level. But this is prevented from happening by the ever-active operations of re-embodiment which, by the special influences brought to bear upon particular groups and by evolution, which admits new entrants to the human kingdom and lets out old inhabitants, differentiate their various evolutionary stages, environments and conditions. A monotonous uniformity of thought and solidarity of aspiration—could they ever be obtained—would be signs of totalitarian compulsion, intellectual paralysis, or moral inactivity. They would not be a social advance, but a social calamity. What is the use of pursuing such an artificial ideal?

It is impossible for all the men and women in the world to think and feel alike. What is repugnantly intricate to one is fascinating and intriguing to another. Consequently it is impossible to persuade them to accept a single ideal, a single religion, a single metaphysic, or a single form of mysticism. This planet is not a nursing ground for the mass production of souls. Each human being represents a divine thought and is consequently working out a divine end. He may be a mere thought of God, but he is nevertheless an important thought to God. We are individuals and have each an individual purpose to fulfil even though the One abides in us all. It is better to be more realistic and less ambitious than to play Don Quixote and tilt at windmills.

199

The existence of so many sects, religions, creeds, and churches is to be traced not only to historical causes—such as rebellion against corruption—but also to psychological ones. Each corresponds to the moral level, mental quality, and intuitive refinement of its members generally.

200

Each man will understand religion in his own way, according to the grade of his intelligence and character. The more ways of approaching God that there are to be found among us, the more opportunity will there be for us to make this approach. A single way might suit one type, but will not suit others. With the offerings of several ways, these too are served. Let us therefore welcome variety and not try to destroy it.

201

The fact that so many different religious sects exist all around us indicates that where choice is free and personal, not reached under social pressure or by family tradition, response to truth shapes itself according to the capacity-level.

202

Salvation is as open to those who adhere to some church or sect as it is to those of no church at all.

203

A single teaching could suit persons at widely different degrees of advancement only by lowering its quality to suit the lowest degree. But it would then no longer be itself.

204

The anti-materialistic teaching will find more response if it suits the needs of the country, the people, and the epoch in which he lives.

205

A union of many religions is a naïve idea, but a tolerant attitude among many religions is an excellent one.

206

The different religions expressed different kinds of temperaments, and different sects within a single religion express different mentalities.

207

The Qualities of a man's character are much more important than the tenets of his formal creed.

208

The protagonists of a world federation of faiths or of a reunion of all Christian sects or of a federation of all rival theosophical societies do not grasp the fact that a marriage of two or more half-corpses cannot produce a living body.

209

The capacity to receive truth is variable from person to person; it is not present equally in all.

On choosing one's religion

210

In this area of religious belief there is, for most people with faith, mere obedience to tradition. Either they do what is correctly anticipated from them, or they do some original thinking for themselves. Thus their religious outlook depends either on surrender to circumstances and environment or on their intellectual capacity. The first group seeks comfort and ease; the second has begun, but only begun, the search for truth.

211

Real thought is rare. How few follow a religion because they have chosen it after independent investigation and reflection, how many slavishly refuse to examine it impartially only because it happens to be popular at the time and in the place where they are born or live! As if popularity were a test of truth!

212

Formal religion does not give enough satisfaction to large numbers of people. Yet open atheism leaves them without hope, in despair at the futility of individual life. Then there are large numbers of others who, unquestioning and complacent, do not trouble their heads beyond their personal and family selfish interests, who observe the forms of their inherited religion in a superficial conventional way and are inwardly unaffected by them.

213

I know that most men depend—and must depend—upon some religious revelation to which they were introduced by their family. In this way a higher faith was ready to hand from birth. But he who awakens to a still higher need, his *own* revelation, has the right to seek for it.

214

Most people have had no revelation, no vision, no soul-shaking inner experience. They must perforce accept the word of someone who has. But unless they are content to remain in the religious denomination acquired by heredity, not by the search for truth, they will be confronted by the difficulty of how to choose among teachers, preachers, and prophets who all contradict one another.

215

There is something radically wrong in rating men quantitatively instead of qualitatively. There is something grotesque in the spectacle of ill-informed conclusions and impulsive judgements on an equality with the broad-based conclusions and well-matured judgements of a trained intelligence and disciplined character. Therefore I do not believe in the fetish of counting the number of followers of a doctrine, and using its largeness as an indicator of its truth.

216

People who belong by birth or choice to any particular cult, religion, or group usually believe that theirs is the highest in theory and the best in practice. This belief usually becomes a mechanical one, so that mere membership in the organization tends to make for less endeavour to find God than if they were thrown on their own individual resources.

217

The irony is that in religion most people distrust the new, and underestimate the unorganized. They feel that in the old, the traditional, and the established religious group they can take hold of what is solid and firm, reliable and safe.

218

Although huge established organizations command respect and claim authority in religion there is a real need of detached independents in this same field.

219

Adherence to any religion may be either a personal convenience or a flaming conviction. It is reckoned enough to be labelled a member of some conventional orthodox and organized religious community to be regarded as having fulfilled religious duty. Because men measure human spirituality by human conformity, history mocks them and punishes their error with evils and crimes, with sordid happenings and brutal deeds. Whatever faith a man attaches himself to, outside the faith of his forefathers, will depend partly on his intellectual level and partly on his personal inclinations. If he is sincere, he will illustrate the difference between the social inheritance and profound conviction motives, as well as demonstrate the superiority of the conscious adoption of a faith after wide search and comparative examination over the mere inheritance of a faith after geographical accident or chance of birth. For the source and form of religious belief have usually been the parents of the believer. Men accept their faith from their fathers and never question it. Yet is what his forefathers happened to believe in religion a valid standard of what is true in religion? What shall it profit a man if he enters a religious building merely because his neighbours expect him to go, or if he takes part in a religious gathering for the same reason that soldiers take part in military drill? It is impossible for those held in creedal chains or organizational straitjackets to keep their judgement free and their thinking unconditional. A respect for the human personality cannot submit entirely to the extremism which would impose a rigid straitjacket of total authoritarianism. Indeed, a man is likely to be harmed by it. This happens as soon as he allows his leaders to imprison him in the tradition or enslave him in the institution. He is then no longer able to benefit by, and is instead robbed of, all the other knowledge or inspiration available outside the little space in which he is shut. The men of this era have to be led closer to the freedom of their higher self. No organization can do this because all organizations necessarily demand fealty and impose bondage.

220

There is a wide difference between people who come by their religion through inward private conviction and those who come by it through outward social convenience.

221

The self-deception into which the masses fall is to start their thought about religion with the presumption that it must necessarily be organized, institutionalized, traditional, and professionalized if it is to be genuine religion at all.

222

People are easily impressed by size, tradition, wealth, prestige. They are overawed by a "great" religion with many fine churches, a long past history, and a well-organized structure. They will follow such a religion even though its ministers are spiritually dead whereas they will not even look twice at a man who is shining with the Overself's light and permeated through and through with the consciousness of God's presence.

223

It is one thing to accept a religion through traditional authority and another to accept it through a search for truth.

224

What faith a man chooses for himself, if he goes so far as to reject his ancestral faith, is partly a matter of temperament, partly of past experience and present opportunity, partly of moral character and intellectual development.

225

The real trouble is that many mistake tradition for religion. When they can learn the profound difference between these two things, when they can appreciate that a social relic is not a spiritual force, they will become truly religious.

226

A worship which is daily, and not weekly, is required of him who is really religious.

227

Freedom from the limitations of membership in organized religion may be good but anchorage in its harbour is in another way also good. Each man decides for himself.

228

At some point down the line of being born by family into a particular religious persuasion, the first ancestor to have the courage—unless he was forced by ruling tyranny or bribed by social ambition—to become a convert must be applauded. He may have been mistaken, his mind weak enough to let itself be misguided, but he did have the faith that he was moving from an inferior religious form to a superior one.

229

It is he who has chosen to remain in the church into which he was brought by birth or to join the one which pleases him better. It is he who must answer for the decision, bear the responsibility. The institution has its own but that is separate.

230

Too often we meet men holding at the same time beliefs which are contradictory. This is mostly pertaining to their respect for science and their reliance on intellect in professional matters being kept from colliding with their religious dogmas and prejudices.

231

In most cases people stay with their inherited creed but in others they seek and find one which reflects their own inclinations, character, or limitations.

232

Where a religion is organized and codified, validated by long tradition, and spread by a large number of people, the question of its truth is not a pressing one to its followers.

233

To keep one's religious affiliation through heredity or habit but to live without daily reverence or active faith—this is not true religion; it is pseudo-religion. Yet this is precisely what conventional hypocrisy so lazily accepts.

234

The herd of men and women are so hypnotized by the prestige of an institution that they never stop to question the truth of the institution. This is why Jesus was persecuted and Socrates was poisoned.

235

The largest followings of religious groups belong to the least rational and least inspired ones. And the followers are there usually because their parents were there, not because they have thought their way into these groups.

236

A wide experience of men shows up the strange fact that they may be well-talented, brilliantly executive, or acute reasoners, yet their religious beliefs will often be kept in closed compartments, unaffected by their mental powers, undisturbed by their excellent judgement, and hence quite primitive and quite irrational.

237

Some men, all too many men, are as stupid in their religious belief and practice as they are clever in their business ideas and activity. If they were to manage their businesses in the same credulous unreasoning and superstitious way in which they follow their religion, they would go bankrupt.

Grading teaching to capacity

238

Why did primitive races bring a highly spiritual wisdom to rest on the same pillow as barbaric superstition? The question is easily answered by asserting "the need of grading teaching to capacity."

239

Instruction in religion and all other subjects must be adapted to the level of the learner, or time and energy will be wasted, while the desired result will not be obtained.

240

Let us not deny the need of so many millions for a personal relationship with their God merely because we have found truth and satisfaction in an impersonal one. Are they to have nothing to look up to because they are unable to stretch their minds into that rarefied atmosphere? Is it not better that they do the more essential thing and acknowledge the existence of a Higher Power rather than fail to worship It at all?

241

The first work of religion is to bring the highest mystical ideas within the reach of the lowest mental capacity. It does this by symbolizing the ideas or by turning them into myths.

242

Unless there is an equal level between the understanding of a student and the communication of a teacher, there can be no complete success in the teaching. Hence a competent teacher first puts himself *en rapport* with the mind of the student. It is because the sages did this that they found it necessary to set up personal gods, priestly guides, and organized sacred institutions for the benefit of the masses. But this must not be taken to mean that the sages themselves believed in such gods, revered such guides, honoured such churches, or regarded them as eternally useful or always necessary and their dogmas valid for all future ages.

243

The simple masses can understand better that there is a God who answers prayers or responds to ceremonial invocations than that God is impersonal and transcendent.

244

The physical and mental images of religion exist because men need, and must necessarily make, symbols of That which they cannot conceive directly.

245

Is it not better to give to those who are unable to comprehend that there is a divine reality—which is anyway beyond human grasp—a symbol which stands for it and which can be grasped by ordinary human faculty or human sense? At the least it will remind them of it, at the most it will help to lead them to acknowledge its factuality.

246

The mass of people who believe in a transcendent power seek for more than a symbol or form to express it. They seek also for a channel, an embodiment, something or someone seeable and touchable through which it can find an outlet.

247

Those who are unable to formulate any concept of the formless Power in which they are rooted, and therefore unable to worship it, must worship a man instead. Hence the saviours and gurus, their religions and scriptures, the churches and temples.

248

In religious myth and legend, in sacred ritual and ceremony, there are symbols and allegories which are useful for meeting the mass-mentality but which offer much more to the educated one.

249

The masses are susceptible to, and impressed by, the colourful pageantry of religious processions, religious symbols, and kindred outward suggestions which awaken pious feeling.

250

The man of developed reason will feel its need less, or even not at all, but the unevolved multitude is moved emotionally and impressed mentally by ceremony. It preserves tradition, satisfies gregariousness.

251

The fact is that orthodox religion is usually a compromise between the truth and the lie, a concession to human weakness to which the truth must be offered wrapped up in the lie.

252

It would be cruel to tell the uninstructed many that the God they worship exists only in their imagination and superstition. But it would be equally cruel to let them always remain as children and keep the truth from them.

253

He should be sparing with his ideas for spiritually elevating the masses. The first aim must be not to sail over people's heads into the clouds. Otherwise he becomes a mere dreamer, while nothing tangible is achieved. It is better to give the masses one ounce of idealism in a pound of realism, and thus ensure its being swallowed successfully, than to give them a full pound's worth and have it totally rejected. No doubt they are spiritually sick, but they must be treated with homeopathic doses where teaching is concerned. This approach illustrates one of the practical differences between mysticism and philosophy. Indeed, it is often possible to tell from the character of its practical proposals for dealing with a deplorable social problem or reforming an unsatisfactory public situation, how far any theory of life is true to the facts of life.

254

Just as young children are more influenced by the world of the five senses than by the conclusions of reason, so many whose adulthood is still largely physical rather than mental are more influenced by what they see, hear, and feel, rather than by reason or intuition. Such persons are far from being ready for philosophy and could never give assent to its teachings. They lack discrimination and are led by appearances. They are impressed by "signs," that is, physical miracles, cures, and demonstrations, as proof of God-given power. Few of them would be willing to forsake their ego-directed lives and take to the way of living which Jesus—in contradistinction from his Church—really preached. But all of them may make excellent followers of an inwardly devitalized mass religion.

255

If, in the past, the truth has been dressed up in ecclesiastical myths, that could not be helped. It was in the nature of things and in the nature of man. It was also in the conditions of communication in bygone ages when most men could neither read nor write. Symbols and fables were useful in the intellectual childhood of the race.

256

Religions which have invented myths to suit the mentality of the multitude, who put up symbols to which they can attach meanings, are behaving quite logically. But man cannot live by invention and symbolism alone. As he grows up, evolves, gets more educated, his need is for the Reality behind them.

257

Many of the Gods worshipped in ancient cultures—Western or Eastern—are simply states of being. They are not to be regarded as living personages but as symbols of that higher state of being. For the masses, their picture and form may represent a useful object of worship, since it is difficult to form abstract conceptions of such states. For us who study philosophy, they represent conditions superior to our present one and to whose attainment we should aspire.

258

The sage could not transmit his knowledge to the masses except by presenting a remote symbol of it, a picturesque reflection. But this caused it to lose its vivid immediacy and its personal actuality. Yet so only could religion be born.

259

The sages had to face the fact that the masses under their or their pupils' care were inferior in mentality to themselves, and that their knowledge of the significance of the universe could only be communicated effectively through the use of symbols, suggestions, and images rather than through plain statements of fact. Hence the whole content of folklore and religion was invested in those days with its sacred character not because of what it said but because of what it did not say.

260

Those who cling to tribal legends and magical rites as essentials of religion, who put them on the same level as theological affirmations and moral injunctions, have never understood religion.

261

We can hope to understand folklore, myth, early religion, and savage beliefs only when we understand that these are the first, faint foreshadowings of philosophic truth created for the benefit of primitive minds by better informed ones. The savage was taught to think in terms of what he could easily visualize; consequently, he was taught to see the invisible in the visible, to feel the presence of spirits (that is, shadowy human or animal forms) as lurking in trees in order to explain their growth and life, as escaping from dead bodies in order to explain that the dead man continued to survive, or gigantically sized and placed in the sky in order to explain the processes and movements of Nature. How else could the intelligent leader teach these ungrown minds the truths that the mind of a man did not die with his body, or that mind was forever producing thoughts of the universe? Thus, these primitive "superstitions" are semi-symbolical and they rest on a philosophical foundation.

262

Religion *as we usually know it* touches only the periphery of the spiritual life. It is truth brought to bed with mental incapacity. It is a presentation to the gross senses of man of what is by its very nature entirely supersensual. Its exposition is not only elementary and narrow but necessarily incomplete.

263

It is a sign of the primitive mentality to believe in the personal actuality of a purely mythical and symbolic figure. Yet such faith is not to be despised and rejected as valueless, since it is a fact that the imagination can take hold of such a personal and pictorial representation much more easily than it can of an impersonal and abstract concept.

264

The easiest way for religion to account for the various forces of nature and laws of the cosmos to simple minds was to personify them. When it came to the Supreme force and Supreme mind, it had to personify that too. Thus, its limited and human conception of God is easier for the masses to grasp than the higher and truer one.

265

The savage mind bases its religion on fear, the cultured mind on faith. This proves the position taken by philosophy, that there is an evolutionary movement in religious concepts as there is in social customs.

266

It cannot be said that these truths have been kept from the masses. Rather, the masses' own limitations have kept them from these truths.

267

Emerson's scorn of the "mummery" of Catholic pageants and processions which he saw in Italy is intellectually understandable but spiritually unwarranted. Such festival shows have this effect, that in the mentally unevolved masses they keep alive the remembrance of historic figures and values in their religion, while in the mentally evolved they provide satisfaction for aesthetic needs or symbolic ones. Whatever promotes a mood of reverence is to be welcomed.

268

The mentality which has not been developed to perceive anything beyond the touchable and seeable, which cannot itself comprehend the abstract and metaphysical, this—the mentality of the masses—has to receive a simpler form of spiritual food. For it there must be the more palatable and easier digested food of dogmatic religious revelation. If from the standpoint of the sage such a religious form is a concession to popular prejudice and kindergarten minds, it is not at all a hollow valueless concession. He will always regard it as most essential to the welfare of the world, provided it is kept within proper limits.

269

Primitive peoples feel and act in response to the *feelings* aroused in them. Civilized peoples behave in the same way but with this addition, that feeling now combines with immature reason and to that extent is controlled by it. This explains why it was easy for the leaders of early races to get them to submit to religion. For religion is an appeal to feeling excited through the imagination.

270

To put the masses in a lower category of development may find supporting reasons—at least in past centuries—but to try to keep them there permanently is unjust. To feed them on myth, symbol, allegory, keeping back the higher truths and not telling them the facts about their existence, is also unjust.

271

Some readers have taken exception to my statement in the eleventh chapter of *The Wisdom of the Overself* that the aborigine should be left alone to worship God in his own way. They point out the great uplift of religious conceptions which has followed the work of Christian missionaries amongst aborigines. My own observations as a traveller would endorse this claim as true in some cases but false in others. There has been welcome advance in some countries but definite deterioration in others. This is apart from social, medical, and educational work of the missionaries, for which I would bestow the highest praise. However, the point I tried to make is evidently not quite understood. I hold only that, just as philosophy should not disturb the advanced religionist's faith but yet should make a higher teaching available to him as and when his faith weakens of its own accord, so the advanced religionist should not disturb the primitive religionist's faith but should make his own higher creed available as and when it might be helpful to do so. This would still leave a clear field for Christian missionary activity in distant lands but it would regulate and limit such activity within wiser borders. When I wrote about the advisability of letting the aborigine alone, this applies only if he is satisfied with his religion. It is not wrong to interfere when he begins to find fault with it. I did not mean to cause doubts about the value of propagating higher and more spiritual types of religion amongst primitive peoples. On the contrary, such propaganda should certainly continue, although it ought to be less offensively, less ignorantly, and less dishonestly practised than it has been in the past. It should be there, on the spot, available for those primitives who are nearing the level where they can begin to profit by it. Between the primitive tribesman, blindly obeying his patriarchal leaders and unthinkingly following his traditional customs, and the modern city-dweller, the difference is unmistakable. It is a difference on the one hand of more liberated individuality and on the other of more developed intelligence. Hence, the kind of teaching which historically suited the one is unsuited to the other. The missionary has his place in the world of religions, and especially so when he is the bearer of a more developed religion, but that place is not, as he thinks, an unrestricted one.

272

We need not accept a primitive form of religious revelation if our own intellect has developed too far beyond such a level. But we ought not despise those who do accept it, who find in it an answer to their need of belief in the higher power. However imperfect and unevolved, it is at base an affirmation that God is.

273

The man whose idea of himself is strictly limited to his little ego, and who is excessively attached to it, will naturally tend to form an idea of God as being a kind of gigantic person.

274

It is not true religion but rather impious irreligion to present the formless, limitless, sense- and thought-transcending infinitude of the Deity as a capricious tyrant and angry giant. To make It into an exaggerated human entity is to minify and slander It.

275

But most people, certainly the common folk, want a human God, one who shows emotion and responds to theirs.

276

It satisfies the demand on the part of the populace for a powerful supernatural being only if God is made masculine in gender, just as it satisfies their demand for a magnified father only if God is made humanly personal. They must have an anthropomorphic deity.

277

The Myth, given out to the populace, to the human mind at a simple naïve and unevolved level, is not intended for nor acceptable to the human mind at a high-cultured level. For this, nothing less than the Fact will do. For the others the Myth is, as a high Tibetan lama said recently (and privately), "like a sweet given to children because they like it so much."

278

Religion of the popular, mass kind makes its demand upon belief, not upon intellect. The priest or clergyman is not concerned with the question whether his offering is true: it is simply a dogma to be blindly accepted, an arrangement which suited the simple illiterate masses of earlier times and still suits those of our times in backward lands.

279

The truth could not be expressed in all its fullness to those whose cultural level was so different from today's. If they were given less, it is because they could not comprehend more.

280

It was perfectly correct for primitive peoples to feel and obey this deep longing to glorify their hereditary rulers and to worship their high priests.

281

We find that not a little in popular religion is nothing more than a thinned-down materialism.

282

The masses are not sensitive to the mystical, nor comprehensive of the philosophical. They must be reached through the physical senses. Hence religion is their path.

283

School the immature to enjoy and appreciate truth, prepare them for it, give them a chance to learn its elementary phases: this is a better way to stop their estrangement from religion.

2

ORGANIZATION, CONTENT OF RELIGION

Clergy

If we are to keep religion inspired; we must keep its ministers and priests inspired; that is, we must keep their *hearts* open to the sacred presence, their minds *alive* to the sacred Truth.

2

Who are the real bishops, priests, clergymen, and preachers of God's church? They are those who show, by the way they live and think, that they have found the spiritual self and follow the spiritual laws. And this is true whether they wear a clerical garb or a layman's suit.

3

Let the churchless man follow his own way but let him not deny the priest's path—it too is a service to those who are helped by ceremony and chants.

4

The objection that no intermediary ought to come between man and God needs to be kept in its place and confined to the limits of reasonableness. That a section of the people should be specially ordained and specially trained in religion and theology as a clergy is not in itself a bad thing, even though it could be abused and turned into a bad thing. That another section should be willing to live a disciplined, ascetic, and secluded life devoted to meditation and study is also not necessarily bad and anti-social, although again it also could become so if the purpose of all this is wrongly understood.

5

To transmit thoughts which have come out of some celestial plane, or feelings which hold a man by their delicate charm, to make one's way into ever-deepening states of tranquillity or of revelation and later return to

point at life's higher possibilities—these also are forms of religious attendance and, in some instances, even of priestly services.

6

Jesus, the first and best Christian, set an example for all later professed
Christians to follow. He did not preach in return for payment. He did not
turn religion into a profession. He even told those whom he sent forth as
apostles to carry no purse. If therefore we wish to understand one reason
why the Church does not represent him, here it is. The apostle Paul made
tents so that he could pay his own way while spreading the Christian
message. Modern spiritual teachers could not do better than follow this
excellent example. Their instruction should be given free. Hence they
should either earn their own living or have their own financial resources.
Thus, the new clergy will not labour for hire but for love. They will draw
no salary for their teaching and preaching, but will draw it from their
worldly work. Having learned how to earn their own living first, they will
be beholden to no one, dependent on no organization, but will have the
freedom to speak as the Spirit of Truth bids them speak. The old idea was
to preach and serve at the cost of the clergy's hearers. The new idea will
impel the minister to preach and serve at his own cost. When religion is
pure, however, there will be no professional clergy. Its ministers will then
have to earn their livelihood from a different source. Thus they may remain undefiled in motive and inspiration.

7

The mere title or position of priest, minister, clergyman does not sanc-
tify a man if he lacks the inner sanctity.

8

I have a distaste for "professional" spirituality. It took some years to
develop. It not only includes the teachers, guides, and ministers but also
the special kind of jargon they use in their communication.

9

By professional spirituality I mean that which is labelled as a priesthood
by an established organization, an authoritative hierarchy, and accepted by
the people as such. And I mean also that which is self-labelled by members
of the laity who take on a title like "Swami," who stand before the public
to preach and teach, who wear a special dress or uniform or robe.

10

All priests should be instructed in the exercises of meditation.

11

Only when meditation is officially restored among the highest positions
in spiritual life will religions be able to rise to their most important level.
Only when laymen can find available, whenever they wish to accept it,

both instruction in the art and retreats where it can be practised with the least obstruction, will the religious organizations be able to render their best service, their best fulfilment. For this it is which makes men connected in the most intimate way possible—within human limitations, of course—with the Overself.

12

It is not only those professional persons like priests, clergy, and monks who minister to the religious needs of men and women, but also the writers and artists, the rulers and leaders, the educators and the authorities, who must teach them the necessity and importance of aspiration towards spiritual goals.

13

Fate has put the priest in the position he holds; the necessity of earning a livelihood doing work on which others depend is an honourable one; and the Church as an influential organization has its definite place in society, a space in which the minister can play a worthy part. If he holds the ideal of service and seeks to infuse a little more light and life into those entrusted to his spiritual care, and if he does this with wisdom and discretion, he may do much good. He should grade his teaching to suit the minds of hearers, reserving for the intelligent few those doctrines which the others could not grasp or would resent emotionally. He must teach fables to intellectual children but the more mature deserve better stuff.

14

Even the clergyman who is trying to reach simple country folk would do well occasionally to drop a hint for the benefit of the few who are ready to receive initiation into mystical practices.

15

Clergymen can render better service to their flocks when they deepen their own inner life.

16

The minister who is able to instruct his flock serves them, but the minister who is able to inspire them serves them better.

17

When religion becomes a professional job, when men make their living by it, its reality vanishes, its hypocrisy appears.

18

It is not enough for a priest to have learning and virtue; he needs also to have inspiration. It is not enough that he performs correctly the outward gestures and ceremonial movements required of him or chants the proper sentences prescribed for him.

19

The ecclesiastic too commonly suffers from spiritual pride, too often makes empty pretense to superiority.

20

There are priests who lose their own faith and become spiritually impotent, so that in the end they preach to empty churches. They cannot help themselves, much less help others, cannot give consolation, much less give truth.

21

Why should we not consider some of the great writers like Plato and Thoreau as spiritual prophets, as holy in their way, and as illuminative to their fellows, as Christ himself?

22

Exaggerated statements by enthusiastic devotees or confused imaginations passed on by naïve ones come from the laymen. For deliberate removals and even insertions responsibility lies with the professional class.

23

Narrow-minded ecclesiastics look with horror at any and every departure from rigid orthodoxy and insist on a mechanical legalistic following of the form of every detail.

24

It is more important in their view to preserve the institution of which *they* are a part than to serve the people.

25

If there is to be an institution or organization and if it must have a head, experience leads the impartial observers to prefer unhesitatingly the elective principle to that of hereditary succession.

26

The benediction of a bishop possesses grace and power only if the bishop himself is an inspired man, not because he is a member of the institutional hierarchy.

27

If the words of a priest or a clergyman contain the message of true spirituality and carry comfort to suffering men, the latter might walk many miles to hear him; but if they do not contain them, they might probably walk miles to avoid him! How many clergymen have said all that they had to say in their very first sermon, since which they have added nothing new? Yet although they have had nothing further to preach, they continue to preach it boringly for the remainder of their lifetime! The people of this hapless epoch seek the bread of an inwardly-ravishing spiritual experience; they are offered instead the stones of inwardly-dulling intellectual gabble.

2: Organization, Content of Religion / 49

28

There are doctrines which belong to the spiritual infancy of the race, others to its spiritual adolescence. A prophet, a minister, or a priest who offers them to spiritual adults makes himself ridiculous.

29

The finished product of the theological seminary who takes his first pulpit with much education but little inspiration, may know his dogmas but is unlikely to know "the peace which passeth understanding."

30

Religion has suffered from the impostures of wily priests and the hollowness of boring services. But it has survived because of the nobility of inspired priests and the truth of fundamental beliefs.

31

If the clergy are to free themselves from this corruption of doctrines, this degeneration of mood, this hollowness of rite, the first step is to free themselves of ignorance of the true meanings of religious doctrine, the religious mood, and religious rites. Then only religion itself becomes intelligent and its following become sincere. It then worships the One Spirit, not any one person.

Church and State

32

If the clergy are to be supported by anyone else rather than by their own work, it should be by the worshippers themselves, and not by the State.

33

No church can keep its primitive spirituality unless it keeps its political independence. And this in turn it cannot have if it accepts a preferred position above other churches as a state establishment. It was not the leader of Russian atheism but the leader of the Russian Orthodox Church itself, the late Patriarch Segius, Metropolitan of Moscow, who admitted that the disestablishment of the State Church in his country by the Bolsheviks was really "a return to apostolic times when the Church and its servants did not deem their office a profession intended to earn their living." Such were his own words.(P)

34

There is no way, opening, or gate to God through the State, but only through the individual human being. The establishment and entrenchment of a State Church is based on an illusion, but the Communist disestablishment of religion *in general* is based on a much bigger illusion.

35

Faith in any religious creed and the following of any religious system should not be imposed by the State nor financed by it nor identified with it, but should be left entirely to the individual conscience and support. Even authorities, as history proves, are capable of making mistakes.

Religious symbols

36

Protestants, Calvinists, and Muhammedans who reject excessive symbolism, such as we find in Hinduism and Catholicism, make a good point in refusing to attach too much importance to the symbol, to the appeal to the senses of the body. But the fact remains that for the mass of people who until lately were untutored, simple, and overworked, symbolism did come within their mental reach and thus enabled them to get something from religion which in higher forms they might be unable to approach.

37

True religion is often fostered in a man by the use of a symbol. If a visible representation of the invisible God helps a man's worship, he is entitled to use it. If he has need of a symbol of the Infinite Spirit—be it man, angel, or Incarnation—to help him feel that It is something more than an abstract conception, that It may become existent and real, then its use is of assistance. If the symbol evokes a higher mood for the worshipper, it is an effective and worthy and honourable device which is unaffected by its failure to do this for others. It is one use of the symbol to lead him from the familiar outer plane of awareness to the unfamiliar inner one, to throw a bridge over which his mind can cross into perceptions beyond its everyday zone. He has passed from the tyrannous rule of exterior attractions to the gentle sway of interior ones. Until the time comes when the external symbol is no longer needed, he would be as foolish to cast it aside prematurely as another would be to refuse it altogether. But if he begins to believe that this image is thereby permeated with divine power in its own right, he begins to go astray. The worship of any false deity is the degradation of reason. Hindu pilgrims make their threefold ceremonial perambulation around smug idols and expect marvel and miracle in return. Reason denounces these futile propitiations of an unheeding deity.

38

Unless he possesses enough intuitional and metaphysical capacity, there is no way in which the believer may make contact with the Real except indirectly through the use of a Symbol. This can mediate between the limited degree his capacity has reached and the ineffable degree that can alone make the contact. The mediation is indirect, however, because it makes use of the senses, the imagination, the capacity to believe, or even of the ego itself. Consequently the result is incomplete. There is no way of completing it without passing first into mystical religion and, later, into philosophical religion.

39

The symbols of a religion may mean much where there is faith in them or else recognition of their true inner meaning. But they may also mean little where there is neither. Yet in the end, one should not stop with adoring them or with despising them, but move on to the reality they represent. For the believer, this is something on the spiritual plane; for the sceptic, it is a figment of the superstitious imagination. Only the actual, firsthand, personal investigation of it will determine what it is, if properly done. And this is what philosophy proposes—and does.

40

The same religious symbol which, at an early stage, helps a man to advance spiritually may, at a later stage and after its inner meaning has been well grasped, become a hindrance to further advance.

41

Beauty and Goodness, as we witness them on earth, are symbols of the divine. The failure to recognize this is responsible for much misery and suffering. The commandment "Thou shalt have no other God before me" meant that the highest of all desires should not be sought among earthly things. It did not mean especially the physical gold, bronze, or other metal images that the unfaithful worshipped—these were only symbolic of those earthly things.

42

To take every descriptive statement in most scriptures only literally betrays want of intelligence, but to take it only allegorically betrays a want of balance. The gods and goddesses of scriptures and mythologies are but popular explanatory principles of the one and only Divine principle. They are more easily comprehended by the masses than abstract metaphysical teachings.

43

In religion, metaphysical *principles* become symbolized by mythological *persons*. Thus Adi Buddha, the primeval Force, becomes the first historic Buddha, while Christos, the Higher Self, becomes the man Jesus. Thus the universal gets shrunken into the local.(P)

44

The dangers and downfall of every religion begin when its symbols are taken as substitutes for its realities, and when attendance at its public services replaces efforts at individual development.(P)

45

Man worships through the particular form which tradition and environment suggest to him. In his ignorance he gives the form more importance than it deserves until it comes at last to stand between him and God, a barrier to be broken down if he would find God.

46

In Christian symbolism the vertical line of the cross stands for spiritual aspiration, and its horizontal line stands for earthly desire.

47

If he is to use his religious symbol or spiritual guide philosophically, he ought to direct his mind to the truth behind the one and the reality behind the other. He should not leave it solely with the outer form.

48

The symbolic meaning of so many religious, ritual sacrifices involving the killing of animals on an altar was that the beholders should slay the beast within themselves.

49

They are right in honouring the sacred symbols of their religion, but wrong in letting those symbols extinguish knowledge of the reality for which they stand.

50

As understood by the masses, the gods—whether of India or Greece—never existed: but their figures were used to create significant myths and helpful symbols.

51

The Symbol which has become overused and devitalized, which is almost dead through being taken too much for granted, may prove inadequate and even misleading.

52

Several antique religions make the Virgin Mother a chief feature. Why stretch the credible so far to accept literally what is, after all, only a symbolism? The pure in heart—that is, the ego-free—shall see God—that is, shall give birth to the awareness of a new life within them.

53

The language used, the fables told as if they were history, may not be acceptable to an honest well-educated mind. But it could still, if it wished, accommodate them and remain within the fold of its traditional religion by taking them allegorically, not literally.

Places of worship

54

The simple feeling of religious reverence which we have on entering a church building, even though we may not believe in the doctrines of the sect to which it pertains, if stretched to a farther extent becomes the deep feeling of mystical communion which we have on entering the advanced degree of meditation.

55

Every temple, ancient or Oriental, if built on a philosophically traditional plan, acts also as a diagram of the human mind, with the shrine representing the Overself.

56

The deep heavy clang of a temple bell reverberates in the inner being of its hearers. The musical chimes of a church bell seek to attract worshippers, and each sound works in its own way as a sacred reminder.

57

It is right that the principal cathedrals, temples, and mosques of religion should be built on a majestic plan to impress those who go there to worship and to express the faith of those who put the buildings up. Such structures are not only symbolic of the importance of religious faith, but also conducive to the humility with which worship should be conducted.(P)

58

A building specifically planned and built for religious purposes only, holding an assembly of people who meet there to direct their minds and feelings towards the divine power, kept orderly and quiet so that its atmosphere becomes saturated with worship, prayers, chants, and meditations—such a building is inevitably more attractive to anyone who seeks to use it for the same purposes.

59

It is right and proper that a building put to a sacred use should be reserved for it and kept apart from profane activities.(P)

60

It is understandable that they would like to keep the serene aura of such a place uncontaminated by negative thoughts and mean, entirely self-enwrapped emotions.

61

In some rose-stained-glass-windowed church one may sense the strong atmosphere of true devotion so acutely that one instinctively falls on bended knee in humble prayer and in remembrance that self is nought, God is all.(P)

62

God is Mind and they that would worship it in truth must worship it mentally. The ostentatious ceremonies set up by paid professionals enable men and women to obtain pleasing emotional effects but they do not enable them to worship God. A building becomes a sacred temple when it ceases to hear phonographic mumblings and when it ceases to witness theatrical mimicries, and when it provides a fitting place where its visitors can engage in undisturbed silent and inward-turned communion with their own deeper Mind.(P)

63

A church's architectural form, a temple's sunward orientation and rhythmic music, a mosque's geometric decoration, and a synagogue's galleried arrangement are helps to each religion's expression of itself.

64

The visual effect of those temples, with their towers and carvings, upon the people is a successful reminder of sacred duties, mental and physical.

65

Temples or churches where men babble of God (whom they have not known) might be better used if men themselves kept silent therein. Then, after a while and little by little, God might speak to them.

66

They too often forget that the temple is not greater than the god.

67

The great height and grand interior of a cathedral or an important church are intended to create a mental impression, on the worshipper, of the importance of religion.

68

Although the mental impressions and emotional reactions which follow entry into a Greek temple, a Christian church, or a Muhammedan mosque are distinctly different, the architectural intention is the same—uplift to a higher plane.

69

The church building should arouse or confirm or strengthen religious aspiration when a man first beholds it and then enters it.

70

Temple: The rows of kneeling people, the chanting, the choir, the painted pictures and figures, the robed priests, the dim coloured lights—all contribute to set this place apart and produce an unearthly atmosphere.

71

What is the use of these temples of traditional religion when the gods have deserted them, when the only things in them are a bit of stone or metal, an idol, when truth and compassion, honesty and sincerity, spirituality and service are absent?

72

The symbolism that is built into the walls of church or temple, that is enacted in its ceremonies and rites, may be translated by a philosophical mind into philosophical meanings.

73

Thought, interest, attraction, wonder, and enquiry concerning God are not necessarily stirred up only in the buildings specifically planned for religious purposes; it may happen elsewhere.

74

One of the Indian seers actually prayed to God asking to be forgiven for having gone to the temple so often, visits which by their very nature seemed to reject the truth that God is everywhere.

Ceremonies and rituals

75

These grave ceremonies and beautiful rituals, which mean nothing at all to those practical men who feel no response to religion, mean comfort, inspiration, hope, mystery, and wonder to those who do.

76

If sacramental worship helps to put you into a reverent mind, take advantage of it. If ritual and ceremony seem hollow and meaningless and powerless, turn aside. But do not condemn them. Others *may* benefit.

77

The controversy between those who believe ritual to be indispensable and those who believe it to be irrelevant nearly always ignores four truths which, understood, dismiss the controversy itself—as ordinarily carried on—as futile. The first is that any means that adapts the truth to the limitation of intelligence which is present in the masses is useful *to those masses*. The artistic symbolism of ritual is such a means. The second is that the idolatry which the puritan objects to in ritual, reappears in his own use of mental images and limiting attributes, or anthropomorphic terms in thought, speech, and literature about God. The third truth is that the puritan's means is obviously adapted to a higher grade of intellect than the ritualist's and that one day the physical worship will have to give way through evolution to metaphysical worship. The fourth truth is that since each means helps different groups of men, its advocates should not attempt to impose it on a group to whom it is unsuited and consequently unhelpful. The diverse levels of human minds must be recognized. If it is wrong for the ritualist to interfere with the non-ritualist who has outgrown this level, the latter needs to be tolerant of the former who has something more to exploit in the lower level.(P)

78

Both Jesus and Buddha sought to remove bloody sacrifices from the institutional religion which surrounded them.

79

Any rite or ceremony which reminds men of their spiritual duties, which instigates them to worship the higher power, which helps them to concentrate on it, which creates the feeling of its presence, and which excites them to love it, has justified its existence.

80

For the mass of mankind and for beginners on the Way, any outer ritual or physical method which turns the mind away from earthly things, which lifts it up from total immersion in the lower interests of the personal ego to recognition of and aspiration toward its divine source, has its place and value in human life. But its spiritual merit depends on the extent to which it provokes a mental or emotional—that is, an inner—result. A mechanical co-operation with the ritual, empty of such a heartfelt result, is useless and, instead of being virtuous, may become harmful by creating a complacency which deceives the worshipper and a hypocrisy which deceives society.

81

Correct ideas of the place of asceticism and the proper form it should take are too seldom held. This is just as true of religious ritual.

82

Liturgical ceremonies which touch the deeper feelings are not less useful than inspired texts which touch the deeper thoughts.

83

The ceremonial observance of festival dates, the ritualistic participation in church or temple services, and the following of liturgical usages have their chief value in being first steps for the masses towards faith in a higher power and fervour in devotional attitudes. If a truly illumined priest is present during any of them and, more especially, if he performs a leading role, this value is transcended.

84

It is not hard to surrender to the hypnotic and repetitious choral chants, to the dim flickering lights, to the authoritatively voiced liturgies. Whether the result be only a spectacular theatrical show emotionally received or a vital communion spiritually uplifting depends largely on the celebrant of the rite.

85

If cold intellectuality looks on these ancient sacraments as mere outward shows, participated in as hypocritical routine, fervent piety looks on them as foundations which have supported the established religion and maintained its importance through the centuries.

86

Respectful ceremonials and huge buildings are not in themselves hollow, empty, and hypocritical materialistic forms, although they may become so with time. They are intended to impress the observer's mind, kindle appropriate feelings, and overwhelm him into submission by the power of suggestion.

87

Animal sacrifices do not belong in any way to the worship of God but to the worship of demons. They come near to, and are even used in, some forms of black magic. Whenever temples were turned into slaughterhouses in the past, and in certain lands still today, religion takes its lowest form, becomes pseudo-religion. Still lower were the rites of human sacrifice. Both kinds are concessions to, or expressions of, the killing instinct so marked in unevolved humans.

88

Have no use for a spirituality that only puts itself on show.

89

If church bells remind people of the existence of churches, and if churches remind them of the existence of religion, both serve a useful purpose. But this is not to say that all must go to an external church. Those who can find the spirit and practice of religion from within themselves do not need to; they may, if they wish, but it is not a necessity for them.

90

No sacred performance, ceremony, or rite gives anyone enlightenment, salvation, absolution, or inner strength without the real presence of the higher power. But this can manifest itself anywhere, and when one is completely solitary.

91

Insofar as a religious rite succeeds in arousing the proper attitude of reverence, enchaining the thoughts to a loftier centre than usual, and bringing the worshipper into contact with a genuinely inspired priest, it deserves an honoured place.

92

No formal rite of circumcision, as in Judaism and Islam, no mechanical baptism, as in sects of Christianity, can have the slightest actual virtue in spiritually affecting a child. All that it can do is to affect him post-suggestively by providing a remembrance in adult years of his dedication to a Faith to be secretly held, an Ideal to be earnestly followed.

93

The real use of any physical ceremony in religion can be only to help the worshipper who is not able to arrive at the same mood by metaphysical understanding.

94

Within one and the same church there should be place for such diverse expressions as those who can find stimulus only in rituals as well as those who can find it only in non-ritualistic worship. There should be place for mystics and thinkers as well as for the simple sense-bound masses.

95

Why not be large enough to tolerate both the ritualistic and the rationalistic in the same system, for each has its place and does its service?

96

The liturgy and vestments are but a door to the Real Presence.

97

We do not hear the voice of God in the priest's voice. We can hear it only within the mind's stillness. We do not commune with God through pageantry and ceremony. We commune through self-relaxation and self-surrender.

98

The magical value of any sacrament lies not in itself but in the faith it arouses, the reverence it suggests, and the reminder it gives. If a man can believe, revere, and remember God by any other means, such as reading, for instance, and if the sacrament has no effect upon him, he is not obliged to participate in it. But if a sacramental form helps him to either the remembrance or the aspiration of divine reality, why should he not take advantage of it? It is true that ritual which helps man to concentrate on a value higher than the material ones is certainly useful to him. But it is not indispensable to him. At the last, no sacramental symbol, no external rite can give what a man's Overself alone can give. Although the chief function of external rites is to direct the mind towards internal ideas, a mechanical ceremony of itself has no moral value. One may ask how far do the collective incantations and public prayers of organized religion lead to any tangible results? The mistake is not in creating or continuing these ceremonial systems themselves, these processions and observances, but in forcing them upon people who have no inner affinity with them, who feel no

need for them and no help from them. Liturgical symbolism and ecclesiastical rite may exalt and satisfy the emotions but they do not go beyond
this. They do not carry out their claim to constitute for the participant a
direct sacramental means of grace. Those who administer such sacraments
are invested with no higher authority than a merely human one. We must
not believe that any paid professional has a better right to assume the
status of intermediary between God and man than does an unpaid ama-
teur. In fact, it often is better to believe the opposite. The confusion of
clerical power with authentic spirituality is a common mistake. There is no
real relation between the two. This is because it is not the ethics of a holy
man which clerics seek to spread, but the power of a worldly institution. It
is not faith in an immaterial reality whose propagation is their prime aim,
but faith in a material hierarchy. When it has become outworn, the inner
mental attitude which gave it birth and the accompanying feeling which
gave it justification are no longer active. Consequently, its followers do
not know why they are following it and act mechanically or, quite often,
hypocritically. A ceremonial observance which carries no inner meaning
and gives no mental uplift to those who partake in it becomes even worse
than useless. It becomes a deception. There is a further danger when
ceremonial symbolism becomes more important than moral principle. It is
then that a religion falls into risk of betraying itself. Philosophy appreci-
ates the services of organized religion and objects only when it loses itself
in mere externals, when it sets up its own ecclesiastical organization and
liturgical forms as all-important to man's salvation. The greatest dangers
to its purity are the corrupt forms that men give to it and the selfish
institutions that men set up in it. The seeds of destruction are implanted
by karma and germinated by time whenever a religious form fails to serve
humanity.

99
If anyone wants the processions and banners, the lights and incense, the
priestly robes and litanies of ritualism as essential to his feelings for religion, let him have them. But if he insists on imposing these things on
others who do not share the same feeling, he acts wrongly.

100
The creed and doctrine of a religion, its rites and sacraments, its communions and prayers, hold or lose their value according to the inspiration
with which they were created, the character and conduct which they demand, the proportion of truth they contain.

101
If it is the business of religion to guide faith and not to supply knowledge, to promote moral feeling and not to stimulate rational intelligence,

it would be well if those who are officially in charge of religious institutions were occasionally to remind themselves and their flocks not to become so immersed in its forms and customs as to forget the ultimate aim of the institution. Ceremonies which become more and more mechanical as they become more and more familiar, also arouse less and less inner response, stimulate less and less true reverence, and are apt to turn religious services into empty shows. To take a human ecclesiasticism for a divine religion or a showy ritualism for divine worship is a sign of intellectual childhood. It is perfectly proper in its own time. But systems and customs must grow up, like the child itself. Formalized religion is too often dead religion. "In the opinion that my body is completely extinct they pay worship in many ways to the relics, but me they see not. . . . Repeatedly am I born in the world of the living," observes Buddha in *Saddharma Pundarika*. There is no nutriment here for matured human minds or true human lives. This is why we neither support any external organization nor encourage the following of any personal teacher. This is why we practise, and counsel others to practise, a balanced individualism.

102

When people work themselves into too much emotionalism in religious dancing or singing, there is departure from, or inability to reach, that inner calm wherein alone the Spirit can visit us. These orgies of religious zeal do not yield true insight.

103

The gorgeous ceremonials and censered picturesque rituals of a religion appeal to those of aesthetic feeling, impress those of simple unsceptical minds.

104

It is partly to prevent the doctrines and teachings from fading out of men's minds and memories that they have been put into ceremony and song, symbol and bible, ritual and record.

105

What is it but a few sounds heard in the ears of men? Without the private experience of a glimpse—even only a single one in a whole lifetime suffices—what kind of conception can they form of it that will be accurate and trustworthy? What meaning can it carry to them at all?

106

For, after all, the really important factor is what happens *inside*, what is felt and thought, and less what is being done and said or sung under the imposed formula of the outside ritual.

107

Incense may be used for religious purposes in ceremonies and worship, but less devout persons use it to help smoke out mosquitoes, while more aesthetic ones find its fragrance and colour attractive.

108

All forms of external sacramental worship become worthwhile if they are used as jumping-off steps into real devotion.

109

All gurus and disciples, ceremonials and initiations belong to duality, relativity.

110

The services of aspiration expressed in song are an excellent feature of some churches and chapels.

111

Throughout the Orient, at least, if not in other parts of the world, rituals, sacrifices, and ceremonies have been a large source of income for the priestly order.

112

It is inevitable that where people tend to exaggerate the external, sacramental form so disproportionately, they will tend to overlook the power within the form.

113

A rite, a ceremony, or an image is of worth to anyone only insofar as it brings him, however slightly, closer to a sense of holiness, a feeling of reverence, and a recognition of mystery.

Relics

114

The exhibition of relics, the erection of shrines, or the creation of memorials, statues, paintings, and sects to record the name of a saint or prophet or holy man is useful to impress his attainments upon the minds of others living long after he has gone, and perhaps to inspire them to do something for themselves in the same direction.(P)

115

They believe that in touching these objects left by holy men or in visiting these places where such men resided, they touch holiness itself. A few even believe that they commune with it.

116

"Spare me, and take your absurdities elsewhere!" exclaimed Goethe a few days before he died in rejection of the belief in holy relics—in this case an Apostolic thumb-bone.

Scriptures

117

If you study the history of religion, you will find that prophets of the highest order, like Buddha, Krishna, and Jesus, did not write their messages in books. Every writer of a religious revelation or mystical inspiration belongs to spheres below that on which the great prophets stood. Their work at best is incomplete and at times imperfect. Therefore we should not look for perfection in it. Nevertheless, it is necessary to help lead people in their journey towards the Ever-Perfect and the message reaches those who are not yet ready for the final quest. To understand this situation, we must understand first of all that the truth is beyond all intellectual formulation. A book is the product of the intellect. The truth in its purity can be communicated only in silence and only to the awakened intuition. Hence the great prophets felt that the pen would be a limiting instrument to use. But why then did they use the instrument of speech which also is a mental expression? The answer is partly that in almost all cases their speech was directed to individuals, whereas books are not, and partly because of their being able to give some measure of help towards the understanding of truth through the impact of auras. The spoken words became merely supplementary to the interior and intuitive help.

118

Among the other chief purposes, it was the work of a priestly class as in Hinduism or of a learned class as in Islam to study and learn their scripture, thus preserving and protecting it. For in those days there was no printing. The scripture itself was treated with the greatest respect as containing the record and memorial of the prophet's revelation.

119

It is better to use the term "inspired book" than the term "divine revelation." The one is more scientific, more in tune with modern psychological knowledge; the other raises religious doubts and theological arguments when the assertion is made that it never originated in a human brain.

120

All scriptures are valuable as inspirers of faith and uplifters of minds but none is essential as the absolute arbiter of creed.

121

They do not understand that in setting up the text of some scripture as the last authority, they are worshipping a graven image as much as Moses' faithless followers did of old.

122

So much misinterpretation of sacred scriptures, and especially of the

Bible both in its Jewish and Christian parts, has been rife in the past that it has been used to support contrary opinions. This shows how much fancy and speculation go into these opinions.

123

The great variety of interpretations of religious texts may reveal only the different capacities of the interpreters' imaginative power in many cases but it may also attest their different levels of awareness.

124

Sacred writings are not necessarily those alone which conventional opinion labels as such. Any writing which uplifts the mind, ennobles the character, and imparts a feeling of reverence for the higher power is a sacred one.

125

From the philosophical standpoint, the entire chapter of Genesis in the Old Testament is both an allegorical legend and a divine revelation at remote remove.

126

The undeveloped mentality may be allowed to take the Book of Genesis as historical fact, in the same way and for the same reasons that children may be allowed to take any fairy tale as fact. But the developed mentality ought to know better, ought to take Genesis as an allegory and its scenes, personages, and events as symbolical.

127

There are several interpretative schools of semi-mysticism which devote their energies and spend their time finding new meaning in old texts. They lose themselves on some scripture and torture it into agreement with their own particular teachings. They might be better employed in finding reason first, rather than finding incorrect imaginary meanings in sacred books.

128

There are mystically minded students who spend much, too much, of their time juggling with esoteric interpretations of scriptural texts or tortuously hatching out from these texts confirmations of their own beliefs. My experience is that most passages of sacred scriptures and most happenings in profane fortune are open to as many mystical interpretations as there are mystically minded persons to make them. Such quotations of divine writ and such ascriptions to divine intervention prove nothing.

129

It is easy to fall into the errors of so many sectarian enthusiasts who see so much more in simple texts than the writers ever dreamed of.

130

Such grave and great distortions, interpolations, and eradications have some scriptures undergone in the course of their history and manipulation, it is no wonder that sects compete in common ignorance with one another.

131

A writing can be as much a piece of religious work as one so labelled, even though it is not dealing with a religious subject. It depends on the writer himself, his attitude and character, his knowledge and grade of consciousness.

132

In these ancient scriptures the religious babblings of primitive men are found strangely confounded with the philosophic reflections of wise ones.

133

Those who find allegorical significances in religio-mystical bibles, or who attach symbolical meanings to historical sacred records, need to be especially balanced and discriminating in such activities.

134

Scriptural texts have accommodated so many different interpretations in the past, and still do, that prudence should precede acceptance, patience should attend suspense.

135

It is a grave error to found man's moral life on the say-so of any tribal collection of outdated stories and maxims. A scripture is acceptable not because it is a scripture, but because and to the extent of the truth it contains. Also, not everyone who knows how to read can extract the true meaning from holy scriptures. No scripture, no gospel ever fell from the skies. Somewhere, some man took up a writing instrument and composed the one with which his name is associated. And because he was a man, however divinely inspired, the production was a human act and therefore a fallible one. A book is not a sacred image. It is not something to be revered merely because its typeset pages are printed in black ink on white paper. If we set it up as an authority, we fall into the fallacy of authoritarianism. Medieval debates about angels dancing on needle points or Mosaic cosmogonies are equally unreal today.

136

Those who think that because a statement appears in sacred scripture such appearance terminates all further controversy upon a question are deluding themselves. They base their unqualified assent upon the undeniable fact that the ancient sages knew what they were talking about, but they ignore the other fact that some of their followers did not. They do not know that the scriptural texts have been peppered with later interpolations or debased with superstitious additions and are consequently not always reliable. But even if they were, still, the human mind must keep itself unfettered if it would achieve truth.(P)

137

The biblical sages have told to all human races, not only to the Hebrew race, truths which, being eternal, are as needed in the twentieth century A.D. as they were in the twentieth century B.C. There is no statement in the Book of Proverbs, for instance, which requires revising and bringing up to date, or which can be dismissed as discarded religious superstition.

138

The Authorized Version of the New Testament is so clean-cut, so forthrightly spoken and yet picturesque, that it comes near to being a work of poetic art. It never forgets its purpose—to tell us the story of a man of God and to teach us what to do with our life.

139

Jesus spoke in Aramaic but the written texts of his teaching came to us in Hebrew, Greek, and Latin. Buddha spoke in Pali but at least half his followers got the written teaching in Sanskrit. The possibility of mistranslation through symbolic, metaphorical, or allegorical expressions being taken literally; or through esoteric-mystic experiences being only half-understood; or through terms with two different meanings being used; or through simple ignorance, is an ever-present peril.

140

The simply constructed, unforgettably inspired sentences of Jesus may be picked out in the four Gospels from those which have been interpolated by later men. Why this interpolation, it may be asked? Because they *wrote down* the words, as we have them today, after original bearers were themselves dead. Because with the passage of years and the passing down from mouth to mouth, remembrance may be faulty. Because human mentality may misinterpret the facts. Because human desire may exaggerate them. Because the fatal influence of an ambitious emperor forced organization and institutionalism on believers to serve his own ends and secured the necessary interpolations for this purpose on the theory that the end—monopoly and stability of power through the union of religion and State—justified the means.

141

Those who wish to understand their Christianity better should make this experiment. Let them procure Doctor Moffatt's translation of the Bible into modern English. It lacks the beauty of the King James Version, and can never take its place, but it amply compensates for that lack by the clearer expression and the fresher insights it gives. The two versions are needed together, side by side.

142

Esoteric meanings of the Bible: "Jehovah" means "Who is and who will be." "Israel" means "to see God."

Conceptions of God

143

The God a man believes in will reflect something of his own moral character, mental capacity, upbringing, tendencies, and education. There is no such person as an unbiased, unprejudiced believer. For God being unknown, the man has to substitute his own idea for direct knowledge. It makes no difference that this idea has been supplied to him by other men, through tradition, authority, reading, or hearing. They projected their own concept onto God and he has enough affinity with them to share their limitations.

144

God has made man in His own image, says the Bible. Man has made God in his own image, says the critical science of comparative religion. Understanding this, we can understand why the African savage imagines God in the form of a magnified tribal chief of terrifying aspect. It is not easy, however, to proceed on a higher plane and understand that it is for much the same reason that highly evolved civilized men have made God a great Artist or a great Logician or a great Architect or a great Mathematician. Yet it really is so. Such concepts represent the Supreme seen under the limitations of the beholder's personality. Therefore they are only partial and inadequate. The Infinite Power not only includes all these aspects but necessarily transcends them. So far as the human intellect can form a complete and correct idea of God it can form it only by bringing the whole personality to the effort and not merely a fragment of it.

145

Whatever men may say or write about the divine will always fall short of the actuality. This is so for three reasons. First, the Real transcends thoughts and their clothes, words. Without personal experience of it, and achieved insight into it, the intellect yields opinion only. Second, each man sees and says from his own standpoint, gives his own reaction to the divine. This is always an individual one. Third, there are many aspects of the divine. Muhammed listed no less than one hundred, without exhausting them. So far their totality has eluded description. Let no one insist on *his* own picture of the divine as being the whole one. Let no one set up *his* favoured symbol of it and exclude all the others from the right of worship.

146

We do not mean that the concept of God is an untenable one: we do not assert that it should be totally dropped. We mean only that in the light of our latest knowledge, as gleaned from such sciences as physics, astronomy, anthropology, archaeology, comparative religion, and psychology, the hour has arrived to restate this concept in a modern way. The concept itself remains, but the semantic content which is put into it must be rectified and purified. The fictions about God which were fashionable in older times have been largely exploded, but the *fact* of God's existence remains what it always must be—the greatest and grandest in the universe.

147

However false a man's idea of God may be, the basic instinct which is behind the idea's acceptance still remains a true one.

148

The God whom they worship may be a fiction of their own brains, but It is not a baseless fiction. The essence of the concept is true enough; only its form is false.

149

Whether he knows it or not (and if he is a sage he will surely know but if he is a religionist he may not), the Christian mystic, the Hindu pundit, the Buddhist monk, the Taoist priest, and the Muhammedan theologian talk of one and the same Principle under different names.

150

Each group gives a different name to the Parent of the universe, calls it Brahma or Jehovah, Allah or Tao, but all groups really direct their worship to one and the same God.

151

The self-existent Principle of Life which is its own source was given the same name by prophets of three different religions: "I AM" is the appellation of God in Judaism, Zoroastrianism, and Hinduism.

152

No dogma is more utterly materialistic than that which would compress the infinite unbounded Spirit into a physical human form, a personal human self, and worship that as a God. Nor could any other dogma so utterly falsify truth than that which would make a single religion, a single church, or a single man be sole repository of God's revelation to the human race. They are not religious truths, they are merely concessions to human weakness and human egos. They are exhibitions of the infirmity of human understanding.

153

The man who goes into a church because he believes that all the other churches are wrong, is going to a kindergarten school. When experience has schooled him through many births, he will learn the first lesson—that God is no respecter of churches but comes to the threshold of all, and nowadays too often to none.

154

The elementary religionist protests that he cannot form a conception of an impersonal God and that It could not exist. The philosophic religionist answers that he cannot form a conception of a personal God and that no other than an impersonal one could exist.

155

When I feel the divine presence in my heart, I acknowledge God as Personal; but when, going deeper in silent contemplation, I vanish in the infinite immeasurable Void, I must afterwards call Him Impersonal.

156

The old theology invested God with the quality of man. It belittled the Infinite power and imputed petty motives to the motiveless. Such a theology really worshipped its own thought of God, not God in reality, its own cruel and pitiful concept of the Inconceivable. Can we wonder that it provoked atheism and led to agnosticism when the human race began to outgrow its intellectual childhood? However fitted to that early stage of our growth, such an idea is unfitted to this mid-twentieth century of our history. We must and can face the truth that God is not a glorified man showing wilful characteristics but a Principle of Being, of Life, and of Consciousness which ever was and therefore ever shall be. There is only one Principle like that, unique, alone, the origin of all things. The imagination cannot picture it, but the intuition can receive some hint of its solitary grandeur. Such a hint it may receive through its worship of its own source, the Overself which links man with this ineffable power, the Divine Spirit within him which is his innermost Self. The personal concept of Deity was intended to satisfy the race's childhood, not to enlighten the race's adulthood. The time has come to do away with such a false concept and to accept the purity of this philosophic truth.(P)

157

Let us not be misled by the wide-flung nature of the theological belief in a personal god. For this single primal error introduces a whole host of other errors in its train. (a) The error of the observed Nature apart from the observer. This error is involved in the notion of a separate Creator. (b) The error of teaching a beginning and ending to the world. If matter ever existed in any form, its underlying essence would never completely disappear, whatever the changes it underwent and however numerous they were. (c) The error of the belief that something—the world—was created out of nothing. (d) The error of the belief that time, space, and motion could have been created, for the same reason. Their very existence implies that infinite duration, infinite space, and perpetual motion must also exist—which would negate their own supposed creation. (e) The error that God is all-benevolent and merciful yet creates an immense multitude of living creatures only for the sake of seeing them endure sorrows and tribulations of every kind, finally crushing them with the bitterest blow of all—death. (f) The delusion that we are entering into communion with this God (when we are only communing with our own imaginings about Him).

158

Words or names like "OM," "Allah," and "Mana" were never invented by ordinary men; they were revealed to seers. They are the true natural expressions for the corresponding ideas of God.

159

The Bible's first commandment is "Thou shalt have no other Gods before me." What is the meaning of a "god" here? It means something which is the object of worship. That thing can be money, fame, or sex: it is not at all necessarily an idol, a force, or a being.

160

What any religion, creed, or cult proclaims about God is almost always true as to God's existence, but is not always true as to God's nature.

161

The primitive man fears God. He seeks to propitiate this distant and awful power by offering sacrifices. The positive value of this view is the recognition that a power higher than himself does exist and does affect the course of his life. The civilized man reverently believes in, and gladly worships, God, who is felt to be much closer and like a benevolent parent. The element of fear is still not eradicated but it is very largely reduced.

162

If the arguments of atheism are studied, they will all be found directed against the idea that God is a Person, the mental image which has been set up and which presents God as an enlarged and glorified semi-human being.

163

Religion worships a Personal God through symbols but nondualism sees and seeks union with what is behind them, the Impersonal Reality.

164

The discovery that God *is* may be beyond our own experience, but it need not be beyond our faith.

165

The divine presence is outside time, and those who seek it through ceremonies, practices, or methods measured inside time can find looking-glass images but not the original presence.

166

Many people have so meditated upon their concept of God, that they have become one with the concept and not one with God, as they vainly delude themselves. The concept is not reality.(P)

167

The idea of a personal God as a loving father naturally appeals to, and greatly helps, the intellectually young. Children everywhere feel acutely the need of, and depend upon, such a parent. But when they grow up and become adult, they learn to practise a large measure of self-reliance. In the same way, with the more advanced concept of Deity, the love remains but the being is depersonalized.

168

It will not avail us to practise self-deception. Let us think for a moment of how many millions of men and women implored God to bring this bitter war to an end during its first year but found God deaf, how many millions repeated this request during its second year with the same sad result. Those who would force this narrow and petty picture of God upon others, deny and blaspheme the true God in the very act. Whoever reflects upon this unsatisfactory conception of a deity subject to racial bias, arbitrary favouritism, and other limitations of human personality, must repudiate it. And if it is not repudiated by millions it is only because they never pause to reflect long enough nor deeply enough on such a matter.

169

They project their own mental picture of their prophet or saviour, and it is this only that they see and worship. This projection becomes a barrier between them and the reality, which is by its very presence rendered inaccessible to them.

170

Tibetan texts admit frankly what other religious documents fail to admit, that the crowds of gods whose forms fill temple altars and wayside shrines are virtually "the play of one's own mind," that all the pageantry of worship, chants, music, and prayers is directed to symbolic figures.

171

We all worship God as best we can. But the ignorant perceive and honour only the veils of liturgy, dogma, and ceremony which enwrap Him, whereas the wise thrust the veils aside and worship Him as He is.

172

It is necessary to remind the orthodox from time to time of what one of the greatest and sincerest of orthodox Episcopalian clergymen reminded his audience in a Philadelphia church. He himself dwelt in the holy Presence and knew what he was talking about when he startled them by exclaiming: "God is not an Episcopalian."

173
The concept of God as Father or Father-Mother is a true one but still only an elementary one. The man who rises to the understanding of God as that in which his own self is rooted holds a truer concept.

174
Most people worship at an idol's shrine even when they honestly believe they are worshipping God. For they accept the imaginary personification of the Infinite Power which popular religion sets before them, and bow before it.

175
The atheist asserts that God does not exist, the religionist claims that He does, while the agnostic declares that both are talking nonsense because it is utterly impossible for the human mind, with all its limitations and conditioning, to get at the truth of this matter, since it can know only its own states.

176
Those who feel they must apply a personal pronoun to Deity should do so. But they in turn should accord equal liberty to others who are unable to share this feeling, and not regard them as apostates or heretics.

177
Those who can only believe in a God who has taken up his abode in some institution, some established organization, are and always have been in the majority.

178
The unconscious belief that there is a divine power back of the universe prevails even in the materialist, the sceptic, and the atheist. Only he conceives of it in his own deficient way, limits it to some force issuing from it, and gives it a different name.

179
There are such wide differences among the ideas about God which men, groping to get out of their ignorance, hold, that they might find it more useful to start by examining their equipment for the task.

180
Whatever evidence in disproof of God's existence is provided by thought can refer only to a personal God of popular religions rather than to an impersonal God of an intellectual elite.

3

RELIGION AS PREPARATORY

The religious life, if earnestly followed and conscientiously sustained, carries the devotee only part of the way towards worship of, and communion with, God. It is only a preparatory school. For both morally and intellectually it is a kind of compromise, yielding to a certain degree of the lower nature's rule and accepting beliefs that violate reason. This satisfies him only because he has not made perfect purity and perfect truth his standards.

2

To deny the immense value of the ordinary religion in its own place and to those who have yet to gain its rewards would be to break off the lower rungs of the ladder whereby men must climb to what is the ultimate goal of all religion.

3

The general line of inner development for the human race is in the first stage right action, which includes duty, service, responsibility. In the second stage religious devotion appears. This engenders worship of the higher power, moral improvement, holy communion. The third stage is mystical and involves practice of meditation to get a more intimate communion. The fourth stage is the awakening of need to understand truth and know reality. Its completed product is the sage, who includes in himself the civilized man, the religionist, the mystic, and the philosopher.(P)

4

Organizations are for most people the only way of receiving religious help or acquiring religious belief. This, however, does not mean that they will always remain so, for a time comes when they are seen for what they are—elementary stages usually, intermediary stages sometimes.

5

When a man comes to the attitude that it is not sufficient for him to receive religion at second hand as a creed or a conviction, when he must receive it directly as an actual experience in his own life, when he can pray with Flemish Thomas à Kempis, "Let it not be Moses or the Prophets that speak to me, but speak thyself," he is ready to move up from the first and lowest grade to the second and middle one. Such a one will then put himself in a position—which he did not occupy before—of being able to move forward to the central point of all religion, which is the personal revelation of the Overself, God's Deputy, in the heart of the individual man.

6

The sceptic, the anthropologist, and the philosopher of Bertrand Russell's type say that religion arose because primitive man was terrified by the destructive powers of Nature and endeavoured to propitiate them or their personifications by worship and prayer. They say further that civilized man, having achieved some measure of control over natural forces, feels far less in need of religious practices. This is an erroneous view. Religions were instituted by sages who saw their need as a preparatory means of educating men's minds for the higher truths of science and philosophy.(P)

7

Codified religion is not the final truth. It is but the vestibule of Mysticism, which is the vestibule of Philosophy, which is the vestibule of Truth. He who tarries in any vestibule is a sluggard, unfit for entrance into the innermost chamber where Truth's treasure lies.

8

Religion as popularly organized, with priesthoods and hierarchs, vestments and incense, ceremonials and rites, liturgies and scriptures, churches and temples, is an excellent first step for most people but not for all people.

9

The religious path is only a way leading at its end to the still higher mystical path. It does not bring its followers directly into the presence of God, as they believe, but rather to the beginning of a further way which alone can do so.

10

Yet the worship that is given by the multitude to an imagined God is not without value. It is an initiation, a preparation, and a training for the worship that will one day be given to the real God. It is an archway through which they pass on their way to philosophic worship.

11

The ancient division of men into three grades of spiritual development was expressed variously in different countries. In India, the *Bhagavad Gita* placed lowest the man whose mentality was inert and dull, next the man whose understanding was coloured by emotion or distorted by passion, and highest the man of clear and balanced intelligence.

12

The ceremonies and beliefs of institutional religions are useful, even necessary, on the level of consciousness for which those religions have been created; but they do not assist the mind to rise to the higher levels of metaphysical and, especially, philosophical religion. For these are concerned with a far higher quality.

13

The Ultimate meaning and social significance of religion will be hidden from us so long as we do not understand that it represents the appeal to the first of the three stages of growth in human mentality. The latter begins with the primitive, arrives at the civilized, and finishes with the philosophic stage. We have only to study the fruits of anthropological research to become aware of this truth. Ultimate truth being beyond the intellectual range of savage society, its wiser leaders unfolded a faith suited to their followers' capacity and needs, a faith which worked perfectly well and was indeed the best faith for such people. It ill becomes us to sneer at their superstitions, therefore, merely because we are totally unable to place ourselves into sympathetic relationship with their primitive environment. Their beliefs became superstitions only when those who led them did not realize that capacity for change and growth must be allowed for when the tribes had outgrown their first faith. Therefore, such esotericism does not mean that the masses are condemned to wear forever the badge of intellectual backwardness.

14

A man on the second level will not be able to accept the ideas or practices of a man who lives higher up on the third one. It would be unreasonable to expect such acceptance.

15

It is as erroneous to take the popular form of a religion as being all there is to it, as to take the symbolic statements of that form in a literal sense. Deeper than this form is a mystical layer and deeper still a philosophic lore.

16

The mission of religion is to take mankind through the first stage of the road to spiritual self-fulfilment. It can succeed in this mission only as it leads its adherents to regard religion more and more as a personal matter, less and less as a corporate one.

Doubt

17

It is not enough for one's religious faith to be fervent; it ought also be intelligent.

18

Simple minds can be taught to accept the symbols of religion as realities and the metaphors of its dogmas as truths, but cultivated minds submit with difficulty.

19

All religion rests ultimately in some kind of revelation—that is, on the appeal to faith. The first impulsive reply of modern man must be to doubt.

20

The reality in religion is true, but what too often passes for religion may be quite untrue. Doubt of what is false in it may be faith in, and consequent upon worship of, the real Deity.

21

The capacity to defy religious superstition is needed if a man is to discover religious truth.

22

The abatement of faith in a particular sacerdotal organization is not alarming in itself, but the abatement of faith in the Supreme Power which works for righteousness is indeed alarming. How many people have forsaken institutionalized religion not because they have lost faith in the existence of the Supreme Power but because they have lost faith in the representative character of the institution itself, not because they do not feel the need of religion but because they feel the need of a purer and better religion? If they have not found any other creed to replace the one they have outgrown, they may still turn for inward solace directly to the Supreme Power itself.

23

One may have truly religious feelings yet still be critical of a religious environment which practises hypocrisy or supports superstition.

24

Although organized religion is rendering a great and necessary service to the mass of people, there are still a few individuals who need a somewhat deeper understanding of the truth which such religion is teaching. If they pursue their enquiries they will not only be able to gain this understanding but also be rewarded by inner peace.

25

At a certain distance along the way, the institution or organization which may have helped him in the past now bars his way. Instead of serving his highest purpose it arouses questions, doubts, criticisms.

26

If he is sufficiently developed as a human being, he finds himself wondering at this existence of his and of his world. And if he becomes serious enough to look around for the answers which others have given to his questions, he can easily become bewildered by the contradictory results.

27

The traditional ancient historical religion into which a man is born, and which he accepts unquestioningly, is comforting and secure in his young days. But with adult maturity and the intellect coming more into play, his faith may become disturbed.

28

Questions about the assumptions of religion, uncertainties about its fulfilment of promises, doubts, and distresses may cause him many a pang during this difficult period.

29

The religious devotee does not care to trouble himself with such questions but all the same he cannot keep them out for all time. The human mind is so constructed that under the pressure of experience or the nurturings of evolution it desires, nay even demands, to know. Both desire and demand may be feeble at first and limited in extent. But they will emerge as inevitably as bud and leaf emerge, and find troubling utterance.

30

Those whose hearts could receive a nobler faith, whose heads could absorb a truer one, need not remain captives to an inferior one.

31

A philosophically based religion would give all its worshippers a chance to move up higher whenever they wished, felt ready, or began to express doubts.

32

There are two ways open: either advance into another religion or sect, or sink a shaft into the religion already held and go down deeper and deeper until its ultimate Source is found.

33

The type of religion which seeks to frighten men by the ever-burning fires of hell is for the naïve. Tradition supports it but education destroys it. By education we do not here mean the memorizing of opinions but the unfolding of the capacity to think rightly.

34

As man's intelligence develops he needs to be fed with religious nutriment beyond the simpler forms and faiths of popular religion. If this is not offered he becomes indifferent or atheist.

35

When religious faith is shattered by some distressing event of the personal life, this very loss may lead to gain. For it may be a prelude to a deepening and enriching of that faith.

36

People seek to escape from the soul's solitariness by keeping close to mass organizations, including even the religious ones of traditional churches. Here they find shelter and gregarious comfort. But a day comes when crisis crashes through the one and disturbs the other. Once again they are left alone with the soul.

37

He must look upon the elaborate ceremonials and simple dogmas as a cradle where his growth began, his limbs first extended themselves. But he cannot stay in the cradle forever if he is to become a youth and an adult.

38

Religious devotion, worship, aspiration, start a man on the way by occupying his feelings. But a time may come when he may wish also to know and understand more about the mysterious object of his devotion. It is then that he must prepare to get into deep waters, must hold his breath and take the plunge into philosophic thought.

39

There is no need for anyone to leave his own religion, but there is a need for him to go deeper into it.

40

The human being cannot be kept forever in the child state, neither physically nor mentally, neither in the home nor in the church. This must be recognized if society is to have fewer problems, less friction, more understanding, and more harmony.

41

The concrete image for worship was originally given for all those who needed something physically visible and touchable to hold their attention and keep it fixed on the idea of God. It was a means of fostering concentration. The masses were helped thereby. For others it was a useful reminder. But more developed minds who are able to grasp a metaphysical or abstract idea, as well as those who feel quite cool to external rites and constantly repeated ceremonies, need not let the less developed ones tyrannize over them and make them hypocritically worship, or take part in, what bores them utterly. They may claim their freedom and replace the idol by the sacred Idea, substitute for the rite an inner reverence for the Higher Power.

42

When a movement's inner life hardens into an organization, when its teaching petrifies into a formulated dogmatic creed, when its advocates and elders and guides become parasites on all the others, it may be time to quit.

43

We may give up hollow religious rites, if they have become meaningless and repugnant to us, and yet we need not give up religion itself. The two are distinct.

44

It is better to go one's own spiritual way and walk at one's own private pace than to tread the path of an organized church in steps set for us by professional priests.

45

To insist on primitive forms of religion being offered to, and honoured by, those who have reached the threshold of mental maturity, is like insisting on grown-up men playing with toys or grown women with dolls.

46

When the questions concern the spiritual meaning of life, the spiritual techniques of communion, or the spiritual nature of man, and when they are strongly and earnestly felt, it is the pressure of the answer itself working upon the mind from within that is forcing the questions into the focus of attention. It may take years before the man can unite the two, however.

47

Those who go to church for reasons of social conformity or self-interest, not for reasons of inner need, are on a lower level of evolution than those who refuse to go to church at all because their intellect cannot bring itself to believe in what is taught there.

48

Whether to conform to orthodox religion or make an open break with it must depend partly on the prompting he intuitively feels and partly on his family, social, and business circumstances. If a rupture might do external harm and create great friction, and if he does not feel a strong urge to make a break, then why do so? In that case it would not be hypocrisy to conform but simple prudence. The world being what it is, it is not possible to live in it and yet achieve complete independence. On the other hand, if the intuitive leading takes him away from obedience to these practices then he should obey conscience.

49

The legal, official, and conventional nature of established churches mesmerizes the great mass of people into the belief that here only is the truth, and that outside them lies false religion. The man who is beginning to hear the call of his higher self may often need to resist the power of this mass-suggestion.

50

Few men can accept their traditional religion in its entirety; they accept it only in part.

51

So far as established religion limits the evil-doing of its followers, it renders a useful social service. But this does not help those who, so far from needing such bounds set upon their deeds, are positively active in doing good. Still less does it help the few who have felt the urge to seek the Spirit's absolute truth above all the things of this world.

52

We may accept much that is given out by a man, a religion, or a teaching without sanctioning everything else that comes from the same source. All of it is not necessarily wisdom and virtue.

53

That which appears as enlightening Truth to one man appears as dangerous heresy to another man. These are not mere differences of opinion but of evolutionary growth.

54

Those who venture beyond the boundaries of established orthodoxy are justified in their exodus if they feel insufficiently or improperly nourished within those boundaries.

55

The free man will not take kindly to rigidly binding dogmas, may even come to feel spiritually suffocated by them.

56

The masses have their ready-made religion; the seeker must form his own.

57

Doubt has shaken the belief in a merciful and benevolent Deity but has not much shaken belief in the Deity's existence.

58

The rise to a higher level from a hollow, merely formal and outward religious life to a simple childlike trust in, and inward devotion to, God is excellent. But those who are unable to put aside their intellects so easily may ask for something more.

59

The Christian who has outgrown conceptions of an elementary nature and needs more substantial spiritual food is faced with his own special situation and religious difficulties. He must begin to get for himself some glimpse of the True Self by way of personal experience.

60

It is no sin on the part of any man but rather an intellectual duty critically to investigate for himself the formalized systems of unyielding dogma which, in the name of tradition, claim his belief.

61

It was a Justice of the United States Supreme Court, Mr. O.W. Holmes, who wrote in a private letter with reference to the orthodox religious doctrines which had been inculcated in him in his mid-nineteenth-century childhood: "But how can one pretend to believe what seems to him childish and devoid alike of historical and rational foundations?" The intellectual eminence which had brought this man to such a high position brought him also to such a questioning.

62

The religious individualist who is unwilling to put his mind under the yoke of any organization, who is unaffiliated with any group, has at least as much chance to find truth as the members of such organizations and groups and, as history shows, most probably a better one.

Inner worship is superior

63

We must distinguish between the ritualistic forms of outward religion and the mental and transmental states, the emotional and intuitional experiences of inward religion.

64

People who turn away from religion, even if they believe vaguely that there is a God, because the distance between both is immeasurable, may be startled to learn that God is also very near, is indeed within themselves.

65

True Spirituality is an inward state; mere religiosity an outward one.

66

Enshrined in the secrecy of everyman's Holy of Holies, hidden in the depths of his heart, there is a point where he may find his indestructible link with God.

67

The kind of religious worship which is expressed through outer things, through physical rituals, objects, sounds and processions and movements, is intended chiefly for those people who cannot practise the inner worship of silent moveless meditation. The first is easier but the other is superior.

68

The only value of theology is a negative but still useful one: to tell the student to ascend higher and give himself up to the practice of advanced thought-free mystical meditation.

69

The public demonstration of one's religion in church or temple does not appeal to all temperaments. Some can find holiest feelings only in private. Those in the first group should not attempt to impose their will on the others. Those in the second group should not despise the followers of conventional communion. More understanding between the two may be hard to arrive at, but more tolerance would be a sign that the personal religious feeling is authentic.(P)

70

Men who imagine that if they take part in the ritual of a cult they have done their religious duty are dangerously self-illusioned. By attaching such a narrow meaning to such a noble word, they degrade religion. We have progressed in religion to the extent that whereas ancient man sacrificed the animal *outside* him upon the altar of God-worship, modern man understands that he has to sacrifice the animal *inside* him. The external forms of religion are not its final forms. Jesus ordered one convert to worship "in spirit and in truth," that is, *internally*. The two phases of worship—external and internal—are not on the same level; one is a higher development of the other.(P)

71

A fourteenth-century German churchman, John Tauler, said: "Let the common people run about and hear all they can, that they may not fall into despair or unbelief; but know that all who would be God's, inwardly and outwardly, turn to themselves and retire *within*."

72

There is a vast difference between the man for whom religion means an organization, a numbered group, attendance at a formal ceremony, a set of creedal beliefs, and an official authority on matters of right or wrong—and the man for whom it means a vivid inner experience, enlightening and pacifying, joyous and gracious.

73

A man must find holiness in his own mind before he can find it in any place, be it church, ashram, monastery, or temple. He must love it so much that he constantly thinks about it, or thinks about it so much that he begins to love it, before he can find its real quality anywhere.

74

Set forms of prayer, fixed formulas, and ready-worded phrases are for the multitudes who have little capacity for creating their own. It makes the going easier for them when they are told or taught what to say. But those who have more capacity should not feel themselves bound so rigidly: they should feel themselves free to express their devotional feelings in their own way and own words.

75

In the deep stillness we learn no creed, are taught no dogma. Only outside it, only among quarrelling men, are we saddled with the one and strapped down with the other.

76

So long as they look for the sources of religious truth, power, hope, and goodness outside themselves, so long will they have to suffer from the imperfections and limitations of such sources.

77

The man who wants something broader than the pettiness of most religious creeds, nobler than most religious ethics, truer than most religious teaching, will have to step out of every religious cage and look where Jesus told him to look—within himself.

78

Those who formerly could not bring themselves to believe that God exists are dumbfounded when they discover that He not only exists but even exists within themselves.

79

Men go on pilgrimage to this or that holy place, city, man, or monastery. But in the end, after all these outer journeys, they will have to make the inner journey to the divine deputy dwelling in their own hearts.

80

Too often religion amounts to coddling the ego of the believers and worshippers, both in its existence in this world and in the next one. This merely creates illusions that will later have to be struggled against for release.

81

The man who accepts doctrines, obeys commandments, follows blindly, shifts responsibility to the organization of which he is a member. But his attempt fails. The karma is not only collective but personal. The man as an individual cannot escape.

82

No religion today can claim to be the sole and true inheritor of its Prophet's message. There is no unity in any of them; there is plenty of dissension and sectarianism when it comes to definitions, creeds, and observances. This really means that the individual follower, in relying on tradition to support him here, is trying to push off—unconsciously perhaps—his personal responsibility for his acceptance of it. But it remains there still!

83

When he no longer looks only to the established tradition offered him by others but also and more deeply into his own inner consciousness, he is then following the way pointed to by Jesus and Buddha and Lao Tzu. For this is how and where the soul reveals itself.

84

If many like to share their religious emotions with others in full public view, they are entitled to do so. But if this activity is done with the desire to be seen, to be admired in approval, to this extent the emotion is adulterated and rendered worthless, because it is ego-worshipping instead of God-worshipping.

85

Those who believe they honour a religion by attending its services and ceremonies are not seldom deceiving themselves. It is they themselves who are honoured by the contact.

86

Men and women go to church, mosque, synagogue, or temple, ostensibly to worship the higher power; but what is the good, if when they are there their thoughts are preoccupied with their personal affairs and are thus not really in the church or holy building, but in their egos? They might as well have stayed at home if they don't intend to make an effort to let go and to look up.

87

It is nonsense to assert that people who come together for worship touch a stronger holiness than those who pray alone. What happens is that two forces are at work: first, the power of society, of public opinion, and the crowd to incite and shame them into attending open services where they see and are seen; second, a central place or building reserved for such visible worship and heard prayer *suggests* that divine influence is active there.

88

The way in which some people flock to join organized groups is often an indication on their part of some unconscious or unexpressed doubt, for it is an indication of their need to strengthen their faith by getting the support of numbers. But this is only a spurious support because the faith is inside them, whereas the group is outside!

89

We can truly worship God without ever entering a religious building, opening a religious book, or professing a religious membership.

90

Prayer which is private and individual is superior in quality and sincerer in tone than prayer which is public and collective.

91

Religion will gain in honesty and lose in hypocrisy, society will gain in peaceableness and lose in quarrelsomeness, when religion itself becomes a private affair—so private that even two friends of different faiths will ordinarily neither display their interest in nor talk about them. Their reverence will then express itself just as well and even more sincerely in private religion than in public worship.

92

If prayers are merely said by rote, mechanically or perfunctorily, little or nothing need be expected from them.

93

The dogma, ritual, creed, and sacramental worship of religion exist only to lead up to this inner phase: they are not ends in themselves.

94

The beautifully carved figure which was to have acted as a symbol to men of their higher possibilities and as a reminder of their duty to realize them, becomes over-worshipped, its correct use forgotten and true place misconceived. In this manner materialism penetrates religion, as it does in several other ways.

95

Whether a man accords his allegiance to Salt Lake City or to Rome, to the Mormon revelation or the Catholic credo, is really of more importance to the institutions involved than to the man himself. For in the end his salvation depends on what he is rather than on what the institution is.

96

When Jesus said, "Knock and it shall be opened to you," he meant knock at the door within yourself. No amount of knocking at the doors of organizations outside yourself will bring this result.

97

The altar at which he humbly prays is deep within his mind; the god to which he gives reverent homage is there.

98

Too many people have been mistaught by religion to evade their obligations and to deny their responsibilities by trying to put them into God's hands merely because it is unpleasant or uncomfortable to the ego to deal with them themselves.

99

The more importance is placed upon the inner life by a religion, the less is development given to ritualism.

100

If you depend too much on the external, you will become weaker to the same extent internally.

101

It has been observed that most religious hymns are about ourselves, few only are about God.

102

They worship their own ego and call it God!

103

It is only by relegating religion from being a public to being a private affair that those two typical religious nuisances—intolerance of other beliefs and interference with other people's lives—can be got rid of.

104

We must take a higher position than ordinary religion offers and come face to face with the mystery that is Mentalism. The nonbeing of the universe, the nonduality even of the soul may be too mathematical a conclusion for our finite minds; but that this matterless world and all that happens in it is like a dream is something to be received and remembered at all times. We are important only to ourselves, not to God. All our whining and praying, chanting and praising, gathering together and imagining that this or that duty is required of us is mere theatre-play: Mind makes it all. In this discovery we roll up the stage and return to the paradox of what we really are—Consciousness!

Mysticism and religion

105

Mysticism is religion come to flower. The yearning for security against fears, which religious belief and ceremony satisfy in an elementary way, is still further and much more fully satisfied by mystical experience in an advanced way.

106

When religion is of the socially visible, publicly attended kind, it serves the people in a limited way. When it is of an extremely private, quiet silent meditative kind, it penetrates their mystical essence.

107

Faith in the soul is the first step and is provided by religion. Knowledge of the soul is the second step, and is provided by mysticism.

108

The religionist has a vague intuitive feeling that there is something higher than the daily round, someone behind the universe, and some kind of existence after death. The mystic has developed this intuition into definite insight into his own relation to this mystery: he knows he has a soul.

109

Religion was devised to assist the masses. Mysticism was designed to assist the individual. When religion has led a man to the threshold of deeper truths behind its own, its task is done. Its real value is attained in mysticism. Henceforth, the practice of mystical exercises can alone assure his further spiritual progress. For mysticism does not rest upon the shifting sands of faith or the uncertain gravel of argument, but upon the solid rock of experience. The first great move forward in his spiritual life occurs when he moves from religion to mysticism, when he no longer has to go into some stone building or to some paid mediator to feel reverential towards God, but into himself. Mysticism is for the man who is not in a hurry, who is willing to work persistently and to wait patiently for consciousness of his divine soul. The others who have not the time for this and who therefore resort to religion must live by faith, not by consciousness. The man who wishes to rise from sincere faith and traditional belief in the soul to practical demonstration and personal experience of it must rise from religion to mysticism. Mysticism seeks to establish direct contact with the divine soul, without the mediation of any man and without the use of any external instrument. Hence it must seek inward and nowhere else. Hence, too, the ordinary forms and methods of religion are not necessary to it and must be dropped. When the mystic finds the divine presence enlightening and strengthening him from within, he cannot be blamed for placing little value upon sacramental ceremonies which claim to achieve this from without. Nor is he censurable if he comes to regard church attendance as unnecessary and sacramental salvation as illusory. If a man can find within himself the divine presence, divine inspiration, and divine guidance, what need has he of church organization? It can be useful only to one who lacks them.(P)

110

If the transition from religion to mysticism is to be conveniently made, it must be gradually made. But this can be done only if the teachers of religion themselves approve and promote the transition. But if they do not, if they want to keep religion imprisoned in ecclesiastic jail-irons, if they persist in a patriarchal attitude which indiscriminately regards every member of their flock as an intellectual infant who never grows up, the transition will happen all the same. Only it will then happen abruptly and after religion itself has been discarded either for cynical atheism or for bewildered apathy.(P)

111

Religion brings the truth *to* him only in part and, too often, in symbol—only from outside himself and by secondhand revelation. Mysticism brings *him* to the truth from inside himself and by personal experience.

112

Without this mystical dimension, religion lies at its most elementary level.

113

Under the half-dead conservatism of religious tradition and dogmas there lie concealed a group of profound truths and ulterior meanings. They are needed today much more than those relics are needed. Yet the irony is that the men who teach those traditions have all the prestige of great institutions to support them whereas the mystic who perceives those undisclosed truths stands alone and has little or no prestige. So the masses continue to echo the empty babble of their religious leaders, or else repudiate religion altogether and become either indifferent or hostile to it.

114

Valuable and respected as the Catholic mystics were as guides to mystical knowledge and practice, most of them still remain biased and unscientific guides. Allowance must be made for this difference of attitude with which they approach the subject, from that with which a modern mind— freed from prejudice, superstition, and organizational ties—approaches it. Even so outstanding and leading a mystic as Saint John of the Cross, who is considered to have reached the goal of complete union, limited his reading to four or five books, of which one was *Contra Haereses*, and confined his writing by his proclaimed intention "not to depart from the sound sense and doctrine of our Holy Mother the Catholic Church."

115

Mysticism is not to be confused with any religion. Mysticism can drop all the religions from its hold and yet be unaffected. No religion can help the true mystic, but he can help any religion with which he cares to establish contact. His presence alone inside any fold will give it more than a momentary grandeur and cause men to look on an old Church with new respect. This is why mysticism can stand on its own feet, and why it does not need the doubtful legends and theatrical liturgies of institutional religion.

116

When a man has outgrown the tutelage of religion and tired of the barren negative period of agnosticism which succeeds it, he is ripe for the tutelage of mysticism.

117

A sincere Church would do everything to encourage, and nothing to hinder, its members taking to the mystical quest. For this would be the best sign that it honestly sought to consummate its own work for the individual benefit rather than its own.

118

The assertion that, in certain cases, heresy can be true religion and orthodoxy false, may seem incredible to those who have not the necessary evidence to prove it. Yet Buddha and Jesus and Muhammed were, in their time, heretics. How many others have died unknown, canonized as saints or revered as sages in the minds and remembrances of only a small number of persons? And how many of them, had it been their mission to declare themselves openly, would have been rejected, calumniated, or persecuted?

119

Mysticism is larger than religion and ought not to be confounded with it; yet paradoxically it takes in religion and does not deny it. It fulfils and consummates religion and does not retard it.

120

We must not confuse the truly mystical life with either a religious one or an ethical one. The latter two are merely elementary and preparatory to the former.

121

More than three hundred years ago, a wonderful little woman took the Galilean at his word. She put all her emotional strength into aspiration and meditation and succeeded in achieving an exalted state by practising a simple method. When her own heavenly peace was sufficiently stabilized, she began to think of others, of how she could help them attain it too. She was not so selfish as to be satisfied with her own satisfaction alone. So she journeyed from city to city and from village to village in religious yet religionless France, lighting the candles of human faith with a divine taper. Such was the spiritual darkness of the time that her success was immediate, and such was her own Christlike power that it was amazing. Crowds flocked gladly to her side, listened eagerly to her words, and endeavoured faithfully to follow her instructions. Her doctrine came to be called "Quietism" because she showed people how to quieten their personal thoughts and emotions and thus become aware of the impersonal heaven behind them, the kingdom within. She was no heretic. She drew frequently from Jesus' own recorded words to explain or illustrate her teaching. Yet she did not speak from dead pulpits in churches but from living ones in the fields. The clergy became seriously alarmed. Such activities could not be countenanced, they said. They petitioned the authorities against her, as the Jewish priests had once petitioned the Roman authorities against Jesus. She was thrown into prison and the jailer turned his key on her dismal abode, where she was shut in for a long period of years. Such was the story of poor Madame Guyon.

She was also denounced by the Church, as were her followers, for

having fallen into the sin of spiritual pride. This was because of the assertion that outward practices and ritualistic acts were no longer needed by
those who could find inspiration within. This teaching is quite correct but
politically wrong. Out of respect for, or fear of, the Church's great power
in those times, as well as out of consideration for the mass of people who
were still unable to rise above their dependence on such outward ceremonies, Madame Guyon could have worked longer if she had worked
quietly and privately, not openly and publicly. She could have instructed
her followers, first, not to talk about the teaching to any person who was
not ready for it, and second, not to communicate it even to those who
were ready without the safeguard of complete secrecy.

Do you wish to penetrate to the essence of this episode? Here it is. A
bishop of that time naïvely let the cat out of his theological bag! He said:
"This woman may teach primitive Christianity—but if people find God
everywhere what is to become of us?"

"What is to become of us?" Six short words but what a tremendous
commentary they contain! When religion was about to become a living
actuality in the lives of common people whose hearts were moved by the
enlightening words of Mme. Guyon through personal realization of its
loftiest truth, when it was ready to inspire them from hour to hour with
inward peace and outward nobility, the official exponents of Christianity
interfered and prevented it because of their selfish fears! They did not see
and perceive the ultimate danger to themselves, and the immediate shame
on their teaching, of such a situation. Well may the thinker have repeated
the poet's lines about the mills of the Gods grinding slow but exceedingly
small, for when the French Revolution broke out and spread its ugly
malignant fury over the land, when the so-called Goddess of Reason was
set up on her throne in the very midst of Notre Dame Cathedral, and
when all France was rocking in the great upheaval which retributive destiny and rebellious demagogues had conspired to bring upon her, fifty
thousand French priests fled from persecution, imprisonment, and even
death. To appear on the streets of Paris in those days wearing the cleric's
garb was to court the punishment of death itself.

122

The mystical phase is to be acquired without dropping the religious
phase, although he may wish to modify it.

123

If religion is to save what is best in itself, it must not only set its house in
order but must admit the mystical practices into its system of instruction.
It must become less exteriorized and more interiorized, more mystical.

Stone-built sanctuaries are many in every town and village of the land. But those that truly light the mind are few. Yet there is one with doors wide open to all, great enough to include every city in the country yet narrow enough to exclude the dull materialist, the ruthlessly cruel, and the poisonously selfish. This is the sanctuary of the inner Self. From this mystical standpoint the institutional side of every religion is its least important side. To understand a religion in this way we must first become heretics; we must cast off conventional views which blind the mind's eyes. We need no longer worry ourselves over the hotly debated question of whether or not Christ was born of a virgin mother, for instance, but we do need to give our time and thought to finding that which Christ represents within ourselves. Christ can live again within our hearts, as he himself taught, which means we must look for him inside ourselves much more than inside a Church building.

124

The disuse of outward sacraments and the distaste for church organization which mark the life-history of several mystics, come from the vigour and independence with which they must shield the growing plant of inner life, and from the reorientation of trust with which they turn from all man-made things to God alone.

125

When spiritual yearnings become more insistent but perhaps more indefinable, it may be that the mystical depths of religion are calling him away from its shallow surfaces.

126

The mystic unfolds his higher individuality. The more he does so, the more he tends to draw away from the organization which acts as custodian of his outer religion.

127

Fanatical religion killed Hypatia, conventional religion lynched Pythagoras, respectable religion poisoned Socrates, authority-worshipping religion crucified Jesus.

128

It is historical fact that a number of those who successfully deepen their spiritual life by contemplation practice may develop anti-ritualistic attitudes. This is why mystics have been tolerated, even venerated, and alternately treated as heretics and persecuted.

129

Ecclesiastic hierarchies do not welcome, even discourage, the claim to personal inspiration in their own times. A fresh revelation of deific power is regarded as a fresh danger. For the new voice may be listened to in place of the old parrot-like repetitions!

130

Because time brings to instituted religions growth, and that brings power, success, wealth, and prestige—with all their corruptions and infidelities—all religions' principles need to be periodically re-established. This is why contemporary mystics and prophets are always needed and why they should be given a hearing.

131

So long as so many of the authorized guardians of religion fail to appreciate the fact that mysticism is the very core of their doctrine, so long will they lack the glowing inspiration, the broadening view, and the beneficial strength which religion at its best can and ought to give.

132

What the religious man feels by instinct or faith, the mystical man knows by experience or revelation.

133

It remains a historical fact that the man who has discovered truth finds more opposition within the formal established church of his religion than outside it, more who will accept it among laymen than among professional ministers and theologians. This is regrettable, because the latter ought to be the first to welcome his discovery. But organizational ego, plus personal timidity or cowardice, get in the way.

134

So long as people are overwhelmed by the official prestige of established churches and overawed by their historic tradition, so long will it be futile to expect wide recognition of, and proper honour for, the authentic revelations of a true contemporary mystic.

135

The individual mystic's lack of status is regrettable but expectable. For it is the penalty he must pay for refusing to be overawed by the dogmas current in his time and the traditions inherited from his people's past. What chance has this teaching when its adherents form only a small unrecognized entirely scattered cult whereas the adherents of orthodoxy are numbered by the million, and even those of unorthodoxy are numbered by the thousand or hundred? Must all importance, all truth, all significance in religion be limited to organized groups alone? Are there no inspired persons and no ordinary individuals who do not choose to belong to any such groups at all? Why should orthodoxy and unorthodoxy, merely because they are organized into churches and labelled as denominations, alone represent the voice of religion?

136

The inspired individual who has climbed Sinai on his own feet and received the Tablets of God's Law with his own hands has merely a small fraction of the power, influence, and prestige of the be-robed representative of organized religion, who knows God only at second hand and through others, who has no inspiration with which to bless men and no real power to save them.

137

What is the difference between Quietism and Mysticism? Quietism is Roman Catholic and seems to have been solely devotional-mantra, repetition japa singing, ascetical in order to find personal salvation, whereas Mysticism is a generic term for all religions and seems to be positive living in God plus illumination.

138

So long as official religions held the highest places, so long the Enlightened, the knowers and the seers, were left to walk alone or to think in secret or to stifle their words.

139

There are austere anti-mystic theologians just as there are hidebound anti-mystic ecclesiastics.

140

The devotional life of religion finds its culmination in the meditative life of mysticism. Devotion can be practised *en masse* but meditation is best done in solitude. Religion can be organized but mysticism is best left to the individual.

141

If we mix the mystical with the religious standpoint, the result will be confusion and misunderstanding. They must be kept apart and in their proper places.

142

Those who have touched the mystical level in what they have deeply believed and deeply experienced are much less likely to be dogmatic, narrow religionists.

143

The gulf between ritualistic religion and mystical religion is the gulf between a metaphor and a fact.

144

It would be sheer folly for even an organized form of mysticism to compete with organized religion. The votaries of mysticism are and will remain a minor group. But insofar as their challenge acts as a successful irritant, they may help orthodox religion to improve itself.

145

The Roman Catholic Bishop of Cochin told me a few years ago that he disapproved of mysticism because it could very easily lead, and had historically led, to intellectual and spiritual anarchy and was therefore dangerous. Another Roman Catholic, G.K. Chesterton, the brilliant English author and journalist, told me nearly thirty years ago that he disapproved of mysticism because it could very easily lead to moral anarchy and evil behaviour, and had indeed done so. Yet both men were quite willing to accept mysticism provided it was fenced around by the limitations and regulations, the dogmatic definitions and supervisory direction imposed by their Church.

146

It is the constant contention of ecclesiastical authorities that mystics who find sufficient guidance and teaching in waiting upon the inner light, who disregard all outward supports, expose themselves to deception and error and the Church to anarchy and disintegration. Their contention is correct enough. Nevertheless the argument is not adequate enough to prohibit the practice of mysticism altogether. For, on the first count, the mystic can be taught how to protect himself against these perils. On the second one, not many people are willing or ready to become mystics and there are more than enough left to keep the Church busy while those who are ready can still be helped by the Church.

147

This insistence on the rigorous following of external forms, together with this neglecting of the internal spirit which should be the main object of those forms, is more harmful in the mystical world than in the religious one.

148

That which religion worships as from a distance, mysticism communes with as an intimate.

149

Many believe, some suspect, but few know that there is a divine soul in man.

4

PROBLEMS OF ORGANIZED RELIGION

On criticism and scepticism

The criticism of religious truths arises not only out of its confusion of pure religion with ecclesiastical religion, but, in the case of other persons, out of a low character rather than a lofty ideal. It is then destructive and unscrupulous, taking meanings and deliberately distorting them to suit its own purposes. It is then sincere only in its selfishness and adequate only in its materialism, not only seeking all the defects of the attitude it proposes to replace but also inventing many imaginary ones. It lives by criticism and feeds on conflict. It cunningly entraps those who are so troubled by present world conditions as to have lost hope, enthusiasm, courage, and faith on the one hand, and on the other those who are so troubled by these conditions as to have become unbalanced, violent, irrational, and cruel. To both, the phraseology of conventional religion, politics, society, and economics has become hollow. To both, the feebleness and foolishness of our entire social structure have become apparent. But both are wrong.

2

Unfair and untrue criticism by sceptics may well be ignored, but too often in the past religions have failed to benefit themselves by looking into justifiable criticism from believers. This failure has strengthened superstition and weakened real religion.

3

Instead of being vexed over the rise of scepticism and indifference or grieved over the fall of religious influence, they should seek the causes and adjust faith to reason and truth.

4

If a teaching can make a man more hopeful when accepted, more peaceful when studied, and more intuitive when applied, then it deserves respect, not scorn.

5

When we speak here of the dangers of atheism and the darkness of materialism, we do not refer to those brave, intelligent men who have protested against superstitious religions and pious exploitation. That which they opposed was not genuine religion at all, but the satanic pretense of it. It is an historic and unfortunate fact that such pretense is too often successful.

6

Every man who receives the Life-Force from his inner being yet denies its existence, who is sustained by the Overself's power yet decries those who bear witness to it, sins against the Holy Ghost. This is the real meaning of that mysterious sentence in the New Testament which refers to such a sin.

7

Each person has some kind of faith; this includes the person whose faith reposes in scepticism.(P)

8

In making unfaith their faith, the scoffing have taken the first step forward out of superstition on a long road whose course will be spiral and whose end will be religious once again. But because the impulse behind this step is so largely selfish and passionate, so negative in emotional feelings and erroneous in intellectual convictions, it is a dangerous one. In getting rid of the evil of superstition, they have invited other evils, equally bad and even worse, to replace it.

9

Whether religion itself be totally eclipsed or newly revived, the fundamental truth from which it rises is always hidden deep in the subconscious mind of man. Life itself, the very drive behind the whole universe, will force the atheist one day to seek it and will give him no rest until he finds it.

10

It would be true to say that the materialism of our time is an agnostic rather than an atheistic one. People are indifferent to the question of whether there is or is not a higher power, rather than being deliberate deniers of its existence.

11

The atheists who see only the weaknesses of religion and not its services denounce it as false and injurious. They seize on the undoubted harm done by religious exploitation and religious superstition as a pretext for themselves doing infinitely greater harm by proclaiming all religious feeling to be mere illusion. They point also to the mental aberrations of individual mystics to denounce all mysticism as an even greater illusion. But to stamp out every manifestation of religious life and mystical enlightenment would reduce man to the level of the brute, albeit a cunning intellectual brute.

12

How pitiful the suggestion of Marx that religion is an invention of human imagination to enable one class—the sacerdotal—to prey on the people, and another class—the upper—to exploit the people, or the assertion of Polybius that it is an invention of society for its own protection to maintain order among men and prevent them from running amok into anarchy by following their own individual wills entirely. That it has been used for such purposes historically is correct, but the religious instinct is a very real thing and rises from a very real source.

13

The theory, based on economics, according to which religion was invented to help despoil the working class is unscientific: it is also unworthy of those who boast that they are led by reason. The very adherence to such a theory proves that they are led much more by strong emotion.

14

He alone can be an atheist who has never experienced a glimpse, or who has been caught and become embedded in a hard dry intellectualism, or in whom ethics and conscience have withered.

15

The egoistic fool, with his intellect puffed up by a little learning, sets out to criticize everything, including the belief in God. Let us be humbler, awed by the thought of the World-Mind's unchanging identity and unbroken infinity.

16

Too often a man thinks that his problem is solely personal, whereas it is most probably common to all mankind. Most men and women have or will have to face it at some time; for the basic problems of the human situation are really few, and part of the work of a religious prophet is to give guidance in a general way as to how rightly to deal with these problems. Those atheistic Communists who reject pure religion along with their rejection of sectarian religion, reject also a hand stretched out to help them. In their madness they ignore every prophet's warning against violence and hatred, against unscrupulousness and greed, and set out consciously to create sorrow for themselves.

17

The spread of atheistic movements is something to be sadly deplored. But if they are the inevitable reaction against sham religion we are forced to accept them as historical necessity. This necessity is, however, quite temporary and if atheism is put forward or permitted to remain as ultimate truth, then it becomes as morally disastrous to humanity as the falsity against which it is unconsciously opposed by the dialectic movement of racial destiny.

18

Those psychoanalysts who would stamp all religious instinct as a sexual derivation and those materialists who would stamp all religious belief as a social exploitation exhibit neither a profound psychology in the one case nor an accurate realism in the other. What they assert is only sometimes and somewhere true, not always and everywhere true.

19

The atheistic leaders of our time have tried to banish the concept of God. They have succeeded in doing so for large numbers of people, especially young people. But what is true in the concept will reappear in men's minds again, for it is eternal. It cannot be banished although it can be covered over for a time.

20

A time comes when he outgrows the elementary doctrines and popular observances, when prayer and ceremonial, scripture and asceticism have no further usefulness for him. But this does not entitle him to denounce them to the world, to destroy their place in life, or to dissuade others from using them.

21

It is wrong of those who feel they receive no blessing, no spiritual gain of peace, from a church sacrament to scorn as superstitious others who feel with joy that they do receive it.

22

"You snivelling priest," exclaimed Voltaire, "you are imposing delusions upon society for your own aggrandizement."

23

If a man believes he is nothing else than a human electrical machine, why should he pay any attention to moral character?

24

It is enough to make two statements about the Russians—first, the government in all its departments officially opposes religion; second, the highly influential Communist Party makes atheism an article of belief before membership is granted—to understand why and predict that either self-reaction or self-destruction awaits them. There may be no future also for the Russian Orthodox Church—narrow, intolerant, and materialistic as it *was*—but religion in a larger, purer, and truer sense must one day return because of the innate need for it.

25

Sceptics find one religion as untrustworthy as another because all religions are founded on belief in the existence of an Unknown and—to them—unknowable Entity.

26

The atheist who believes that morality is supported by religion to help keep the populace obedient may be partly right and partly wrong. But he falls into error if he believes that religion was invented solely for this purpose.

27

The illusionist religions, which reject all values and virtues in the world in which we humans have to live, give us little to hope for or live for. It is not surprising that most of the masses under their influence have lived a half-animal existence.

28

In Germany and Austria there were in 1933 over a million members of Freethought organizations; in Czechoslovakia in 1938 there were a million persons who declared themselves to belong to no religious body.

29

The outdated scepticism of earlier science and the moral ineffectualness of the later Church have helped those Communists who brand religion as an instrument of intellectual domination and indirectly of economic exploitation.

30

God is invoked on every side but there is no sign that he has ever been involved in our affairs, say the sceptics. If he reigns, he does not rule!

31

All too many have shaken themselves free from religious superstition without having replaced it by religious truth.

Cycles of inspiration, decay

32

The history of most religious organizations is a history of pure motives mixed with impure ones, of spiritual aspiration mixed with human exploitation, of reverence mixed with selfishness, intuition with superstition, and prayerful petition with arrogant exclusiveness.

33

History shows that nearly every religion moves through the same time-worn cycle of phases—from purity and reality and fellowship through organization and literalness and external expansion to hypocrisy and exploitation and tyranny. All religious influence historically passes through these stages of rise and fall. It begins by expressing an elementary portion of divine truth and by promoting a simple standard of human morality. It ends by opposing the truth and defending immorality. In its purity and vitality, it suffuses the hearts of its votaries with goodwill towards other men and hence draws them closer together. But in its degradation and devitalization it poisons the hearts of its slaves with intolerance towards other men and thus sets them farther apart. The declension of a religious movement begins at the point where the external organization of it begins to replace the internal feeling of it. The intuition is then gradually forgotten and the importance of funds, buildings, officials, prestige, and power rises egoistically and ambitiously in its stead. In the end the inner reality is all but lost, only its mocking shadow remains. It might be said that in its early unformed state, the movement spiritually exhilarates men but in its later institutional state it materially exploits them. It is therefore necessary to make a clear-cut distinction between a religion in its original pure form and in its later corrupt form. Time corrupts every religion. The history of Christianity confirms this cyclic nature of religion. It arose outwardly amidst bitter suffering and violent death; it began to fall inwardly amidst gilded prosperity and exaggerated pomp.

34

By "religion" is meant here not any particular one but the entire cluster of authentic sacred revelations throughout the world. No particular world-religion is referred to in our criticism. What is to be said is true of them all, although more true of some and less of others.

35

The vitality of a religion is most apparent in its primitive unorganized form, as the purity of a religion is most apparent in its apostolic phase.

36

As the inward sense of being dedicated followers of a Way, a Truth and a Life fades away with the efflux of time, so religious vision narrows, moral aspiration slackens, declarations of rigid dogma are insisted on, the abidance by a group of outward customs and rules is enforced, individuality is crushed as heresy, the zeal for self-improvement is replaced by the zeal for meddling with the affairs of others, petty differences are exaggerated, and pure creative spirituality is killed. Every established religion seems historically to pass down through such a degenerative process to a dry sterile condition. It seems not possible to keep the movement on the high level at which the prophet started it.

37

Neither the minds that gather around a prophet nor those who diffuse his influence and teaching in later centuries are likely to be equal to his own. To that extent, therefore, their understanding of him and his teaching is likely to be inferior to his own. This distance from him has the one advantage, however, that it brings them more on a level with the multitude whom they themselves wish to influence or convert.

38

Dull followers in the generations soon to come falsify his ideas, and selfish ones degrade them. Such is the disagreeable truth about every prophet's fate. Receiving the pure teaching is a sacrament but upholding its degenerated forms is a sacrilege.

39

If you realize the extraordinary length of time of the real history of man, and not merely the history which is taught in schools, you will realize also that many religions have come and completely disappeared. Why should we think that these religions which we now know must continue to exist permanently? They are only tools which are used by God so long as they are effective but thrown aside when they are worn out.

40

Time is like a river which is forever flowing onwards, which can never turn back, and which sweeps religions and races before it. This is why those who look for a triumphant and lasting revival of any particular religion deceive themselves. Revivals have occurred and will occur, but history shows how transient they are and philosophy shows why this must be so.

41

People are being deceived by the renewed vitality of some old religions, by their conversions, activities, and literature, into believing that they are witnessing a veritable and durable renaissance with a long bright future before it. This is particularly true of Christians, Hindus, and Muslims. But what are they really witnessing? It is nothing more than the dying flicker of sunset, the sudden blaze before darkness falls.

42

History teaches the same story about all the religions. They begin as faiths, freely held in the heart; they culminate as creeds, imposed like shackles upon the mind. The myth of an almost ecclesiastical infallibility is maintained by the church leaders in their own interests.

43

There comes a time in the life of each traditional religion when it becomes the enemy of true religion. History tells us this; psychology predicts its inevitability.

44

Although atheism appears when religion makes much more fuss over the appearance of virtue than over its reality, mysticism also appears when sufficient time has elapsed to demonstrate the intuitive barrenness of such decadent religion as well as the moral danger to its followers.

45

After the death of the guru, we see the hard outlines of a new sect in the making, the forming of an ecclesiastic hierarchy with new episcopate and new priesthood, the increasing disposition to detect heresy or schism and shut out those who exhibit the capacity, if not the courage, to think for themselves, the rise of personal ambitions and the seeking of private advantage. The honest, let alone passionate, pursuit of truth gradually vanishes.

46

When men transfer their faith to another religion, cult, or system of thought, it not only shows that the force behind the new one is greater than that behind the old one, but may also show that the World-Idea, which includes karma, is itself the force promoting the successful rival.

47

In those first few centuries when Christianity was a pure and vital religion, the name Christian meant one who believed in the existence of this higher power and surrendered his heart to its loving presence. The name Muslim (our western "Muhammedan") had much the same meaning in the early days of Islam's history. It signified one who had submitted his lower self to the Divine, resigned his personal will to the higher will of God. Such submission was not regarded as being only moral; it was also psychological. That is, it was to rule consciousness as well as conduct. Hence it was a difficult achievement following a long endeavour rather than a mere verbal assent made in a single moment.

48

When convention becomes stagnant and kills the living element in custom or religion, it suffocates the growing element in man's soul.

49

Creeds will come and go, being at their best the results of the working of human minds striving to comprehend divine glimpses. They are necessarily imperfect.

50

Most religions were constructed gradually, shaped by time and history. This is most true of Judaism and Christianity, least true of Hinduism and Buddhism.

51

The corruptions of religious doctrine and the conventions of religious society keep out the true spirit of the prophet behind the religion itself.

52

Little sects may become large churches. The movement towards truth may become an institution which hinders truth. The persecuted Christians of the fourth century became the persecuting Inquisition of the fourteenth. Given enough time white may turn black.

53

There are two chief justifications for the existence of a religion: (a) its influence upon the character and actions of people for the better; (b) its dim intimation of world meaning. But when a religion fails to prevent wickedness or to convince men that their existence has a higher purpose, it deserves to decline—and does.

54

The impulse which originated each existing religion has largely worked itself out, leaving stark error and pseudo-religion as its current offering. Even the error has come in the end to assume the form of an authentic tradition!

55

The visible difference between religion in its primitive purity and in its aged decadence is the best argument for the periodical need of a new religion.

56

Not only Buddhism but also Islam and Judaism originally banned the artistic representation of man's form in religious symbolism. Why? Because it commonly led to worship of idols, of the form of the human formulator of that particular religion.

57

If during a prophet's lifetime legends spring up which are only half-true or even wholly untrue, what is likely to happen after his death? This is one reason why religions are said to be based on faith.

58

The debasement of a religion usually runs parallel to the increment of its organization.

Accretions, distortion, corruption

59

A study of religious origins will reveal that much which today passes as established religion is merely accretion: it was added in the course of time. Tradition—now regarded as sacrosanct—was once innovation. It is often the opinion of later men overlaid on the Master's words.

60

The farther we get from the Prophet's time, the more difficult it becomes to discover exactly what he taught. Sects multiply in his name, each with a different doctrine. Imaginations and interpolations, distortions and caricatures become part of the received teaching. As if this were not enough, personal ambitions and institutional exploitations add to the confusion.

61

The defect in human nature which makes it stress the person rather than the power using him, the letter rather than the spirit, is responsible in part for the deterioration of religion. Let men beware of a personality worship which is carried blindly to idolatrous extremes. Let them beware, also, of unquestionably receiving ideas about religion which have been propagated by its ministers and missionaries. It is not group effort but individual effort that counts on the quest. The prophets and teachers helped people in groups and churches only because of the need of economizing their own time and energy, not because this was more efficacious. Those who quote Jesus: "Where two or three are gathered in my name, there shall I be in the midst of them" in rebuttal, are self-deceived. Words like these were never spoken by Jesus. They were interpolated by cunning priests. The populace, a term in which from the standpoint of intelligence we must include different members from all social strata from lowest to highest, is led to accept contradictions and obscurities out of a regard for religious authority which paralyses all independent thinking.

62

It is a tragedy of all history that the names of Men like Jesus, who came only to do good, are invariably exploited by those who fail to catch their spirit and do more harm than good. Formal entry into any religious organization relates a man only to that organization, not at all to the Prophet whose name it claims. No religious institution in history has remained utterly true to the Prophet whose name it takes, whose word it preaches, whose ethic it inculcates. A religious prophet is mocked, not honoured, when men mouth his name and avoid his example. No church is a mystical body of any prophet. All churches are, after all, only human societies, and suffer from the weaknesses and selfishnesses, the errors and mistakes, inseparable from such societies. It is a historical fact that where religious influence upon society has bred the evils of fanaticism, narrow-mindedness, intolerance, superstition, and backwardness, their presence may be traced back to the professional members and monkish institutions of that religion. Priestcraft, as I have seen it in certain Oriental and Occidental lands, is often ignorant and generally arrogant. Throughout the world you may divide clergymen and priests into two categories—those who are merely the holders of jobs and those who are truly ministers of religion.(P)

63

If you want the truth as it was really taught, remember that you will get from the historic official teaching of the later followers a tampered, interpolated, excised, weighted, and moulded doctrine.

64

When the truth of recompense is perverted, it becomes fatalism. Then the aspirations to evolve personally and improve environmentally are arrested, while responsibility for inaction or action is placed outside oneself.

65

More and more as I came to understand religion, to separate its truths from its fables, I discovered how the Master's teaching had been corrupted or distorted, truncated, or stressed in the wrong places. This happened more in some faiths than in others, and differently in one from the other. It happened in Judaism and Buddhism, in Islam and Christianity.

66

The theologians must take their share of responsibility for the enormous extent and power of materialism today, for their absurd squabbles about unreal or remote issues and their silly dogmatics about matters of which they can *know* nothing have repelled large numbers who seek to use their God-given faculty of reason and their capacity to observe facts.

67

There is a long distance from the rhetorical urges intended to create religious frenzy to the calm statement intended to evoke religious intuition.

68

Worse than the degeneration of doctrine has been the degeneration of ethics. A man best proves what he is by his conduct, an institution or society by its deeds. For verbal preaching may be mocked by contradictory practice. The expounders and hierarchs of religion are rightly expected to set good standards for the supposedly weaker masses, but sacerdotal cupidity and ecclesiastical intolerance, the ignoble lust for power and the ignorant hatred of other faiths, have far too often disappointed expectation.

69

The institutions, the credos, the scriptural documents even, of a religion are man-made. Even if and where they are made under divine inspiration, it may not have been present all the time.

70

What is left of a religion after thousands of years of man-handling by biased or prejudiced parties should be received with critical, independent judgement.

71

The temples and churches, the synagogues and mosques of old established religions have become empty of true spirituality, their thresholds profaned by lack of genuine interest, true faith, or real obedience to religion's dictates. The basic commandments of the founders of religion, simple though they be, are seldom given the importance they deserve. In short, the sacred name of religion is violated daily, year after year, century after century.

72

The only way to retain Faith is to regenerate it. Churchianity must become Christianity. Its failure became plain during the War, when a situation existed where the Japanese nominal followers of the peace-bringing Buddha spread murder and pillage across Asia and where the German nominal followers of the love-bringing Jesus spread hatred and aggression across Europe, in some cases with the sanction and under the blessing of their local priests and national High Priests and in all cases without a firm protest and resolute opposition by the whole weight of their organizational influence against such betrayal of what both Buddha and Jesus stood for. Here history but repeats itself. It was not the atheists who crucified Jesus but the priests. It was not the atheists who drove Buddhism right out of India but the priests.

73

People are easily deceived by the stature to which religions have grown into thinking that they have achieved assured stability. An institution which has reached great size has not necessarily reached great success. It is necessary to look beneath the illusion of numbers and the skin of popularity. Spiritual degeneration and decrepitude are still what they are even if they are spread among millions of people. When we try to understand the causes of such disintegration, we are inevitably led to the conclusion that religion wrongly understood and wrongly expounded breeds distrust, exploits ignorance, and disrupts society. How do ordinary people arrive at their understanding of a religion, then? They arrive at it through the guidance of official exponents. Therefore the latter bear a larger responsibility for the downfall of their own faith than they usually realize. They have often invoked judgement of God on others; have they ever observed how history has invoked the judgement of God on them? So far as the mission of an institution consists in assuming the austere role of a prophet and making the glowing message of such a man freely available to simple toiling folk, so far as its presence in society acts as a check on human character, which would otherwise degenerate and permit evils more serious than existing ones to spring up, it possesses something which the people profoundly need; it has a most valuable service to render for which it must live, and it can face its critics as indifferently as Jesus faced his persecutors. But so far as the institution has come to mean something glaringly different or has come to constitute a professional means of livelihood for certain individuals, merely by seating them on the chair of sanctity, or has associated itself with pointless dogmas which outrage human intelligence, it has certainly become something so unchristian and useless that the continued fall of its influence need surprise none.

74

An organization is required to transmit the services of religion whether it be an elaborate Church with three continents under its wing or an obscure sect with a single preacher located in a small room. The personnel of this organization constitute its living value, for theirs is the duty of giving right guidance to its followers. If prelates and priests understand the higher purport of religion they will slowly uplift their flock and deem it their duty to serve rather than to enslave them. For instance, they will gradually replace the notion of an angry or cruel God to be propitiated through devotional communion. If however they fail to understand this purport, they will misunderstand it. And as they are notoriously and tenaciously conservative, they will apply this quality—so admirable when it bespeaks loyalty to true and virtuous things—in wrong directions such as the dissemination of outworn, unimportant dogmas or the support of barbarous customs, untenable doctrines, false history, and worthless rites—nearly all of which do not belong to the faith in its primitive purity but are mutilations or accretions originating from the mediocre minds of ignorant interpolators or the selfish hearts of greedy interpreters. This will lead slowly to the next step, which is to use the organization primarily for their selfish benefit. When this happens the people naturally lose their faith in them as well as in the rites and dogmas, the ethical value of their religion wanes, and enemies arise both inside and outside its frontiers to bring it crumbling to the ground in the long course of time.

75

Religion as shaped by history is not the same as religion as propagated by the prophet.

76

If religions lose their original inspiration, if their texts get corrupted and their priests get worldly, it is relevant to enquire whether such deteriorations can be avoided. The imperfections of human nature warn us that *total* avoidance is impossible.

77

How many a prophet has been crucified afresh by his alleged followers who persecuted and oppressed in his name! How often has his teaching been caricatured by giving it a false application to serve personal interests or support emotional hatreds!

78

Religion is supposed to raise a man's moral quality, diminish his hatred, and curb his selfishness, but too often in history it has failed to do so. But it is not only religion that is at fault: it is also the stubbornness of man himself.

79

When a religion, suffering from decay and inertia, asks us to give reverence to tradition more than we give it to God, it fails in its own mission.

80

When the ceremonies and forms of religion have become a tangled network, when the primal simplicity of its sanctities has been lost underneath the fussy elaborations of its dogmas, it becomes sterile and unhelpful: from the highest point of view, such religion becomes irreligion.

81

If the immature are taught nothing better than the incredible and half-credible assertions, the foolish tales they have hitherto been told, why wonder that religious faith and church attendance turn into religious hypocrisy?

82

It is right and proper to continue a good tradition, to keep a spiritual inheritance from the past which has intrinsic worth; but it is not right to demand enslavement to such tradition and inheritance so that nothing new may enter or be said.

Sectarianism

83

The atmosphere of pure religion is as different from the atmosphere of sectarian organization as a natural flower is different from an artificial one.

84

Religion which wills to lead mankind into spiritual consciousness has failed to do so. Why? Because it has led him into organizations, groups, divisions, monasteries, ashrams, sectarianism, and centres. These have become the important things, not the spiritual consciousness.

85

We may honour, even revere, a place in this world, an epoch in spiritual history, a man who has been graced by enlightenment; but to depend on any particular one only is both unwise and sectarian.

86

He only has the fullest right to talk of God who *knows* God, not his idea, fancy, belief, or imagination about God. He only should write of the soul, its power, peace, and wisdom, who lives in it every moment of every day. But since such men are all too rare and hard to find, mankind has had to accept substitutes for them. These substitutes are frail and fallible mortals, clutching at shadows. This is why religionists disagree, quarrel, fight, and persecute both inside and outside their own groups.(P)

87

Since truth can be looked at from different standpoints, since it has different aspects, it is desirable that there should exist a variety of doctrines and views. Where the attempt is made to congeal it into a fixed creed, for all time, a sect is created and sectarian prejudices are introduced.

88

A sect is not open to truth: it closes the door upon what it has, will not scrutinize whether it be truth or not, will not admit new formulations. And by sects I mean groups with many millions of adherents or a few hundreds. The larger they are, the more accustomed to power they are, and the less open they are when traditional formulations no longer meet contemporary needs.

89

No membership of any church, temple, or ashram will save you if it becomes a cause of narrowing down ideas, relationships, mind—of sectarianism.

90

It is the wrong idea they have of the sect which constitutes their enslavement, not necessarily the sect itself. With a free mind they can use its organization safely.

91

Why has every historic religion divided itself into sects, why has no religious and no mystical organization yet escaped being severed by sectarianism or cut by schism? The answer can be found partly in the different needs of different types of human individuals, and partly in the imperfections and weaknesses of human character. It is because men have not risen into the full truth, because their understanding has not been freed from egoism nor their feelings from bias, that they fall into mean and petty sectarianism. In this pitiful condition, they imagine God to care only for members of their own sect and no other! The work of adverse forces seeking to pervert, materialize, or nullify the original inspired teaching must also be taken into account.

92

Those who look for an earthly heaven and spiritual millennium round the corner of the widespread adoption of some cult are sure to be disappointed. Their credulity shows they understand neither why nor how cults are formed, nor what human nature still is. That people will shed overnight their conventional forms of religious subservience on the one hand, and their selfishness and violence, their ignorance and uncontrol on the other hand, is a naïve belief which only naïve unphilosophic cults could foster.

93

It was a seventeenth-century clergyman, Christian Hoburg, who dared to publish a pamphlet, albeit pseudonymously, which contained such statements as "All Churches are sectarian" and "Christ is unknown to all the Churches."

94

All the revolts against orthodoxy, against organization, against dogma, acquire an enthusiastic following which ultimately ends up with another orthodoxy, another organization, another set of dogmas.

95

My plaint against them is that they are parrots, endlessly repeating and babbling the answers which original minds gave thousands of years ago. They are quite noncreative, and too often quite sectarian under their pretense of non-sectarianism.

96

Not only do organized religions split off into sects, but there are further splits of sects within sects.

97

There are benefits and disadvantages in old, established, traditional religions. But if the disadvantages stay too long or become too strong, they obstruct the basic purpose of religion. If their doctrines hamper religious aspiration or tyrannize over men, they are rendering a disservice. If symbols are taken too literally they may bind men to idol-worship and they may become substitutes for reality. Even an effort to propagate non-sectarian views, to cull what is good or essential from various quarters—as theosophy was to a large extent an attempt—even such a movement is likely, in the end, to become itself sectarian.

98

Schisms are found inside most religions: they are not less free from the ego's activity than politics and commerce.

99

Most blind followers of a sect do not attempt to understand the metaphysical and practical problems involved but simply take sides against the one who is being personally vilified.

100

The earnest pleas of Saint Paul could not stop dissensions among the faithful during his own lifetime: "I beg of you, brethren, be perfectly united in the same mind and in the same judgement." It has not stopped them dividing into bickering sects and contending cliques during the many centuries since his lifetime. Only when we understand the limitations of religion shall we understand why his plea was a utopian dream.

101

A religion might possibly gain universal support one day, but unless its devotees had touched and kept the philosophic level, sects would eventually appear within it to break the uniformity and disturb the harmony.

Intolerance, narrowness, persecution

102

None save Mind Itself can know what Mind is. No person can form an idea of Mind which is at all adequate. No one can create a mental picture which is correct. No one can formulate a concept which corresponds to the actuality of Mind. All results suffer from human limitations. If accepted by any religious creed they become idols worshipped in vain. If this be so it becomes clear that religious intolerance and religious persecution are evil human failings masquerading as virtues exercised on behalf of faith in the true God!

103

The notion that some sect, some people, or some race has been chosen to fulfil a special mission upon earth is a notion which is to be found in every nation that a philosopher can visit and in every epoch of history that he can study. It is a foolish notion and a recurring fallacy. It is such teaching which has kept false ideas and foolish emotions stubbornly alive. But it will persist and go on persisting because it appeals to peoples' vanity, not because it is based on any facts. Josephus lengthily argued that Plato derived his wisdom from Hebrew lore. Nowadays the Hindu Swamis tell us that Plato borrowed it from Indian lore. 'Tis all opinion, mere opinion—the truth is that the light of wisdom can shine everywhere, on any race and at any time. No single nation or land possesses primal inspiration.

104

The devotee believes that his God is the only true God, and other people's Gods are inferior or false. His ego is thus still in the way, despite high experiences.

105

So long as each institutional religion asserts that it alone has the truth, or has more truth, or more closeness to God, or that it is the most important vehicle used by God, so long will it continue to divide men, foster prejudice and ill will, even create hate, along with whatever good it is, or is capable of, doing.

106

Every man is entitled to his own personal opinion. It is his private possession. But when he wants to communicate it to others as a universal dogma or, worse, to impose it upon them as a universal faith received from God, we are entitled to remind him that he ought to keep his affairs to himself.

107

In the end the powers of karma fall crushingly upon those who, for selfish motives, have suppressed truth and supported falsehood.

108

Jesus would have been the first to realize that the love which he enjoined on his followers was essentially the same as the compassion which Buddha enjoined on his own. Yet, uninformed, or informed but biased, religionists seek to decry the Oriental teachings by proving the alleged superiority of the Occidental—as if Jesus was not Himself an Oriental! The real secret of this attempt to classify Jesus among the Occidental races is that they happen to be Occidental: in short, it is the dominance of their egos which leads to the confusion in their concepts.

109

If prejudice favouring an inherited creed denies the full truth, bias against it blocks the path to such truth.

110

All such denigration of other spiritual paths or of other spiritual tribes is as unnecessary as it is inexcusable.

111

The history of religious bigotry is associated with the history of religious persecution. If the first is denied entry, the second cannot appear.

112

The higher power bears no labels but men invent them and, later, their descendants begin to worship the labels instead of the power. Hence religious conflicts and wars: hence, too, religious ideas and atheistic movements.

113
Wherever there is persecution *within* a religion of those who differ from the ruling authority of the period, it usually covers the fact that the persecutors are greater heretics than their victims. For the Founder did not come to preach hatred and cruelty—there is enough of that in the world for God not to need to send someone to increase it—but virtue and goodwill. So the persecutors, even if successfully established and long established, are not preaching *his* message, but their own, which contradicts it.

114
The overleaping of these sectarian labels can only help the dissolving of the sectarian frictions, quarrels, persecutions, and intolerances which in the end turn into tortures, inquisitions, hatreds, and wars.

115
If we study the history of established state religions, too often we find that the priests or clergy of the religion have been able to stir up the fanaticism of ignorant crowds to persecute or to eliminate those who dare to believe otherwise and are foolish enough to state their beliefs publicly. It must be pointed out that this tendency is most pronounced among those who follow the three Semitic religions: Judaism, Christianity, and Islam, in the order of their historic appearance. It is all to the credit of Buddhism and Hinduism that tolerance is almost a tenet of their religions.

116
When the acceptance of religious faith stirs up animosity, creates hatred, and fosters persecution, it is then no better but even worse than its rejection.

117
Criticism is the inevitable karma of superstitious credulity as hatred is the inevitable karma of unjust persecution. We heard much of the persecutions of the Russian Orthodox Church by the Bolsheviks after their revolution but little of the persecutions by the same Church before the revolution. Those who understand how karmic retribution works unerringly will find the following little paragraph, taken from a leading St. Petersburg newspaper, *Novoye Vremya*, during the year 1892, very significant. Dealing with accounts given by Prince Mestcherski of certain suffering endured by the Christian sect called "Old Believers" at the hands of the Orthodox State Church, in Siberia, the paper writes: "The treatment of the Buddhists is still harsher. Says the Prince, 'They are literally forced by the police, at the instance of the local clergy, to embrace Christianity. All kinds of means are resorted to; they are captured in the woods, hunted like beasts and beaten, force even being employed with pregnant women.'"

118

What strikes us most poignantly is the absence of sympathy, of love in the widest Christian sense, for all those outside each little sect. For the incompatible difference between the lofty kindness enjoined by Jesus and the petty meanness practised by the sectarians in his name is heart-saddening.

119

Religion has hardly been successful in bringing men to the most elementary and merely negative duty of refraining from killing one another. At Ayuthia, the former capital of Siam but now overgrown by jungle, I saw a lone large statue of Gautama the Buddha sadly looking out at the ruins of the city destroyed by a Burmese army two centuries ago. And both antagonists claimed to be Buddhists! At Shanghai, I saw another Buddha statue amid the debris of a wrecked temple in the suburban district of Chapei, the scene of battle in 1937, yet both the Chinese and Japanese antagonists here were partly Buddhist, and the Buddha made non-killing a prominent tenet of the ethical code which he laid down for all his followers, for monks and laymen alike.

120

Too many men have used the word God to cover their cruelties, or their follies, or their own selfishnesses!

121

The absurdity of insisting on name-labels, the narrowness of joining religious groups, attains its summit when immortal life is proclaimed as our destiny only if we belong to a particular group!

122

The journey from the narrowness of dogma to the arrogance of infallibility may take time for a religious institution to finish, but when it is finished a further journey may begin. And that is to intolerance, totalitarianism, and finally persecution.

123

The religious temperament has its puzzling contradictions. The Holy Inquisitors would have been hurt if told that they had repudiated Christ, would insistently have asserted their devotion to him. Yet for religious reasons they broke men's bodies on the torture wheel, tied them to the stake for burning. The gentle inhabitants of Tahiti shed tears copiously when Captain Cook flogged a thief on his ship, yet for religious reasons they practised human sacrifice while their priests killed their own children. A Jewish king in the early pre-Islamic Arabia persecuted those among his subjects who were Christians. Later Christian kings in Europe persecuted their Jewish subjects, while Muhammedan kings in the Middle East persecuted Jews and Christians alike!—all in the name of religion.

124

If the *Bhagavad Gita*'s statement means anything at all, it means that we ought to be tolerant to other people's worship, to the form in which they symbolize God. Pliny understood this very well when he wrote: "You are going to Athens. Respect their gods."

125

When conversion is followed by enthusiasm, this is natural, often inevitable. But when it is followed by fanaticism, the convert is put in danger and others even more so.

126

It must be remembered as a mark against exaggerated valuation of, and trust in, religious institutions and religious authority, that the Holy Inquisition not only burned or tortured infidels but even the Franciscan Brothers, good Christian Catholics who happened to become victims of the prejudice of one particular medieval Pope.

127

It is very difficult to find any organized form of religion which does not exaggerate its own value, or denigrate other forms.

128

A truly universal outlook would be free from the subtle possessiveness which wants to draw others into one's own particular fixed cult or creed and keep them there forever chained. This kind of religious attachment is not less binding, not less shutting-in to horizons, than those other, and more obvious, forms of personal, material, or emotional attachment.

129

Fanaticism is often allied with superstition using the authority of religious texts, customs, or traditions. So it passes unscrutinized and self-deluded, too often preoccupied with externals and trivialities.

130

They hold their opinions too ferociously to hold them on a basis of reason.

131

The sacred foolishness of those teachers of the path of religious devotion who reject all the other paths is still better than worldly foolishness, but it cannot form part of the philosophic ideal.

132

Where doctrine is elevated above life, it inevitably leads by a series of fatal downward steps to guarding itself by persecuting those who hold opposing views. This happened in medieval Catholic history. It happened in early Reformation history, and it happened even in American Presbyterian history.

133

The Romans, who brutally slaughtered the assembled Druids in Britain, were symbolic of the retribution which eventually punishes priestly fanaticism and of the challenge which inevitably comes to priestly superstition.

134

They are fools who do not know that though they burn ten thousand heretics this day, God will implant the same idea, if it be a true one, in ten thousand minds tomorrow.

135

So long as ecclesiastical leaders falsely teach their flocks that their own particular religion is the only one acceptable in God's eyes and that all other religions are bereft of His grace and light, so long will religion continue to give birth to strife instead of peace, prejudice instead of tolerance, hatred instead of love.

136

The Israelites did not have a monopoly of the "God's Chosen Race" belief. Milton, in his "Areopagitica," proclaimed that "God reveals Himself first to His Englishmen." Hegel, however, asserted that it was the divine decree for the Germans to lead the world. And, until Hitler's hordes smashed through their land, not a few of the mystically inclined Poles passionately believed that theirs was to be "the Messianic race." In the Far East, the Japanese cherished similar beliefs until American bombs initiated a process of revisionary thinking.

Naïve sentimentalists or distorted thinkers manufacture romantic impressions about their race religion history or country. Some dream golden-age, Eden-idyllic fantasies about the past or future that have no basis in fact. Perverted wishful thinking asks for illusion—and gets it!

False theory breaks down before personal experience of the present fact as it actually is. This is often quite painful but how else is the real truth to be established when the sayer of it is disregarded or disbelieved?

Superstition

137

We need religion, yes assuredly, but we need it freed from superstition.(P)

138

When the faculty of reverence is diverted from its proper object—the divine Power—and perverted to a base one, it becomes superstition.

139

Theological arguments which use empty words without mental substance, sacred names of non-existent entities, can be classified as superstitious.

140
Do not lose your wits over religious fables which were intended to help ungrown minds—that is, most minds—or to soothe and comfort half-grown ones needing new interpretations and better explanations. There never was a "Golden Age" where all people lived happily together, nor is there now an "Iron Age" where they all live miserably together.

141
Every superstition is a truth corrupted. Therefore when we say that religion ought to purify itself, it need in many cases only turn its superstitions inside-out to set itself right!

142
Superstition is a costly luxury which the mood of this age cannot afford to set up; it is harmful to genuine religion and useless to genuine devotees. False thoughts are so plentiful that they lie ready to the hand of man; hence he finds it easier to pick them up without effort, rather than to exert his own mind to independent thinking. In the absence of the inspiration of true religion men will accept the degradation of untrue materialism, though it is noteworthy that the younger clergy have abandoned the teaching about the creation of the universe and the origin of man which they had inherited.

143
There is no excuse for such unthinking complacency. If the powerful suggestions of tradition and environment persuade us to believe certain things heedlessly, to go on believing them throughout a lifetime is to shame and deny our thinking power. Much of what passes for religion is mere superstition. Religion raises us whereas superstition degrades us. We must seek the true face of religion under the false mask of mere spiritual legalism and hollow theological casuistry. We must cast away the accretions and have no use for what is sectarian and self-seeking and superstitious in religion.

144
Scepticism is the inevitable swing from superstition. The moral code that comes with the superstition goes with it, too. This is the worst danger of false religion.

145
There is a very real difference between right faith and superstitious faith.

146
Where religion lets itself support the superstition which, if allowed, grows like a parasite upon it, it begins to practise deception upon itself and imposture upon society. It lets go of Truth at its own peril and to its followers' harm.

147

Because millions of people share a superstition does not make it a truth.

148

The perversions of truth have been numerous. But the materializations of truth have been even more numerous. In Japan the guru of a certain Zen sect gave thirty blows with a wooden stick to an unfortunate disciple. This beating was considered to be a precious opportunity for the disciple to gain Satori (Enlightenment)! In India many a pious person or holy man who arrives on pilgrimage in Benares is told by the priests there that by bathing in the River Ganges and putting his head under the surface of the water, he will then gain spiritual enlightenment!

149

When a religious dogma prevents people from searching for the true cause of their distressed condition—whether it be personal trouble or physical disease—and hence from searching for its true remedy, it is nothing more than a superstitious belief masquerading as a religious one.

150

Puerile superstitions have intertwined themselves with every religion, or even taken their place along with golden wisdom.

Dogma

151

We have only to study history, true history, which requires a wider reference than is customary, to discover how religious dogmas develop, how private imagination and personal opinion go into their creation. They are human, not divine.

152

There are religious dogmas which are quite unreal, others which are quite inane; yet, this said, the general residue of religious teaching is solidly and substantially true. Some of it may be wrapped in mystery, which those who want to go farther can unravel with the help of mysticism or philosophy. All of it contains a perceptible message of uplift, of hope, of comfort and of guidance.

153

In the old days metaphysics fell asleep through too much reclining in the arms of my lady Church; if it woke up with the Renaissance that is because this theological flirtation was stopped.

154

False doctrines promulgated in logical form under the title of theology, false beliefs bequeathed from generation to generation and holding crude superstition: these we can well do without, but when getting rid of them, exercise discrimination, take care not to get rid of the true doctrines which theology contains and the worthy beliefs which tradition passes down.

155

It is more prudent to assert that you have some of the truth than to assert that you have the fullness of it.

156

Every organized religion must have dogmas. It could not be what it is without them. Even its first basic assumption—that there is a God—is a dogma. There is nothing wrong in its adherence to dogmas. What is wrong is adherence to false dogmas, to those whose truth is denied by the realities of existence and life.

157

Where any of the doctrines of a religion are unable to survive the tests of reason, examination, factuality, and evidence, they hide away in a part of the mind where the tests cannot get at them. This is called "resting on faith." It is a way of defending them from certain defeat. Instead of permeating the whole outlook, they are compartmentalized.

158

It is a more truly religious man who does not put his religion in fetters, manacled to hard dogma, cruel canon law, and intolerant practice.

159

These creeds and systems are interesting as records of human faith and thought, imagination and invention, but they are useless as paths to salvation. They may give comfortable hopes to their devotees but they do not repudiate the ego which fosters illusions and creates sufferings.

160

All these mystical symbolisms and metaphysical allegories become in the end obstructions which get in the way of a clear understanding of the truth.

161

It is possible that the minister of an orthodox church may be a truly enlightened individual. How, then, it will be asked, can such a person coordinate the abstract Truth of Philosophy with the popular belief of the divinity of Jesus Christ? One answer might be that he privately interprets "divinity" in a special way but publicly follows the orthodox interpretation, because of what he believes to be the necessity of making use of the best available means for leading mankind nearer to Spiritual Reality. Outwardly he might elect to appear as a representative of, say, the Church of England.

162

If the metaphysical foundations are unsound, we need not expect the moral superstructure to be safe from criticism.

163

Where faith has a false basis and a wrong direction, it may one day weaken or even collapse.

164

Those who have the heroism to turn away from outworn creedal dogmas are the real followers of their Redeemer or prophet, the real believers in God.

165

When petty quibbles about surface details and trivial idiosyncrasies of behaviour are placed on a level with the highest ethical standards in importance, we must assert our critical judgement. When external formalities are made to matter just as much as internal virtues of character, we must use our sense of discrimination.

166

When religious faith is inculcated as an attitude towards the unknown and unseen, it is rightly inculcated. But when it is advanced as the right attitude towards the irrational and impossible, it is wrongly advanced.

167

To teach the masses one thing publicly but to believe something very different privately is an attitude which has a great and grave danger—it tends to obliterate the distinction between a truth and a lie.

168

Religious teaching will be all the better when it is freed from life-prisoning and mind-fettering dogmas.

169

A belief for which there is supporting evidence ought not be put in the same category as an unfounded belief.

170

Some religious doctrines are stiflingly narrow and create a desire for the fresh air of reason and science, humanitarianism and compassion.

171

The doctrine of relativity may be applied anywhere and shows that there are no unquestionable creeds, no indisputable dogmas.

172

We can absorb the religious spirit, its emotional reverence for and intellectual fidelity to the Higher Power, without absorbing its commitments to crystallized dogma.

Institutionalism, exploitation

173

I do not know of any organization or institution which attempts to work for mankind in a religious or mystical way which has not its weaknesses, its limitations, and its evils, for remember, every organization and every institution is in the end composed of human beings and in them there is always this dual age-old conflict of good and evil.

174

In the beginning an organization is "pure," that is, seeks earnestly and sincerely to perform its proper function. In the end, its original ambition realized, its success established, it deviates into other purposes. It becomes power-hungry, tyrannical, selfish, more interested in its own perpetuation than in serving the early ideal, more eager for membership and money than in the common welfare. And this is as true of religious as of political organizations, trade unions, and commercial associations.

175

Without some organization there may result intellectual anarchy, moral indiscipline, and emotional chaos. It is also true that the man who accepts a traditional form, joins an organized group, or enters an established church benefits by the help of the tradition or institution. Hence, we are not against teachers and groups which fulfil or even only sincerely strive to fulfil these legitimate expectations. But neither in past history nor present experience are absolutely sincere institutions ever found on earth, although they may be found on paper. It would seem that to set up an organization is to introduce fresh sectarian limitations; that to institutionalize a revelation is to render null and void its spiritual inspiration; and that to totally submit faith, reason, and will to one man is eventually to invite exploitation and accept superstition.

176

The degradation, falsification, commercialization, and exploitation which men, making use of institutional religion, have made of a prophet's mission, speaks clearly of what these men themselves are made. The fact is that they are not fit to be trusted with the power which institutionalism gives them. Religion is safer and healthier and will make more genuine progress if left free and unorganized, to be the spontaneous expression of inspired individuals. It is a personal and private matter and always degenerates into hyprocrisy when turned into a public matter. The fact is, you cannot successfully organize spirituality. It is an independent personal thing, a private discovery and not a mass emotion.(P)

177

When religion identifies itself with an ecclesiastical organization and forgets itself as an individual experience, it becomes its own enemy. History proves again and again that institutionalism enters only to corrupt the purity of a religion.(P)

178

No religion will keep its original purity or inspiration if it fails to keep out its organization's own ambitions and thirst for power or wealth.

179

In religion inspiration dwindles as organization grows. Men come to worship the visible organization itself instead of the Invisible Spirit—that is to say, to worship themselves.

180

Institutional forms render their service by helping a body of teaching to survive, by giving permanence to a tradition, by enshrining and preserving valued memories.

181

Any ecclesiastical organization or any prophetic person who claims *exclusive* knowledge of higher things, *exclusive* communication with heavenly spheres, goes beyond whatever real mandate of authority it possesses. None has the right to make such a claim. Instead of honouring the organization, the latter is dishonoured by it, by its arrogance and falsity.

182

Beware of religious institutions. They are dogmatic, self-loving, unable to transcend their limitations.

183

How would old established ecclesiastical circles, of whatever creed, receive their prophet today? A little knowledge of history, of human organized society, with a little practice of imagination would soon supply an answer.

184

The true Church is an invisible one. It exists only in the hearts of men.

185

The true Church is an interior and invisible Idea, not an exterior and tangible institution.

186

Every attempt to organize religion harms it. It must be spontaneous if it is to keep its purity, personal if it is to keep its reality.

187

No system, no doctrine, and no organization can hold truth without squeezing out much of its life.

188

A religion must be transmitted from generation to generation, so its ministers and scriptures come into being. The purity of its doctrines must be maintained: so sects heresies divergencies reforms and dissents are resisted.

189

It is somewhat sad to observe, in the study of history, that the very purpose of creating an organization to preserve, to guard, and to keep pure a new religion too often becomes with time the very cause of the opposite condition. Additions are made to texts, truths are cut out from them, while the organization regards its own preservation and power as more important than anything else.

190

If there is any lesson which history can teach us, it is that absolute power always corrupts. Such unchecked domination proves in the end, and in the religious world, as bad for the dominator as for those dominated. It breeds weaknesses in him and retards the spiritual growth of his victims. This is not less but even more true when it is exercised by a group, for the risk with the creation of all institutions and organizations is that everything is thereafter done more for the sake of the institution or the organization than of the principle it was embodied to spread. That this risk is very real and almost unavoidable is proved by all history, whether in the Orient or the Occident, whether in ancient times or in modern. It is not long before a time comes when an organization defeats its own ends, when it does as much harm as good, or even more, when its proclaimed purposes become deceptive; external attacks and internal disputes increase with the increase of the organization. No religious organization is so all-wise and so all-selfless that, being entrusted with totalitarian power, it will not yield in time to the temptation of abusing that power. It will practise intolerance and paralyse free thought. The history of every religious monopoly proves this. Thus the individual's need to follow whatever faith he pleases, to think and act for himself, to find the sect that suits him best, is endangered by the monopoly's demand for blind obedience and blinder service. The organization which begins by seeking to spread truth ends by obstructing it. The inheritors of a message of peace and goodwill themselves bequeath hate and bitterness.

191

We do not need to be much learned in the chronicles of both Asiatic and European history to note the unfortunate fact that as religious institutionalism spreads and strengthens itself, religious inspiration shrinks and weakens itself. The original impulse to authentic communication with

God becomes gradually changed into an impulse to selfish exploitation of man. The climax comes when the ecclesiastical organization which was intended to give effect to the sacred injunctions of a seer or prophet not only fails to do so, but actually tries to prevent its members from trying to do so themselves. His purpose is perverted. His teaching is degraded. Thus religion, which should be a potent help to mankind's evolution, tends to become and does become a potent hindrance to mankind's evolution. For such a degradation the karmic responsibility lies heavily on its paid professionals.

192

History has shown that a monopolistic religious institutionalism invariably falls into spiritual degeneracy and inevitably ends in intellectual tyranny. The setting up of autocratic government, episcopal authority, and professional clergy is sooner or later followed by a train of corruptions and abuses. Jesus denounced the religious institutions and religious hierarchy of his time, and drew his followers out of them. Yet hardly had he passed from this earth when they began, in their atavistic reversion to traditional ideas, to recreate new institutions and new hierarchy. If it be asked why the spiritual teacher who knows the harmfulness of these ideas is not heeded by those who believe in him, the answer is first, that belief may be present yet understanding may be absent and, secondly, that the innate selfishness of men finds too easy an opportunity for exploitation through such ideas to miss falling into the temptation of propagating them. Were the truth of any religion really clear to people, all the bitter controversies and bloody persecutions of history would not have happened, and all the innumerable commentaries of theology would never have been written to prove what was so plainly evident.

193

While religion is intimately associated with ecclesiastical organization, it will be intimately associated with money and power needs also. In such a situation it can no longer remain true to its purer self but must inevitably deteriorate.

194

The harmony among religions is a fact, but unfortunately it is not a fact easily seen nor frequently supported by religious organizations in whose interest it is to oppose it.

195

If you wish to know one sign of the difference between a true religion and a half-true or untrue one, remember that the latter seeks power over men whereas the former never does.

196

Institutions are necessary to society; it is only when they become tyrannical or dictatorial that they serve evil purposes.

197

Where religions have failed it is through their institutionalism; where they have succeeded it is through whatever individualism still remained in them. Romantic illusions may keep these institutions alive, but the darkening gloom of our times shows that human welfare cannot be preserved by illusions.

198

"Thou shalt have no other God before Me!" warns the Biblical Commandment. Yet the ignorant still give to the Limited—an organization or a man—the worship which they ought to reserve for the Unlimited—God—alone.

199

For those who have little time and less inclination for the work of study, reflection, meditation, and aesthetic appreciation—namely, for the toiling masses—an attempt is made to accommodate their needs and limitations by providing them with popular religion. But human nature being what it is, sooner or later the institutions and organizations associated with religion become either semi-commercialized or turned into instruments of power. A modern Japanese thinker even went so far as to criticize them by accusing them of "stealing Heaven's Way."

200

An institution or organization is only a background for the men who work in it. It helps or hinders them, elevates or degrades them, but they are the more important factor.

201

We must separate, in our minds, institutional religion from personal religion, the outward structures they have built up historically from the inward atmosphere they have created individually. Persecutions and pogroms come more often from the first, yet without these institutions how would the texts, the teachings, and the reminders be passed down?

202

To give religion a merely institutional significance is to take the incidental for the essential. The churches and sects of religion are its least part; the influence on character and intuition is its greatest.

203

The doctrine of an apostolic transmission of divine authoritative power through human ministry and episcopates is one instance of such false but widely accepted belief. Man will never be saved by any official church.

204

When an organized religion places power over humanity before service to humanity, it loses its way; and when it becomes an instrument of persecution, it prepares its own eventual doom.

205

The sects seeking to get adherents, to commit new members to their dogmas or opinions, are not for him. For nineteen hundred years priests, captive clergymen, and pale theologians have been deliberately endeavouring to persuade people that the kingdom of heaven is to be reached within a professional organization called the Church, *and nowhere else*, as though they could be saved in a mass. Had the ecclesiastics honestly said that their organization existed to help people find the kingdom within themselves and therefore had a perfect right to receive support, nobody could cavil at them. But they have deliberately transplanted the emphasis in their own interests, and followed their master only from the safe distance of a sermon.

206

The organization which gathers round such a prophet, especially after he has left his body and cannot control them, may become an obstacle and, to some extent, even a traitor to his real value and true message.

207

When a religion organizes itself to conquer the world, the world instead conquers the religion. History tells us this time and again.

5

COMMENTS ON SPECIFIC RELIGIONS

Ancient religions

In the Mithraic cult of the Middle East, the sun was united with the Earth, fertilizing it. We call Mithraism a religion of sun worship, but the hidden God behind it was the real object of worship. Yet the final end of all the solar activity—fertilization—was not forgotten. Spirit and Matter became one, daily life of the human being became his spiritual life. Then only did the results of this fertilization—the living crops—appear. Zen *sahaja*, natural *samadhi*—this is what they mean.

2

The sacred places where Druidic priests worshipped were chosen according to knowledge—geographic, astronomic, religious, ritualistic, symbolic, and magnetic.

3

It is something in history to ponder over that in the Alban hills, a few kilometres from Rome, there was once a Temple of Orpheus where, 3000 years ago, the Orphic mysteries were celebrated, where Orphic religion prevailed with its tenets of rebirth, fleshless diet, the quest, and inner reality. It is arguable whether the two other religions which followed it in that area have brought a better message.

4

The dualism of the Persian religions—Zoroastrianism and its kindred Mithraism—is ethical but the dualism of Indian religions is metaphysical. These are two quite different definitions. But in the case of the Christian Manichaeans, whose doctrine Saint Augustine followed for a time and later renounced as a heresy, there is a strange mixture of the ethical along with the metaphysical.

Bahaism

5

Granting the fact that an incarnation has been given a special mission by God which will affect millions of souls and that he must therefore be charged with special divine power, I am unable to see in what way he can be superior to other prophets who have come into close communion with God. It would seem that he would still come within the category of Muhammed's well-known statement, "I am only a man like you." Yet the status which the Bahai faith seems to assign to Baha'u'llah is nothing less than the divinity in the flesh. How can it be possible for even Baha'u'llah to have communed with the uncomprehensible, inconceivable Godhead directly if, as he says, that Godhead is beyond all human conception? Surely no man, however saintly he may be, can escape this limitation?

6

The criticism of the differences in my books from some of the teachings of Baha'u'llah and Bahaism are partly due to misunderstanding and partly to actual divergence. The latter arises, I believe, from the fact that in these days the Bahai faith stresses organization and institutionalism, whereas in the early days it was like primitive Christianity and primitive Islam, free from these later accretions. Although history shows that every religion has followed this course, I still consider the essence of religion to be mystical and not institutional.

7

To the extent that the Bahai faith has dropped the mystical side for the organizational, to that extent it has suffered inwardly however much it has expanded outwardly. In this it follows the history of most religions, which grow and spread their influence in the world at the cost of the purity and spirituality which should lie at their core.

Buddhism

8

Buddha, this godless yet godlike man, rejected most of the Gods in the Hindu pantheon, threw aside the sacrifices, rituals, prayers, and priestcraft current in his time. Buddha is worthy of every admiration because he showed men of rational temperament, men who find it difficult to believe in a God according to the common notion and who are not devotional by nature, how to attain the same spiritual heights as those do who believe and who are religious. He made room in heaven for the rationalist, the free-thinker, and the doubter of all things. Again, those whose familiarity with the Buddha is limited to his statues, with their characteristic attitude of contemplation, often form the wrong notion that he spent his life in inactivity and meditation. On the contrary, he lived strenuously, like Saint Paul, teaching and travelling incessantly, limiting his meditation to not more than an hour or two every day. If Buddha formulated the tragedy of existence, he did not permit his resultant pessimism to paralyse him into mere apathy.

9

That Buddha, like Jesus, wanted to reach the populace, there can be no doubt, except in the minds of the prejudiced. First, he went to extraordinary, most unusual lengths to repeat his teachings from different aspects, so as to make his meaning clearer. Second, he recommended his monks to use the ordinary dialects of simple people whenever they preached Doctrines which were both complex and subtle in themselves and needed simplification anyway.

10

If Buddha did not, like most of the other Indian teachers, affirm the existence of God, he did not deny it. But the reason for this position can be found in his environment, in the Indian scene—too much superstition masquerading as religion, too little respect for reason and fact.

11

The Buddhist can readily get rid of the charge of atheism by referring to the doctrine of Buddha concerning "Amitabha"—"the infinite light of revelation . . . the unbounded light, the source of wisdom and of virtue, of Buddhahood." It corresponds to the Christians' "Logos," the Word, "the true Light that lighteth every man that cometh into the world."

12

It is amusing irony that the very rites and ceremonies which the Brahmin priests tell the masses will advance their spiritual progress were denounced by Buddha because they hinder spiritual progress!

13

It is not the prophet, not the seer, but the men who come later who found churches, establish organizations, and turn religion into a vested interest. Thus when Buddha was dying his attendant disciple, Ananda, was alarmed, according to the ancient records, and said: "The Master will not pass into Nirvana before he has arranged something about the Order?" The Buddha replied: "It would be one who would say, 'I will lead the Order' or 'The Order looks up to me' who would arrange something about it. But I did not think so. Why then should I make any arrangements about the Order?"

14

Although Zen was founded as a Buddhist sect, the Zen attitude toward humanity is far from the Buddha's, with his tender compassion. When I discussed the menace of another global war with a distinguished Japanese Zen leader, he coldly remarked that if it removed most of mankind it would be a good riddance of a nasty race! He felt no distress at the suffering involved. He seemed to look down at it as if the war were a little quarrel among little insects like destructive termites.

15

It is true that the Buddhist way is one of self-discipline and the Christian way one of discipleship, but this is so in appearance only and not in the highest schools of both ways, which are naturally esoteric; the latter approach each other much more closely. The Mahayana school, for instance, has many parallels with the Christian and has as much right to be regarded as authoritatively Buddhist as has the Southern School of Buddhism.

Christianity

16

If you want to learn what Christianity originally was, you must put together the pieces of a jigsaw puzzle, collecting them from the Protestant, the Roman Catholic, the Greek Orthodox, the Manichaean, and the Coptic Churches. Then you must add further pieces from the Alexandrian, the Russian, and the Syrian traditions.

17

The close relation between new faiths and old ones can still be readily traced in Asia, where the vestiges of the latter continue to flourish by the side of the former among aboriginal tribes. It can be traced, too, in African Egypt and Ethiopia, in lands even more accessible to the Western student of theological archaeology, by anyone who cares to venture into the Coptic churches and to examine the Coptic tradition. He will find it in many of the externals and theoretic dogmas of the simple primitive cult of Coptic Christianity, a cult whose propitiations of burning incense, unimpressive mass, cymballed music, and priestly blessings are replete with characteristics that were familiar enough to the Pharoahs. Christianity, which arose in a region midway between the Orient and the Occident, significantly moved westward first and then spread across Egypt, where it silenced the superannuated sanctuaries more quickly than in any other land. In fact, although the worship of Jesus was so quickly triumphant in this colony of Rome, it did not officially supplant the worship of Isis or Jupiter until the reign of Constantine two and a half centuries later.

18

The fact that Jesus was born in the Near East and not the Far East gave the religion that bears his name a geographical advantage and a historical familiarity which help to explain why Buddhism and Hinduism spread in all other directions except Westward. And the fact that the European-American mind is much more outward bent and much more attached to the personality than the tropical-Asiatic mind explains why Christianity had much more affinity with and appeal to the first mind.

19

Christ spoke to the Roman world, and to some of those parts of the Near East which were then included in the Roman Empire. Buddha spoke to Asia. Saint Paul and Timothy felt themselves "forbidden of the Holy Ghost to preach the Word in Asia." In short, Christianity is for the West since its civilization grew out of the Roman one.

20

The spectacle of so many sects, hostile to one another, teaching dogmas that Jesus never taught, raised probing questions in the minds of many Orientals who spoke to me about the matter.

21

The Oriental ideas about the spiritual goal and methods of spiritual practice as they appear in most Buddhist and many Hindu sects are not likely to appeal to Occidental seekers. For they seek the dissolution of human personality, either through merging into an inconceivable Unity or through disappearance into an indescribable Nirvana. As a rolling wave dissolves in the sea, as a wisp of smoke vanishes in the air, so does the separated human life enter its ultimate state. Few Westerners are prepared to renounce their own identity, to sacrifice their inborn attachment to personality for the sake of such a vague goal—one moreover which seems too much like utter annihilation to be worth even lifting a finger for! To most Westerners it is unpleasant and terrifying to look forward to such an end. For who gains by this goal? The man himself certainly does not. The absolute Unity remains what it was before; so it does not gain either. If we enquire why the goal is acceptable to the East but objectionable to the West, the answer will be partly found in the latter's religious history.

By seeking to perpetuate for all eternity the same human personality in the spirit world, too many orthodox church interpreters of Christ's teaching have misinterpreted it. For Christ taught in several clear sentences the giving up of self, the denial of personality. These theologians reduced this preachment to the practice of charity and unselfishness but kept the ego as something precious, whereas Jesus asked not only for these moral virtues, but for the immeasurably more important metaphysical-mystical virtue of rooting out the ego itself. The moral improvement of character is thus substituted for the metaphysical destruction of ego.

22

A more sympathetic study of the other Oriental religions, especially the Indian ones, would help Christians to understand better, and interpret more correctly, their own religion.

23

Those who support the sending of missionaries to foreign countries do so in the belief that they are honouring Jesus' words, "to publish the gospel to all parts of the world." But the world in his time and speech is not the world of our own. This is shown clearly by Saint Luke's allusion to it: "In those days there went out a decree from Caesar Augustus that all the world should be taxed." Here "world" stands for the empire of the Romans. It does not include the Chinese, for instance.

24

Those who are not yet ready for any other than a Christian path would not be helped by Hindu and Buddhist literature.

25

The gospel story is not a transcript from the Indian story of Krishna, as some of the critics suggest. A few of the similarities are certainly there but the explanation is a mystical one.

26

The British soldier and sailor all unwittingly prepared the way for the British dissemination of Bibles throughout the world. The British Empire has been one of the carriers of the Christian scriptures.

27

Those who know little about the origin, history, and development of religious opinions would receive a shock, or rather a series of shocks, if they were to inquire into the development of the principal Western faith and if they were able to lay hands on the necessary material. But let them be warned that they will not find such material in official sources. There was once a very voluminous literature which contained the true Christian teaching, but it was completely exterminated by the official church as soon as the latter's triumph over these so-called heresies was established. How ironical it is that reincarnation, the very doctrine which is today regarded as a heresy—that is, a perversion of true doctrine—was originally regarded as an authentic one!

28

A Christianity once existed which has long been condemned and forgotten but which is as much nearer the true teaching of Jesus as it is nearer him in time. We refer to the school of the Gnostics. Their defeat and disappearance does not lessen their truth. The Gnostic Christians of the third century accepted the pre-existence and earthly rebirths of man. With this doctrine there came naturally the law of recompense, which warns men to heed more carefully what they think and do, for the results will return equally and justly in time.

29

Gnosticism was banned as heresy by the Church Councils, its books destroyed, its teachers persecuted. The truth in it was banned indiscriminately along with the untruth. The differing sects in it were treated all alike. That during Rome's luxurious and decadent periods some sects said we should give to the spirit what is of the spirit and to the flesh what is of the flesh, and practised immorality, is true. But it is also true that other sects presented the struggle by good forces against the evil ones in most dramatic and forceful terms. Its recognition of the meaning, place, and importance of "Light" seen in meditation was a prominent and valuable feature of Gnosticism.

30

Those Christians who were closest to Jesus' time did *not* set up two categories—those in the world and those living withdrawn from it outwardly, with the second as superior. It was monks who later made this division.

31

In the third-century pagan world, hate and envy prevailed. The propertied classes were hated by the poor, the working classes hated the middle class, while the army was hated by all classes. Christianity preached love to neighbours, philanthropy towards strangers, as the Emperor Julian, though hostile, reluctantly admitted. It would bring these mutually antagonistic classes together, as the Emperor Constantine saw. Pagan religions and philosophies revealed this, too, but failed to practise it, had become cold. This is one of the reasons, apart from the alleged visionary experience of a cross in the sky, which persuaded Constantine to adopt Christianity as the official religion of the Roman Empire.

32

The early Christians who spoke of being "in Christ" were men whose intense faith, devotion, and sacrifice had lifted them into the Overself consciousness.

33

The most intellectual early Christians were those who abode in Alex-

andria, for it was the greatest Mediterranean centre of philosophical learning before Christianity appeared in it.

34

Chrysostom was born about 347 A.D., Tertullian about 150 A.D. The
latter was the first of the Church's Latin Fathers, well educated, a brilliant
scholar, with numerous friends among the learned, and a wide knowledge
of the tenets teachings and customs of his time.

35

The Christian thought of Clement and Dionysius is close to the higher
philosophic thought of the Indian Rishee-sages. And this is not surprising
when we remember that they got their ideas in Alexandria, which was then
having regular commerce with India.

36

Was not the most important council of all the Council of Nicaea, which
finally settled Christian doctrines for a thousand years, but which foolishly
dropped the tenet of metempsychosis as heresy after it had survived the
first five centuries of *anno domino*; was not this great gathering composed
of men who mostly could neither write nor read, who were stern extreme
ascetics, fanatical in character and behaviour, narrow, intolerant?(P)

37

When the Romans ruled there were few means of communication, and
even these were slow and difficult. Nor were there newspapers and printed
books. The message of Jesus spread along Roman highways but even so
took a few hundred years to find its hearers.

38

In symbolism of the Trinity, God signifies the World-Mind, Christ the
Overself, and the Holy Ghost the Kundalini.

39

"I indeed baptize you with water unto repentance; but he that cometh
after me is mightier than I, whose shoes I am not worthy to bear: he shall
baptize you with the Holy Ghost, and with fire."—Matthew 3:11.

Water has been universally used in sacred literature as a symbol of the
emotional nature of man. The fluidic character of both is the reason for the
use of this symbol. What John called "baptism by water" means therefore
such a cleansing of the dominance of his animal passions, desires, and
appetites. Consider further that it is the tendency of water always to flow
downwards in obedience to the law of gravity, and then note the striking
contrast of the tendency of fire, whose sparks always soar upwards. "Baptism by fire" therefore refers to a process on an entirely higher level, not to
a merely negative purification but to a positive illumination. Light is one
of the effects of fire. The work of John the Baptist was concerned with

clearing the way for Jesus, the light-bringer, a preparation that was not only outward and annunciatory but also inward and purificatory. John collected "followers" for Jesus; they were the masses who sought physical help and emotional comfort in their troubles and sicknesses. But Jesus, when he came in person, not only gathered all these followers but also collected "disciples"; they were those who had no necessity to seek such help and comfort, but were attracted by the Spirit itself as it shone through Jesus. They were the few who received the baptism of fire and by the Holy Ghost. Many people became followers but few became disciples.

There is, further, a difference between the baptism by the Holy Ghost and the baptism by fire. The baptism by the Holy Ghost arouses and awakens the potentialities of the dynamic Life-force, raising its voltage far above the ordinary. This process is usually accompanied by thrills, ecstasies, or mystical raptures. It represents the first awakening on the spiritual level as it filters through the partially cleansed emotional nature. Baptism by fire represents the next and highest stage after this event, when, the thrill of the new birth has subsided and when, in a calmer and steadier condition, the intelligence itself becomes illumined in addition to the feelings, thus balancing them.

40

In Love (for the highest) in Wisdom (of intuition and Intelligence) and Power (the creative energy of the Overself) we find the inner meaning of the Holy Trinity.

41

Christianity's most solemn ritual—the celebration of the Holy Eucharist—which symbolized membership by a common meal, was partly taken from the pagan Mysteries. This is the part that was brought in during a later century.

42

The public confession of sin, "sharing," as one cult calls it, is unnecessary and leads in the end to exhibitionism. The Roman Church, in the wisdom of many centuries, rightly has made the confessional a private affair, heard only by the priest, and even then the penitent only half-sees him through the gauze curtain in the booth.

43

It is a misunderstanding of the benefit of confession or sharing, which has value only if done with or before a superior person. With others it is futile or harmful.

44

Ought he not enter the confessional booth to denounce not only his sins but also his stupidities? Is it not a duty of human beings to display intelligence?

45

That the cross was a mystical symbol used in the ancient Mysteries was known to Plato. In the *Republic* he wrote: "The just man, having suffered all manner of evils, will be crucified."

46

Jesus did not construct any religious system or creed, Church or doctrine. Others did that when he was no longer there to say Yes or No. Christianity was therefore *their* creation, not his.

47

A reincarnated Jesus appearing in our century would not be able to recognize his original message in the orthodox sects of our time.

48

These three doctrines—now turned by the Church for its own motives into three dogmatic superstitions—were, and are, sacred truths before being corrupted. They are the Crucifixion, the Atonement, and the Trinity. Trinitarianism in its present form was never taught by Jesus. It came into Christian doctrine centuries after he lived.

49

Nowhere does Jesus in the publicly available sayings included in the New Testament order the formation of a clergy or preach the need of a church or lay down a ritual. Instead he gave clear precise instruction on how to pray: "Enter into thy closet, and when thou hast shut thy door, pray to thy Father which is in secret." But Paul thought differently and founded what is now misnamed Christianity.

50

The Inspired Prophets did not themselves personally organize religion. What they did was to give inspiration to those individuals who could respond to it. It was their followers, men acting on external methods, men with limited capacity, who organized and eventually exploited institutions. Indeed these followers had no alternative but to use such methods, not possessing themselves the inner depth of the prophets. The truth is that nobody has ever really organized religion, for it is a private and personal affair between each individual and his God. It is men who have organized themselves for purposes derived from their religious feelings—which is not the same as organizing religion itself. All such organizations are man-made throughout, as is also the authority they claim. There is no record in the New Testament speeches of Jesus that he himself appointed apostles. Consequently we must believe that they appointed themselves after he was no longer present among them. The basic claim of certain Churches to be a continuation of this apostolate has no ground to support it in Jesus' own statements. It is because of this claim that the Catholic Church does not theoretically recognize the right to freedom of worship on the part of other religious organizations, although in actual practice it gradually found it expedient to grant that right on practical grounds. "My kingdom is not of this world," declared Jesus. We may easily identify to which world these institutions belong, which were later organized in his name, by noting the official status which they secure in "this world." This explains the historic opposition occurring at times between the true spirit of Jesus and the worldly behaviour of his Church. It is regrettable that most people confuse an institution with the man upon whose name it may be built. There is no indication that Jesus ever wanted an organized church, but there is every indication that it was his followers who wanted it and who made it. Unfortunately, the masses do not understand this but are easily deceived into thinking that they are in touch with Jesus through his Church when in reality they are not so at all. To find Jesus they must go deep into their own hearts. There is no other way.

51

Search all the words of Jesus and you will not find the word "religion" uttered once in reference to what he was teaching. It was a way of positive living, although men have turned it into a mere social convention.

52

The truth about Jesus and about his teaching is hard to find today. For it is buried under a man-built mountain of deliberate falsification and superstitious accretion.

53

Jesus is honoured in every Christian Church by name, by chanted hymn, and by carven figure. Why does it not also honour his tremendous teaching that the kingdom of heaven is within man himself, not within the church?

54

The great Galilean was put by God among very little men. What he told them was beyond their comprehension, so they emotionalized it, sentimentalized it, organized it, and produced an all-too-human and undivine thing.

55

The severe impact of Jesus' phrases, stripped of embellishment and free from rhetoric as they are, shows up the lengthy lucubrations of official religionists for what *they* are.

56

Nowhere in the parables, nowhere in the spoken words of Jesus is there any teaching showing that he wanted an ecclesiastical hierarchy established or that he instituted a system of sacraments.

57

The so-called Holy Inquisition was quite unholy and more akin to those who persecuted the early Christians than to Christianity itself.

58

When men become enslaved by their religious symbols to the extent that they are willing to murder other men for them, or even to imprison them, when this slavery blinds their better sight and renders them fanatically intolerant of all other views, Nature deems it time to liberate both— the first from their sin, the others from their suffering. When ecclesiastics become intolerant and forget the first virtue of all religion—which is goodwill towards other men—and when they begin to persecute good men who are unable to agree with them, they not only put others in danger but also themselves. Jesus is one authority for this statement, for he warned all mankind that they would reap the circumstances sown by their conduct. Another authority is the ever-open bloodstained book of history. A good deal of true Christianity burnt itself out in the medieval fires which its more ardent advocates lit for each other and for those unfortunate infidels who knew nothing more of Christ than his name.

59

When the earth was regarded as flat, it seemed plausible to believe that God was a super-Person somewhere out in the heights of space, separate from His universe and beyond its limits. The philosophers of Alexandria never accepted this view and were later persecuted by those who did— ignorant religious fanatics.

60

The figure of Jesus has been molded into fictions by credulous, imaginative, or professionally interested priests—fictions that were acceptable to the marvel-loving taste of posterity. But no marvel could be greater than what he taught—the entry into the kingdom of heaven, which is nothing else than a conscious return to the true nature of man. Thousands of theologians have scrutinized his personality and estimated the worth of his teachings, but most of them have deluded themselves because only those who have come within the orbit of a living sage can possibly understand him or his words, in their truest significance. Jesus made an impact on the spiritual life of the West, but that impact has never been properly evaluated because it cannot be perceived in the light of Church organization but somewhere else—in the hearts of men. Although he did not properly belong to our own planet, he gave us the emphatic assurance that we too might win his realization and attainment; we too might uncover our true selves and enter the Light. Professors come and write their academic footnotes to his work, but he must be viewed for what he was—not the organizer of a Church but the planter of living, unseen seeds that fertilized in their own special way in the nature of Western man. He owed and demanded allegiance to no particular sect or school, and he paid fealty to no earthly master. He stood out only under the auroral light of divinity which shone down upon his life. He descended like an angel to dwell in the tabernacle of flesh at a time when religious life was but a guttering candle.

61

Jesus emanated love, Jesus brought truth, and Jesus incarnated forgiveness.

62

Whether Jesus was merely human or really divine is a question which may worry others but which does not trouble me. He had something to communicate and did so. He had affirmation to make, a gospel to give which supported so many people for so many centuries. That men have demeaned his message, exploited his person, and twisted his words is regrettable but, men being what they are, expectable. It is good that he came, for clearly they needed him.

63

Whether we put Christ's telling Truths into hard syllogisms and heavy intellectual dogmas which enter the mind or simple but noble phrases which are felt in the heart, we must accept them.

64

Most Christian churches and sects have claimed a spiritual monopoly. The main foundation for this claim is the sixteenth verse of the third chapter of John where the Evangelist says that Jesus is "the only begotten son of God." But nowhere in the New Testament does Jesus himself make the same assertion. On the contrary, he went out of his way to tell men, "The works that I do shall ye do also," thus refusing to put himself in a unique separate and unattainable species, which would make it impossible for other men to imitate his example or hope to attain his understanding.

65

The belief that Jesus was specially created, as no one before or since has been, is unacceptable. The belief that Jesus was one among the other great souls invested with special power is both acceptable and reasonable.

66

"Why callest thou me good?" asked Jesus. "There is none good but one; that is God." If these words mean anything, they mean that he is still a human being, however close and harmonious is his relationship with God, and that he is not to be deified.

67

When Jesus declared that he was the Way, he spoke as the infinite Christ-self in every man, not as the finite person Jesus. He meant that whoever sought God, the Father, had to come through this higher self, could not find him by any other channel. This only was the Way.

68

The Sermon on the Mount is truly representative of Jesus' teaching. It holds first place in the literature of the world; it contains the essence of practical Christianity expressed as finely as is humanly possible.

69

Jesus' Sermon on the Mount is not merely a pretty speech. It is a discipline. Therefore, it is only for his disciples. The masses who seek benefits or follow convention, not being ready for the effort, cannot be called disciples.

70

When Jesus told his adult hearers that they had to become children before they could enter the kingdom, he made what must have sounded an astonishing assertion to them. What did he mean? How are we to interpret and apply his words? There are two ideas worth noting here. First, a child enjoys living. Second, a child thinks, feels, and acts spontaneously. Both these factors are combined in its direct awareness of life, untrammelled by hesitations or obstructions imposed from without and unfiltered by colourings or opinions imposed from within.

71

I had heard from different sources—Hindu, Buddhist, Nestorian and Indian Christian—of this legend which is current in the Western Himalaya region and in Chinese Turkestan, that Jesus came as a young man to India and spent several years there before returning to Palestine.

72

We hear much of Jesus' being the friend of sinners and outcasts. But the fact was that he was also the friend of good people and society's supporters. It is true to say that his mission was chiefly to the populace, the common people, but that did not mean that he was hostile to those classes whose grammar and diction were superior and whose possessions and status were higher.

73

It is hardly credible, to those who understand, that Jesus ascended quite literally and physically "to heaven." This assertion can be credible only to those who ignore Jesus' own statement that "the Kingdom of heaven is *within* you," those who look to the *sky* for its abode. For the same reasons, Jesus' second coming is also not to be taken literally, visibly, and physically, but inwardly as an experience in the heart.

74

Christ's supposed despairing exclamation on the cross, and also his last uttered words, "My God, why hast thou forsaken me?" have been wrongly translated, according to the Nestorian Christians, one of the oldest sects, whose Bible in the Aramaic language in which Jesus spoke gives the phrase as: "My God; For this was I kept," meaning, "This is my destiny."

75

It is one more of life's singular paradoxes that such a man as Jesus, who incarnated essential goodness, who would not wish to inflict the slightest hurt on any creature, who came here among men to be appreciated, even revered, so that they might draw the return back-flow of spiritual life-current to revive a materialistic world, met so much insensitivity. So many saw nothing superior in him but denigrated him, attacked him, vilified him, and sought his death.

76

It is utterly impossible to find in the first drawings, carvings, or pictures of Christ any reference to his suffering on the Cross.

77

The orthodox view of the Bible is untenable, according to philosophic tradition. It is really a collection of books written in different centuries by men on different levels of inspiration. It mixes half-history with myth, and legend with allegory and poetry. The tribal memories of the Hebrews are put on the same level—which is a mistake—as the inspired revelations of their seers and the Mystery teachings they learned in Egypt and Chaldea. The orthodox view of Jesus is equally dispelled by philosophic insight. The man Jehoshua, who was the real figure behind the legendary one, lived a hundred years before the supposed date. Although much of the teaching associated with his name in the New Testament is actually his own, not much of the life there given is actually historical. The narrative in its pages is partly an allegory depicting a disciple's mystical journey ending in the crucifixion of his ego and partly an excerpt from Jehoshua's biography. There was no violent death, no physical crucifixion in this biography.

78

We need not torture our reason to accept these parts of the New Testament which seem incredible. If we give some of them an allegorical meaning, as being taken from the mythology of a mystery cult, and reject the others as the results of deliberate tampering with the text, as obvious interpolations, we shall be able to justify all the more our faith in the credible parts. For with them is interwoven the genuine historical narrative of the real life of the man Jesus. The result is a mixed composition, where the Annunciation and Crucifixion are not to be taken literally, but Jesus' preaching and his disciples' apostolate are. The biographic Jesus must be separated from the symbolic Christ, for the one is an earthly figure and the other a mystical concept.

79

Consider how vain, how puffed-up these mortals be when they declare that nothing less than the One Infinite Power—the Absolute Itself—deliberately incarnated as man to help them. Surely if it had such intent it would act more in accord with its own laws of progressive development and send here another mortal but a more advanced one. Such a man could be found on a more advanced planet. And this is what happened. Jesus came here from a higher planet. There was no need for God to intervene directly.

80

Benedict de Spinoza's mathematical mind led him to put into apt mathematical symbol this same criticism: "The doctrine that God took upon Himself human nature I have expressly said I do not understand. In fact, to speak the truth, it seems to me no less absurd than would a statement that a circle had taken upon itself the nature of a square."

81

There are a number of alleged portraits of Jesus, some passed down traditionally and others made in our own time by psychic means. They are not in agreement with each other. But this contradiction is resolved when we understand that each is the fruit of the artist's own idea. They are imaginative conceptions.

82

Jesus was not an ordained minister, yet his preachments have outlived many centuries. He was only a layman, yet he brought more reverential feeling for the higher power to more people than thousands of clergymen combined.

83

Jesus said: "Except you eat the body of the Son of Man and drink his blood, you have no life in you." In the Aramaic idiomatic and colloquial language the phrase means: "endure suffering and work hard." Also, "Eloï, Eloï, lämä säbächthänï," could not possibly mean, in the case of a man so advanced as Jesus was, "My God, My God, why hast thou forsaken me?" In the Aramaic common speech it becomes clear, for there it means, "My God, my God, for this (destiny) I was preserved."

84

There has been much miscomprehension of Jesus' proclamation that the kingdom of God was immanent. It did not refer to a future event but to a present fact; it was not prophetic but Vedantic. The kingdom is "at hand" always; immediacy is its correct attribute.

85

Not once in all his recorded sayings did Jesus ever refer to, or use the word, Hell.

86

Jesus is the Greek transcription of the Hebrew name Jehoshua. Christus is Latin, Khristos in the Greek, which is a title meaning "anointed," as Buddha, meaning "enlightened," is a title, and Gautama the name.

87

During the course of my studies I have been shown three portraits of Jesus which seemed to be immeasurably more authentic than the oversentimentalized, utterly unrealistic ones which the Western world self-deceptively takes so seriously. Yet all three were sufficiently different from each other for each to present a different aspect of his personality. The first was a drawing quickly made by Jacques Romans, a clairvoyant friend who died when he was nearly 100 years old. I do not know what became of this portrait. The second was an oil painting by another clairvoyant, Boyin Ra, which his widow showed me in their Swiss home. The third is a fresco in the Assembly Hall where Canons meet in Chapter of Monastery of St. Mark, Florence, by the Dominican monk and visionary Fra Angelico. In the drawing, the aspect shown was that of a man in absorbed communion with his Father. In the canvas it was a man confronting the world fully possessed by the strength of the Spirit. In the fresco it is the Christ of the Crucifixion, extraordinarily sad—for the human race. Thus the first typified Prayer in depth, the second, divine Power, and the third, mysterious melancholy, Pity. Yet they were of a *real* man, not a fanciful one.

88

In ancient Rome as in modern Europe, in Attica as in America there were, and are, humanists who reject religion as such but concede its usefulness in restraining the baser expressions of human character. If they cannot denigrate Jesus, they deride his spiritual message. They may accept him as a good man, as an ethical teacher, but not his revelation that God *is* and that man may commune with Him.

89

Jesus went to the length of denouncing as hypocrites those who were outwardly faithful in performing religious practices, but who were secretly sinning in thought.

90

Christ's mission was addressed to the common man with limited intellectual attainments. I have said so in my book *A Search in Secret Egypt*. That is why he did not publicly teach the metaphysical truths.

91

James, the brother of Jesus and an Apostle, was a vegetarian. But the theologians and historians ignore this fact which was testified to by the Judeo-Christian Hegesippus, who lived in the century following and had contact with the Palestinian circles of the Apostolic time. Moreover Hegesippus asserts that James had been brought up in this way since childhood. Does this imply that the family circle was vegetarian?(P)

92

The first need for Christian theology is to separate the teaching of Jesus from that of the unfortunately canonized Paul, who never even met him and who began to organize a Church, spread a doctrine, and formulate an asceticism of his own. This gained power and prevailed far too long, being the chief contribution to keeping people from the true Christianity.

93

If Paul had not busied himself with turning Jesus' inspiring message "The Kingdom of Heaven is within you!"—meaning it is within you *NOW*—into an ascetic message of long-drawn war against the carnal body; if he had listened better and learned more from that flash which lighted his road to Damascus, instead of returning to the bias and prejudice of his innate nature, he might have given history a higher, less Judaic, version of Christianity.

94

Some of the statements of Saint Paul are on a religious level and are very questionable; others, on a mystical level, are representative of his own but not of general experience; while still others, on the philosophical level, as in his remark to the Greeks about the Unknown God, are quite confused. But he was used to spread Christianity despite this, because of his fervent missionary temperament; and so his preachments were mainly effective and serviceable to the cause, even though they led in the end to a vast organization which was never mentioned, desired, or suggested even once by Jesus.

95

It must be said, and said quite plainly, that the Western and Near Eastern worlds would have had a better history, and Christianity would have had a stronger foundation, because truer, if Saint Paul had never been converted but had remained a Jew. For the vision on the road to Damascus, although a genuine one, was totally misinterpreted. It was a command (to stop persecuting Christians) of a solely personal nature; but he went much farther and not only began the construction of a new world-religion but shifted its emphasis from where Jesus had put it (the kingdom of heaven within men) to Jesus himself, from faith in the Christ-consciousness to faith in a crucified corpse.(P)

96

The apostle Bartholomew preached in India—this is stated by the Early Church Father Jerome, and by Eusebius in his *Ecclesiastical History*. Others add that he also taught in Persia and Egypt.

97

Quote from Saint Paul: "In Him we live and move and have our being." In Mind we have God, man, and the universe. All are of Mind, pure Being, pure Consciousness, so in Mind we humans live, move, and have our being. Is not this a mentalistic statement equivalent to the religious statement of Saint Paul? The fact that the saint arrives at it through his own personal experience and that the mentalist arrives at it either through his own deep reflection or personal revelatory experience does not alter the identity of the basic idea.

98

Pantaenus, who went as a missionary to India in the very early Christian times, was not an ordinary missionary: he was a Gnostic, a Christian mystic.

99

When pure religion descends upon the earth and makes its way among men, two things will happen. It will dissolve the false belief of the populace that they already possess it, and it will receive the opposition of religious institutions with pretensions to represent it. It was Saint Paul who started Christianity on the road which turned it into Churchianity. But he derived his Christian knowledge at second hand. He knew less about the work which Jesus sought to do on this earth than about the work which he himself sought to do. He is the true founder of the Christian Church, its first great propagator, but he is not the truest interpreter of Jesus' message. It is the Church's personal self-interest, however unconsciously present, which has made the apostle Paul the most praised Christian teacher and the most frequently mentioned one in all the sermons and writing of the clergy. Never having met Jesus, he should not be blamed for never having fully understood Jesus' teaching. The grave consequences of this misunderstanding appeared later in the form of obstacles which interposed themselves between Jesus and his true work, and which succeeded in diverting and distorting it. They were organization, dogma, hierarchy, and literalness. Where Jesus tried to create Christian individuals, Saint Paul tried to create Christian groups. This opened the door to hypocrisy, externalism, materialism, ritualism, priestcraft, persecution, and deterioration. The realizable kingdom of heaven within man had to give way to an unrealizable kingdom of God on earth. The way back to true religion must therefore lie through making a fresh start with new ideas and a fresh approach through individual self-development.

100

Without Paul, Christianity could never have had any future in Europe and would have remained and died in obscurity. Paul brought it to Greece and Rome and put it into formulations that reached the non-Asiatic mind.

101

That Saint Peter was the proper successor of Christ, with all that this assertion entails for church and bishop, is at least debatable.

102

Saint Paul had passed through the initiatory revelation given by the Greek Mystery schools, and the results show in his writings.

103

The Catholic Church is nearer to philosophy than most Protestant sects. Its mystical meditations, ascetical disciplines, metaphysical activity, and secret doctrine are some points of contact, despite its ritualism and anti-mentalistic theology.

104

Reverend C.O. Rhodes: "Protestantism makes no provision for the contemplatives and loses much as a result."

105

The contrast between the Catholic and Protestant missionary in Asia is striking. The latter has divided his allegiance, part to wife and family, part to mission. The former is free and fully devoted. The Protestant carries the double burden—family welfare and mission welfare.

106

What is your attitude towards the Pope? This is a question I am sometimes asked. My answer is: I have much respect for him as an individual. I believe he is a man who lives in prayerful fellowship with spiritual forces. I might even be willing to accept the claim that, historically and legally, he is the successor of Saint Peter, but I have not studied this point. Unfortunately, I am unable to respect His Holiness as an institution, for I am unable to accept the claim that he is the Vicar of Christ on earth. Christ's true church is not built with hands and his representative is to be found by each man in his own heart alone. [We are uncertain to which pope this para refers.—Ed.]

107

I am equally unable to accept the Roman Catholic doctrine that true saints have existed only within the Roman church and that all others are impostors, lunatics, or self-deceived.

108

Although I personally do not belong to this or any religious organization, I sympathize with Quaker ideals, respect the Quaker ethos, and admire the Quaker individual. But although the Quaker form of worship is quite lofty from the religious standpoint, it is not lofty enough from the mystical one. Its silent meditation is good, but its congregational meditation cannot attain the profound depth possible in private and solitary meditation. Moreover, its expression in uttered speech of what "the holy spirit moves us to say," although helpful from a religious standpoint, is a hindrance from the mystical one. For it disturbs the individual concentration.

A community which has always been told by its rules that the corporate form of worship is the primary and necessary one cannot leap suddenly into the blinding glare of full truth. It has to travel first from the quarter-truth to the half-truth, and so on. The Quaker method of group meditation is such an advance. It represents a loftier view of the meaning of worship because it shifts the emphasis from outward sacrament to inward holiness, from swallowed creed to quiet "waiting on the Lord." But from the true mystical standpoint, this group form is only a concession to traditional human habit and gregarious human weakness. Nevertheless, if anyone feels that membership of a religious body is essential to him, then I would recommend him to join the Society of Friends, or Quakers, as they are more popularly called. Not that I am satisfied with all their doctrines and methods, but that I consider there is more honesty and more safety amongst them, less exploitation and less insincerity than amongst any other religious denomination I know. That there is no paid class of professional clergy in the Society of Friends is undoubtedly one of the factors which contribute to this purity.

109

When Pope John announced his project for a convocation, it was a history-making piece of news. His prophetic vision showed him the need for his Church to rethink, renew, reactivate, and reinspire inside itself, not only its own body but also outside in its relations with the other Churches. The Vatican Councils which followed the Ecumenical movement are signs of the times.

110

The Eastern Orthodox Church allows the lower ranks of priest to marry, but not the higher ones. This is because the fathers considered celibacy a prerequisite to enlightenment. "Acquire chastity," enjoined Saint Ephraim, the Syrian, "that the Holy Spirit may come to dwell in thee." (The latter's writings are much read in the Mount Athos monasteries, which helps to explain why women are forbidden to visit them.)

111

What the Methodist finds at his church through group singing is not quite the same as what the Quaker finds at his Meeting-house through group silence. The one method is purely emotional, the other is passively intuitional. Both Methodist and Quaker are uplifted but there is a difference in the quality of the result.

112

Luther carried out the work for which he incarnated—the purifying of a once great religion from the selfishness and sinfulness and commercialism which had made it a hindrance that spoiled its helpfulness.

113

If men like Cardinal Newman, T.S. Eliot, G.K. Chesterton, and Graham Greene turned away from Protestantism to Catholicism despite their brilliant minds, it was not in quest of the truth but *to escape from truth*. They were poets at heart and in the Holy Church found satisfaction for their feelings. The beauty of its ritual, the mystery of its dogma, and the music of its chants appealed where intellect resigned itself to incapacity.

114

Whereas the Greek Orthodox Church gives its liturgy the primary importance, the Protestant Churches give it to the Bible.

115

The younger Luther learned much from German mystics, but the mature Luther rejected them. What he eagerly absorbed at one time he completely discarded at another time. What was truth earlier, he called "vain fantasy" later.

116

The Calvinist's stubborn ascription of salvation wholly to grace is as extreme and one-sided as the yogi's ascription of it to self-labour. It is not less extreme than the Calvinist view of fate, with its iron hardness.

117

Jesus said that the kingdom of heaven is within us: he did not say that the Church is within us.

118

Christianity in its beginnings was a mystical religion. Its only hope of recovery from the ailments which afflict it now is to return to the road it has deserted.

119

They need not look beyond Christ and Christianity for these verities but they must learn to understand Christ and interpret his message on a deeper level than the professional hierarchies have been able to do.

120

The only way in which the individual can find Jesus today is to seek for him within his own heart by the means of constant prayer and study, together with the faithful carrying out of his teachings in all daily life.

121

The initiated early Christians understood well enough that the Christ was no other than their own higher self, the Overself. This was true then; it is true now. The Christ-Babe must come to birth in a man's own heart before he can become a real Christian. The true Christian, as distinct from the merely nominal one, feels this force which enters his heart, but it is something very different from, and much superior to, mere emotion.

122

The woman of deep Christian piety who has striven to follow this path knows well that in the Christ-Self within her heart she has her greatest treasure. Its Presence is the God she is to worship. She will have learned in the past the mysterious value of tears—tears of spiritual yearning, as well as tears of worldly grief.

123

The Church that Jesus actually founded was not an ecclesiastical organization, complete with its credos, liturgies, rituals, robed prelates, and imposing buildings of its own, but a deeper awareness of being and a better outlook on life. It was therefore an unseen Church, laical rather than clerical.

124

The message of Jesus, which was so largely a call to repentant deeds and changed thoughts, is needed today by us all much more than it was needed by the Jews of his time.

125

The noble life of Jesus inspires sensitive men as few lives have done. The benign sayings of Jesus afford them matter for heartfelt ethical reflection during the peace of eventide. The terrible sufferings of Jesus have taught his weaker kindred how to bear their own personal misfortunes with strength, courage, and dignity. The true followers of Jesus have spent great sums and given much food, clothing, shelter, and education through varied praiseworthy charitable enterprises.

126

There are several matters which are not dealt with by the personal teaching of Jesus. Is it not proper therefore to regard them within the general spirit of his teaching? And where there is only a single uncertain mention of such a matter, is it not safer again to interpret it within the light of that same internal spirit rather than within the letter of mere external logic? If we do this, we will find it impossible to give to the word "church" the meaning which the materialistic mind historically gives to it. The true Christian church was an invisible one.

127

When religionists realize that Jesus' simple and eloquent sayings are more important to them than Jesus' unhistorical and less significant doings, and when they begin to look into the inward mystical experience which found expression in those sayings, they and their cause will gain much, while the dissensions and schisms, the rivalry and dispute among their churches will grow less.

128

Is it not heresy to the orthodox to proclaim that potentially every man can know, and unite with, the Christ-consciousness, and thus in effect *is* the Christ-self?

129

If the teachings of Jesus, for example, were correctly interpreted, if the teachings of the churches which use his name were freed from the ignorant accretions and veiled materialisms which he never taught, the Western people would then be so effectively helped by their religion that it would undergo an intellectual rebirth.

Hinduism

130

If the Roman Catholic faith teaches that Salvation is the highest and most desirable aim in human life, the Hindu faith teaches that freedom from rebirth is such an aim.

131

Religion teaches mythology as historical fact. The Hindu holy book *Vishnu Purana* tells of a king who massacred the male children in his country in a vain search for the divine Krishna, whose fortunes, it was predicted, would menace his own. The Jewish scriptural tale of the infant Moses and the Egyptian scriptural tale of the infant Osiris escaping from exactly the same danger are significant. We have here versions, different in time and altered by time, of one and the same event, whose original is lost in the prehistory of Central Asia. Or, alternatively, we have an equally ancient myth whose inner meaning needs to be fathomed.

132

The Hindu religion does not have congregational worship. Its temples are for the individual devotee. Its priests serve him alone, not a group of devotees.

133

Coconut is a sacred fruit, used in many or most Hindu religious ceremonies. It represents the human head, hence bloodless sacrifice. It is believed to be the only fruit without seed.

134

The study of comparative religion shows that Hinduism's "Divine Mother" is simply the Creative Energy of the universe. The name and form are merely symbolic, but have been taught to the simple masses of a pre-scientific age, being better within their grasp.

Islam

135

Sheikh Al-Alawi: "The acts of worship were prescribed for the sake of establishing remembrance of God." Here a Sufi teacher puts in a short pithy sentence the chief service of most religions.

136

Non-Islamic people react with horror and contempt when they learn from history that those who rejected the Islamic religion when proffered to them by invading armies were then given an ultimatum: "Die by the sword or become a slave for life!" But the background to these incidents needs to be seen. The Arabia of Muhammed's time was inhabited by semi-savage tribes: Islam was originally an attempt to lift them forcibly to a higher, more civilized life, and a higher view of religion. That Muhammed's followers later tried to impose Islam on more developed peoples, especially Christian and Hindu people, was wrong.

137

During the minutes of prayer, Muhammedans the world over turn concentrically in the direction of Mecca. The physical unity which they thus achieve is a fit emblem of the spiritual unity which all men will one day achieve—for all must eventually turn toward the Overself.

138

Christian Europeans who came into contact with the Saracens and learned some Sufi truths and practices started the Rosicrucian movement. The rose was a Sufi metaphor for the mystic exercise (meditation in some form). The Cross was added by these Europeans.

Jainism

139

Jain meditation is for self-contemplation or for purifying ideas and emotions or for loving and reverencing an ideal still beyond us, an ideal embodied in some historical sage but which is realized for the time being through mental union within oneself.

Judaism

140

Christ came as an obscure prophet, teacher, avatar (call him what you wish) and did not attain sufficient fame to be written about in any of the contemporary Roman imperial histories. Yet this obscure man's teachings became known throughout the world. And yet he was repulsed by the Jews, who in turn were repulsed by the people with whom they lived. Why did the Jews turn away from him? Was it not because of their failure to recognize the stronger light which he had brought them? And was his failure not due to their excessive nostalgia in looking back to the times when they were a free nation? Was it not due to their excessive fidelity to their ancient religion, to their lack of flexibility?

141

The synagogue at Nazareth which expelled Jesus and the synagogue at Amsterdam which expelled Spinoza—are these not symbols of the failure of official religion to raise itself above its own selfishness and take up its true mission? Are they not reminders of its inner bankruptcy?

142

The Jews, whose original prophet-seers must have comprehended the meaning of pure Spirit, who were forbidden to make any graven images for themselves, have made several in the form of the spirit-suffocating letter of their Torah, their Talmud, their Old Testament, their traditions and customs. All this, intended to uplift and purify, not only failed to do so but prevented them from recognizing Jesus for what he was.

143

An unpublished paper on the history and solution of the Jewish problem by P.B. gives the spiritual meaning of the mission to humanity of the Jewish people, their opportunities and failures in the past, why they were persecuted, and the great opportunity which will come to them to close their whole tragic history and enter a new, happy phase—if they will follow the advice given to them. Had they accepted Jesus two thousand years ago as a prophet from their own line, they would have saved themselves much misery. Now it is a mockery that Jesus is not followed even by so-called Christian nations. It is too late (and no longer timely) for the Jews to accept Jesus. Where, then, are they to look? The problem is stated and a solution attempted in this paper. This is the only one that would be successful as well as the only solution that is divinely commanded. [To date, this paper has not been located.—Ed.]

144

Both Buddha and Solomon were not stupefied by their royal luxury: each noted the sad side of life. "The heart of the wise is in the house of mourning; but the heart of fools is in the house of mirth," bemoaned the Israelite.

145

It is interesting to note that the philosophic ideas of the French eighteenth-century Enlightenment writers got their basic thought from Spinoza's critiques of the Hebrew Bible, despite their personal dislike of the Jews themselves. Voltaire was decidedly anti-Semitic.

146

YHWH, in Exodus 3, was the name given, to Moses, by that Presence which spoke to him out of the bush, and its derivation followed—the Hebrew root for *being*! That it became the narrowed concept of a tribal anthropomorphic god—Jahweh—is the inevitable historical consequence; that is what the tribe could take and be satisfied with.

147

Once I wandered into the prewar Ghetto of Venice—a small and uninviting quarter where the Jews were formerly made to live by law, and where a few still resided because they were too poor to live in a better place. I thought of this dark race, its long and painful history, and the words of Charles Lamb rose in my memory: "The Jew is a piece of stubborn antiquity compared to which Stonehenge was in its nonage." I saw the Wandering Jew shambling through the centuries. I pondered on his meaning. And these were my thoughts:

They could not altogether escape their strange destiny, which took them out of their native land and forced them to wander though half the world. It was their own stubborn conservatism which brought them among strange peoples, still clutching tightly to their own worn-out creed and not as missionaries of Jesus' loftier development of it. Thus instead of bringing light as they might have done, had they responded to the sacred call, they brought merely physical goods, for their cosmopolitanism found its full scope in creating and financing the import and export trade of many countries.

In a curiously distorted and obviously inferior manner, the Jews have played a historic role which is an indirect reflection of the higher role they could have played as the first wholly Christian nation. They carried earthly goods to the different nations when they might have carried unearthly ideas.

The legendary story of the Wandering Jew has a profound esoteric significance. Even the Jewish claim of being a chosen race also possesses a similar significance, albeit it is one which the Jews themselves have failed to grasp. If they are no longer a chosen race, it is for them to reflect why this is so.

The more cultured among the early Christians understood that the Overself—whom they called Christ—was the real object of their worship, the ultimate goal of their mystical endeavour, and that the man Jesus was but its Voice—like those other voices with which the Word periodically breaks its silence for the guidance of bewildered mankind.

6

PHILOSOPHY AND RELIGION

Differences, similarities among religions

The genial tolerance which affirms that all religions express something of the truth is justified. But whereas some express only a little, others express much of it.

2

The esoteric traditions have come down from remote antiquity into a large part of the Oriental and Occidental hemispheres. In most cases they were well guarded. A thorough study of them shows that they hold many dissimilarities. If some of these are due to the changes which are inevitable from one century to another, or in transposition from one climate to another, others are clearly due to irreconcilable standpoints and contradictory revelations.

3

The differences exist, and in great number, but they are mostly on the surface. The agreements exist and concern the more important matters; they are mostly at a deep level.

4

If some forms of religion are sensuous, if others are austere, all forms are expressions of some aspect only and hence incomplete.

5

In most of the creeds, cults, and systems there is some truth, a little in one, more in another, but also some error or some limitation of outlook. This is why they are all in disagreement with one another.

6

This cacophony of different and conflicting religious teachings may turn one man away from religion altogether but another to deeper and more detailed study of them.

7

We may try to make religions more tolerant by pointing to their points of agreement: this is laudable. But what is gained by ignoring or belittling the points of difference?

8

Different religions are or should be different attempts to lift mankind out of materialism.

9

Because they are different approaches, this need not mean they are antagonistic ones.

Comparative study, practice

10

No little coterie or large sect may rightly claim the sole knowledge of God, or the sole communion with Him. The very claim cancels itself out quite automatically, the mere statement of it is contradicted and refuted by the large volume of evidence gathered together in the studies of Comparative Religion, Mysticism, and Philosophy.

11

The well-informed observer, scholar, traveller knows that each cult, religion, sect, movement is but one of many. It contributes what it can to truth but it has no right to claim that it alone has all the glory of truth, or that no other has any truth. There have been insights in widely scattered groups in widely different centuries.

12

To search widely as well as variously in the records left by those who seem to have some insight is a wise procedure. How much better than remaining imprisoned in the limitations of a single geographical culture, a single period of thought! How much more likely to lead to broader, truer understanding of life!

13

His religious feeling should be broadened by comparative study of other faiths. It should be wide enough to take them in amicably even though he demurs at some of their tenets or deplores some of their history.

14

The subject of comparative religion, born in the previous century and developed in our own, attracts attention from the curious but serious study from the earnest. It is a fit and worthy field for questers, who should widen it to include comparative mysticism and metaphysics. But they should study only the best in each system and, annually, the best of the best. The worst is there, but let others, non-questers, wallow in it.

15

He will become truly religious if he ceases to remain sectarian and begins to take the whole world-wide study of religious manifestations for his province.(P)

16

Whoever limits himself in his search, faith, and acquaintance to a single book—the Bible—limits the truth he finds. Such is the position of those sects with narrow outlooks like the Lutheran Church, the Calvinists, the Jehovah Witnesses, and several other churches. They silently proclaim their own lack of culture when the bibles, texts, hagiographs, and recorded wisdom of all lands, all historic centuries, and all languages are today available or translated or excerpted.(P)

17

If anything will ever show it, the comparative study of the world's religious mysticism will show that truth, grace, spirit do not come through the historic Jesus or the historic Krishna alone, nor through the historic Christianity or the historic Hinduism alone. They can be confined to a single religious dispensation only by those who refuse to make this study or, studying, refuse to discard bias and divest themselves of prejudice while doing so. Today all who study widely and honestly know as clearly as can be that God's message has been here all the time, however impaired or imperfect its forms may be and however different his messengers may be.

18

Few take the trouble to discover what is authentic in religion and what is not. It would be a long tiring process requiring several years of extensive study involving history, theology, psychology, plus personal practice in several forms of worship, plus experience in varying moral values—and all this over wide areas of the world and through the centuries, for without knowledge of comparative religion the investigation would be an incomplete one. Ignorance is much easier. This is why scientifically minded persons become sceptics and piously minded ones become superstitious.

19

There ought to be religious education in the schools; the mistake in the past has been to narrow it down to a single creed or sect. It ought to be widened, to include the history and teachings of the world's chief religions, as well as those of persons without organized established churches.

20

Education in even elementary and certainly in secondary schools should give the pupils at least a little notion of comparative religion. This could at least be confined to biographies of founders of the world faiths together with those of celebrated saints and mystics from different lands and cultures. At college and university levels, carefully chosen tenets from their teachings could be added, and some discussion of the theologies or philosophies involved. In all this instruction the religions dealt with are to be described fairly and explained without prejudice, not criticized or judged.

21

If some pious persons raise the head in prayer, others lower it. If many Christians let their knees go down to the floor, some Muhammedan dervishes bring theirs up to the chest. If Catholics and Protestants sit on benches or chairs during church service, Greek Orthodox congregations stand during their service. Hindus and Buddhists squat cross-legged in meditation, but Indian Jains stand. All these outward forms have been shaped by tradition and so historically: fanatical insistence on them misses the point—what is going on in their minds and hearts. Not only the facts revealed by the studies of comparative religion and comparative mysticism show up the silliness of fanaticism, but even more the correct understanding of those facts.

22

If any one religion is to be taught to children and youth at State expense, then all representative religions should be taught likewise. Let it be a part of such education to know not only the life and teachings of Jesus, but also the lives and teachings of Buddha and Baha'u'lla, Krishna and Muhammed. Only so will religion in its purity rather than in its corruption be instilled. Only so will the young be liberated from the quarrels and prejudices created and kept alive by the selfish monopolies and vested interests which exploit religion for their own benefit.

23

The economy of Nature is spacious enough to have room for all these different ways and means to the common end. They are not competing rivals. A true perception accepts them and is thereby made tolerant toward them.

24

History has presented us with too many spiritual guides, prophets, sages, and saints in too many lands and through too many centuries for any single cult to claim a monopoly of revelation wisdom truth. No human formulation can give us all the fullness, so we profit by them wherever they appear. But partisans, with narrow views, ignore history and neglect the study of comparative religion.

25

The philosopher successfully reinterprets in the secrecy of his own mind the dogmas, rituals, and beliefs of every religion that history, scriptures, circumstance, or study brings into his life. Thus, too, he is able to save the truth of religion when others impatiently reject that along with the falsity of religion. It is true that the comparative study of religions, in a spirit of sympathetic detachment from all and prejudice against none, is rare. But it is a useful part of philosophic study. The rational investigator can take no scripture as finally authoritative but must take all scriptures on their merits. He understands that a religious message is partly shaped by the character and tradition of the country in which it has been delivered. Taking into consideration the various beliefs of human development, he finds it desirable that there be room for variety in religions and for freedom in thought. The Inner Voice has spoken differently to different people. The variety of religions proves not that they cancel each other out but that they arose in response to a variety of needs. Nobody will be kept out of the kingdom of heaven because he does not belong to the orthodox religion which prevails in the place where, by the accident of his birth, he happens to live. Nobody will get into the kingdom of heaven because he does belong to the orthodox religion. The right of entry will depend on quite other and quite nobler qualifications.

26

The study of comparative religion ought to be part of all educational systems to foster knowledge, replace narrow fanaticism by a reasonable tolerance, and combat superstition or persecution.

27

Such a comparative study can bring the evidence needed to dissolve ignorant intolerance and to combat religious hatred. It will show up the foolishness of denouncing heresies when most founders were, like Buddha and Jesus, themselves great heretics from the standpoint of the prevalent religions. It will show the case for a reasonable freedom of thought so that different types of people may find the path, the goal, and the form which suits them. So long as they are good morally, beneficent and helpful, there is room for most creeds.

28

So far as they are genuine expressions of the impulse to worship the Higher Power, all religions have a rightful place. But where human ambition and greed, ignorance and superstition, fanaticism and unbalance have entered into them, they render disservice or do actual harm. The study of comparative religious history is valuable.

29

There is hardly a people which did not have a large or small fragment of the higher teaching in its possession. Egyptians, Chinese, and Greeks in early times, Persians, Spaniards, and Germans in later times, were among this number. Anaximander, teaching in Europe more than two thousand years ago, ascribed the origin of the universe to a First Principle which was "the boundless, the infinite, and the unlimited."

30

When a man begins to exercise independent thought and independent judgement, when he becomes sufficiently informed through the study of comparative religion to note how devastating are the disagreements and inconsistencies with each other, he will have only one possible conclusion open to him. The various beliefs about God and the different statements about religion are as likely to be wrong as right, but the personal experiences of God are all *essentially* the same. But this conclusion reached, he passes through it out of the religious level and rises up to the mystical one.

31
Those who are really intent on finding truth will search for it as widely as their circumstances allow and think about it as often as their time allows.

32
Truth can speak for itself. It has done so since the earliest recorded times—thus incidentally defeating the theory of religious evolutionism— and has done so even in our own time.

33
The study of comparative religion is one thing, the study of comparative history of religion is another; but both demand from the student enough willingness to try to be unprejudiced.

34
The study of comparative religion must be an independent, not a partisan one.

35
The study of comparative religion along with the history of religions, and the inclusion under these heads of little-known, unorganized sects or inspired individuals, is the first step to open the eyes of blinded humanity. When most people are insufficiently educated about their own religion, it is not a surprise that they are ill-informed about that of others. Nor can this study stop there. It ought to be broadened to include the mysticism and metaphysics behind and beyond religions.

36
Comparative religion will become more scientific as it is freed from the prejudices brought to it from the images previously stamped upon other religions by half-ignorant missionaries trying to make them look childish or foolish. The spiritual insensitivity of agnostic or atheistic investigators reflects back from their encounters with other people's spiritual experiences.

37
The liberating power of the study of comparative religion comes into effect mostly outside the academic centres, outside the colleges where it is

taught with a bias towards the particular religion prevailing in the country, along with a prejudice against the other religions outside it.

38

Welcome knowledge from the four points of the compass but be carefully selective in what is absorbed. Avoid sectarianism but do it wisely.

39

It is not even enough to make a comparative study of religions and mysticisms, of metaphysics and systems and practices through the centuries and around the world. Discrimination in what is found becomes necessary, evaluation and critical judgement become essential. It is then that unexamined dogmas and rigid sectarianism with the stifling attitudes they generate are more likely to be dropped. In the end a higher kind of knowledge, the intuitional, coming from a higher level of the mind, must penetrate it all. This is the beginning of the most meaningful events.

40

This larger outlook which the study of comparative religion gives to a man may set him free from being confined to dogmas of a single creed or the practices of a single religion. If he feels happier with this liberation why should he not abide by it? Why should he build walls around his faith and customs? Why must he go only into a church and not into a mosque, only into a synagogue and not into a temple? Why should he not feel free to go into all of those if he wishes—in other words, to be able to worship anywhere in any place at any time?

41

He is safe in selecting those tenets, those mystical revelations, those moral disciplines and personal regimens which form a common basis to all religious cults and systems; they are at least the best beginning.

42

Religion as profound conviction and religion as a social inheritance are vitally different. Philosophy examines religion as profound conviction because it is not the monopoly of any particular race or land but is the possession of all. There is no single religion with which philosophy identifies itself. It cannot accept what is not proved true; it may not regard a belief as false but it cannot use it as true. It does not deal in *a priori* reasoning; it assumes nothing and is thoroughly agnostic at the start. Faith and philosophy are like the lion and the lamb—they cannot easily bed together! Consequently, philosophy's approach to religious questions is comparative in method and eclectic in spirit.

43

Anthropology is another of the subjects which can yield some of its substance to the student of philosophy. So far as it traces the evolution of the God-idea and of morals from primitive to civilized, it may usefully be studied.

44

All these intellectual and imaginative activities in religion like historical research, theological speculation, and Sanskrit, Greek, or Hebrew interpretation are proper in their own place; but their value ought to be recognized as being quite limited, if contrasted with the value of direct insight.

Philosophy completes religion

45

The Quest takes him through three levels of experience. First, he travels through religious beliefs and observances. Then he discovers mystical ideas and practices. Next, he sees that the personal consolations of religion and the intuitive satisfactions of mysticism are not enough. So he adds to them the impersonal quest of truth for its own sake and thus enters the domain of philosophy.

46

Philosophy does not cancel or deny the sublime teachings of religion but endorses and supports what is incontrovertible in them. The rest it corrects or rejects.

47

In every act of religious worship—however blind it be—there is a dim realization of God's existence. It is the business of mysticism to get rid of much of this dimness and of philosophy to get rid of it altogether.

48

The statements of religion ask for our belief: they may or may not be true. The statements of mysticism ask us to seek experience of their factuality. But the statements of philosophy confirm belief by reason, check reason by intuition, lead experience to insight.

49

If we look at man's inner life from the point of view of the whole cycle of reincarnation, popular religion will be seen to be a preparation for philosophy. The idea of a personal God is admitted and belief in it is encouraged, because it is the first step towards the idea of and belief in an impersonal God. Belief that the good or ill fortunes of life are sent to us by some outside being at his whim is useful as leading the way eventually to the understanding that they come to us under the operation of eternal universal law. This is one of the reasons why philosophy does not criticize or oppose popular religion on its own ground and why it leaves it completely alone and never interferes with it.

50

A man may be holy without being wise, but he cannot be wise without being holy. That is why philosophy is necessary, why religion and mysticism are not enough, although excellent as far as they go.(P)

51

Between those who feel too weak to go farther than the simple reverence of church religion and those who feel strong enough to enter the philosophical quest in full consciousness, there is every possible degree.

52

Only those who are able to drink the strong wine of philosophy can forsake religion without losing by, or suffering for, their desertion.

53

These fine teachings may quickly be distorted by popularization or greatly cheapened when brought within reach of the common understanding. If their integrity is to go in order to make concessions to the sensate mentality, if their truth is to be adulterated in order to accommodate the mass mentality, then whatever is gained will be less than what is lost. The higher truth can and should be translated into the vulgate for a mass audience—and the attempt is being made—but no unworthy compromises should be made. After all, if men want to learn the partly true, partly false, they can do so from a hundred sources. But if they want the wholly true, how few are the sources to which they can turn! Let us keep at least these few inviolate.

54

To insist on carrying religious dogmas into philosophic truth, for example, is to insist on carrying the child-mind into adult life. Each has valuable work to do in its own place but may become useless or even harmful when set up in judgement of what is beyond its frontier. Religion is important, mysticism is important, metaphysics is important; but if we fail to distinguish between the relative degrees of such importance, if we do not estimate them separately against the larger background of philosophy, we are liable to fall into the common error of confusing their categories and values, and thus deceive ourselves.

55

The religious codes are judgements or opinions, and are absolutely necessary at the popular stage; but on the philosophic level, where truth contains the highest possible goodness as an accompaniment, inspiration from the Higher Self produces a nobler conduct.

56

From the standpoint of social need, we must be the advocate and friend of religion when it performs its proper duty of keeping men within ethical bounds. But, from the same standpoint, we should be the opponent of religion when it becomes a farcical, hypnotical, hollow show, or when it slays and tortures men for holding other beliefs. But mounting to a higher level and adopting the standpoint of what is the ultimate truth, we can be the impartial observer of religion, for then we shall see it is but an elementary stage of man's journey on the upward mountain road leading to this high goal. Whoever seeks the last word about life must not tarry at the starting point.

57

Religious institutions have always been unfriendly to philosophers. This is because they have feared philosophy.

58

When a man of superior intellectual attainments, moral stature, or intuitional feeling ends a period of doubt or search, of darkness or agnosticism, by attaching himself to a sectarian religion, and especially to a sectarian religion which attempts to impress the senses by sacerdotal pomp and ritual, as well as the mind by claims and dogmas, it is a confession of the man's mental failure, an indication of his intellectual retrogression, and an advertisement of his moral cowardice. Such a man should have gone onwards into either the mysticism of truth or the metaphysics of truth. There must have been some weakness either in his character or in his intellect which caused him to fall back so far.

59

Philosophy does not effect a conversion from one religious point of view to another, but a confirmation of what intuitive feelings and ideas are trying to tell the man.

60

Mentally disturbed or emotionally hysterical persons can neither find Truth nor produce beauty, except during temporary lucid periods. Religious cults founded by them can only attract their own kind. Art created by them can only find acceptance because of supposed daring originality. Both are unhealthy and increase the existing confusion. Truth is eminently sane. Reality is breathtakingly beautiful. Popular externalized religion must rise into internalized mysticism, but the first must avoid the danger of superstition and the second avoid aberration. This is why both attain fulfilment in the safety of philosophy.

61

They come to religion seeking consolation; he comes to philosophy seeking truth; the two aims are quite different. But in the end the philosopher experiences consolation and the religionists take a step towards truth.

62

All the outer forms of religion, all the outer rites affect their sincere devotees emotionally, but within the higher part of the ego only. But all the *samadhis* of yoga, and certainly the insights of philosophy, escape this limitation by cutting completely through emotion into its deep calm core—the real being.

63

Because religion is an easier approach, because it requires only a devotional attitude whereas philosophy requires both a devotional and an intellectual one, the one feeds the multitude, the other an elect.

64

Here is religion without ritual, inspired ministration that wears no vestment, and church attendance without leaving home.

65

Popular religion is able to do so but philosophy cannot speak directly to all persons. It can open its lips only in the presence of those who have been made ready by life to receive it.

66

Both religion and mysticism are self-enclosing activities. The defense against fears which religion offers and the transcendental experiences which mysticism offers provide personal satisfactions. But philosophy can only offer truth. It is not directly concerned with substituting one emotion for another, even if the new one is on a higher level, nor does it care whether the man has pleasing or displeasing experiences through following it.

67

Philosophy shows how a teaching which is purely religious can be re-expressed in a non-religious way.

68

If they look less to ecclesiastical institutions for spiritual satisfactions, it is not because they feel less spiritual need. It is because their needs have deepened, because they want to come to the principal points of the matter rather than the tedious, obsolete, arguable, and questionable ones.

69

The mass of men need something visible and touchable and perhaps audible if they are to believe it really exists—hence idols for primitive people, rituals and ceremonials for more developed people. But for the advanced ones, an idea needs no such symbol, as they can grasp it by mind alone.

70

A theosophy, a mixture of what is excellent in all the religions, is a breeder of tolerance and fellowship among them, a stage on the way, but still not the ultimate level. For that the seeker needs to penetrate in depth, beneath religion to mysticism, beneath mysticism to philosophy.

71

For one person who will respond to the call of philosophy, there are perhaps a thousand who can hear only the call of religion.

72

That most people are only in the first degree of religion is not their fault; they cannot help it and are not to be blamed. They are simply what their past has made them. If others have risen to the higher degrees of mysticism or philosophy it is because they have a longer fuller past behind them. Young plants are not to be reproached because they are not old trees.

73

The teaching which is suited to those who are well on the way to the final stage of spiritual development is not much help to those who are only at the first stage.

74

To rise up from the religious level calls for some metaphysical faculty, a sensitivity to subtle ideas. The mind's more abstract level must be used. Those unaccustomed to it should not let themselves be discouraged. Each attempt made at intervals helps to open the way.

75

The philosopher does not have to sing hymns, mutter mantrams, attend churches, or take part in rituals and ceremonies organized by priests and clergymen. All that is useful, necessary, and essential to the masses—for it is the limit of their spiritual exploration. He, however, has ventured much farther and he cannot stop within these narrow borders.

76

Once the individual has risen above the levels of religion it would be sheer folly to fall back into them.

77

There is no liturgy and no ritual, no hierarchy and no institution in philosophic worship, nor are they needed.

78

The philosopher joins with the atheist in resisting superstition. But they part again when this resistance is directed against atheism itself—the greatest superstition of all.

79

No doubt individual students have their own beliefs but for these they must accept responsibility themselves. Since philosophy seeks to know the Real, it is not concerned with beliefs.

80

Philosophy neither elevates any man into God nor drags God down to any man's level.

81

Religion is satisfied with the spiritual fact diluted by myth and legend, philosophy wants the fact only.

82

Ungrown and immature minds would be bored by the illuminations of philosophy. For a philosopher to argue with them combatively would be a waste of time—theirs and his. There are so many creeds, systems, and sects which are really preparatory to philosophy and which are more useful to them at their stage. When they are ready for something more fundamental, they will find their way to it.

83

Mankind is led by easy preparatory stages towards the highest philosophy. Only when they are well grounded in true religion or mysticism and sound metaphysics is the full and final revelation made to them.

84

There are some persons who could not be stopped by worldly attractions from seeking something entirely unworldly, who longed for an understanding that was true and a consciousness that was real, stable, transcendental, and peace-bestowing. They tried orthodoxy and unorthodoxy, faith and unfaith, cults and leaders, organizations and solitariness. In the end they found their peace, or rather the first step to it, when they found philosophy.

85

Thus the vaguely felt, dimly apprehended, and always symbolic truth of religion is developed into clear full direct knowledge by philosophy.

86

It is not interested in forming just another sect, in building up one more denomination.

87

That worship which the followers of popular religion give blindly, instinctively, and often mechanically is given intelligently, scientifically, and consciously by the adherents of philosophy.

88

Those who are attached to the religious creed into which they have been born have no need to discard it merely because they wish to avail themselves of the knowledge and benefits provided by philosophy, for by applying its light to the creed, to the forms and the symbols, they will find much more meaning and depth in them. Properly interpreted they will not be found contradictory. But what has been added by ignorance, miscomprehension, wilfulness, or superstition will be shown up for what it is. The Founder's great message will remain untouched, his access to the eternal verities will be vindicated. In the case of those who had previously turned away from their traditional religion into a blank agnosticism, or even a stronger atheism, their doubts will be removed. So philosophy alone serves both groups! If it refuses to support false beliefs, it equally refuses to support false negations of religious belief. It sees quite clearly through religion and atheism and can nourish the follower of both.

89

There is nothing in religion that philosophy really displaces. It simply supplements and completes, corrects and inspires mature understanding, and leads the individual to *experience* the blessed inner peace which religion, per se, can only *allude* to.

90

Religion signifies an intellectual descent when compared with Philosophy *only* when it is *separated* from Philosophy, which earnestly sets itself the task of evoking the presence of a new Faith in the hearts of men. Prayer, worship, communion, reverence, and faith in God are indispensable parts to the philosophic life. Philosophy is, for those who are willing to live it as well as to study it, a religion. They acquire the religious spirit from it even if they never possessed it before. They increase their religious fervour if they did possess it before. They finish up with a sense of their helplessness, their smallness, and their dependence. They finish up with prayer. Thus religious worship, so often denounced as the first superstition of primitive man, becomes the final wisdom of matured man.

91

Why walk into the prison of another sect? Why not walk out from all sects into freedom?

92

Because philosophy includes and extends religion, it necessarily supports it. But it does not support the erroneous dogmas and misguided practices which are cloaked under religion's mantle, nor the human exploitations which are found in its history.(P)

93

The attitude of philosophy towards proselytizing Euro-American converts to yoga and propagandizing Ramakrishna Mission swamis is naturally sympathetic, yet wisely discriminating. It refuses to associate itself solely with any particular religion, whether Eastern or Western. Hence, it is uninterested in conversions from one religion to another, unconcerned with the defense or attack, the spread or decay of any organized religion. Those who especially link it with Hinduism alone or Buddhism alone are wrong. But although philosophy has no ecclesiastical system of its own, a philosopher is free to support one if he chooses to do so. This may happen for social reasons, or family reasons, or special personal reasons.

94

Because most religions theoretically turn people towards a power holier than themselves, however high or low their concept of that power may be, there is no ground for intolerance, fanaticism, or persecution. But because these things do exist, we must ascribe their origin to the human faults of upholders of religion and to the sectarian ambition or selfish aims of its organizations. Such an atmosphere is suffocating to would-be philosophers, with their pursuit of calm, their attitude of goodwill, and their doctrine of evolutionary levels. They are perfectly willing to let others follow their own way of worship, so long as it is not morally destructive or utterly evil.

95

If religion is for the consolation of man, philosophy is for the improvement of man.

96

How far is the distance between the pale apathetic faith of a nominal religionist and this wholly intensive devotion of a philosophic life!

97

If philosophy confirms basic religious feeling, it does not do so to serve any particular sect, institution, or creed. On the contrary, it frees one from the narrowness too often associated with them.

98

Buddha said, "Proclaim the Truth"; he did not say, "Convert others to the Truth." It is for the philosopher to make it available, to open up a way for others, but not to count the gains or weigh the harvest.

99

Judged from the philosophic level, the old religious forms which are disintegrating and the new forms which are striving to replace them are both gravely imperfect.

100

Philosophy does all that religion does for a man, but it does more. It not only restores or reinforces faith in a higher Power, gives each life a higher meaning, brings consolation and support during trouble, and ennobles one's treatment of other people, but also explains the deeper mysteries of the nature of God, the universe, and man.

101

The disciplinary revelations of the Overself displace the ethical regulations of established orthodoxy and render them unnecessary.

102

Religions and cults seek to get people into their particular folds. Philosophy seeks to get them out of all folds.

103

There is hope for these teachings so long as they do not become embedded in an organized church, so long as the movement of public appreciation remains individualistic, so long as no orthodoxy gets established with its accompanying pronouncements of anathema upon heresy.

104

The religious feelings of a philosopher are not less existent than those of the outwardly pious; they are deep and delicate: yet they are untouched by sentimentality.

105

Compulsory belief in particular religious dogmas has done harm as well as good, has led to much bloodshed and hatred. Philosophy instills an air of tolerance which operates against such religiosity.

106

The principles of philosophy are its clergy. They serve its little flock, minister to its higher needs, and support it in times of stress.

107

In the presence of sectarianism, with its rivalry and recrimination, philosophy remains aloof and silent. Unlike the sects, it is concerned with universal truths that will always be valid.

108

There are no labels in the kingdom of heaven, no organizations and no ashrams either. He who affixes a label to his name, be it that of Christian or Hindu, Advaitin or mystic, affixes a limitation also, and thus bars the gateway leading to the attainment of Truth. The study of philosophy mercilessly demolishes every possible division which the history of man has established.

109

It does not seek the convinced sectarians but tries to get the ear of the intelligent laymen who are dissatisfied with orthodox doctrine.

110

The current of religious conversion, exciting though it be at the time, is likely to exhaust itself as emotion subsides. The inward growth which comes with philosophy is slower moving and deeper rooted but more lasting. The change it makes cannot be undone, the peace it leaves cannot be taken away.

111

It is not religion itself that he has outgrown but *organized* religion, not truth that he has denied but arrogant claims to monopolize truth. He does not want a heaven which is really a prison.

112

Those who have passed through the disciplines of body, intellect, and emotion are no longer on the same level as those who have not. They need a teaching appropriate in every way to their higher development.

113

All that is finest and all that is really essential in religion is not negated but carried to its fulfilment in philosophy.

Philosophy and "the faithful"

114

It is unphilosophic and imprudent to disturb anyone's religious faith. It is only when the course of events or their own mental development creates doubts and disquiet—and even then they must come seeking more satisfactory answers to their questions—that higher teaching can be given. But even then the manner in which the latter is presented is important—that is, try not to bring it into collision with those parts of their faith which they still hold, be constructive and not destructive. In that way the new teaching can be presented as a higher octave of the old one or used for reform of the old one.

115

Intolerant religious organizations which would allow no other voice, however harmless, to speak than one which echoes their own must in the end fall victim to their own intolerance; for as men through their education and contact with more developed persons come to perceive the Truth, their hostility and enmity to those religions are inevitably aroused. They will then either fall into agnosticism or into sheer atheism, or they will find their way to other and truer expressions of what religion should be if it is to fulfil its highest mission. Therefore, it is not the work of a philosopher to reverse, correct, or otherwise disturb other people's religious beliefs. If the latter are faulty and if the organization propagating them is intolerant, he may be sure that given enough time others will arise to do this negative and destructive work; and this saves him the trouble of these unpleasant tasks. His own work is a positive one.(P)

116

He will not disturb the faith of those who are satisfied with their own religion or of those who feel sure they have the truth. His ministrations are only to those who humbly call themselves seekers, who do not arrogantly feel they have arrived at the goal of truth, who are bewildered or who approach him earnestly.

117

Because of the absence of intolerance from his character, the philosopher neither desires nor attempts to impose his ideas upon others. He gives them the intellectual freedom he wants for himself.

118

He will accept the fact that a variety of attitudes and a diversity of views must exist among mankind, since the life-waves behind mankind are themselves so varied in age. The result of this will be a large willingness on his own part to let others believe what they wish so long as they do not try to force these beliefs compulsorily where not wanted.

119

They attend the church synagogue mosque most piously but the experience of the Deity as it really happens (not the ego-inflating joyous semi-mystic experience of popular religion and conventional mysticism) would frighten them away if described in advance. For it involves the disappearance of the ego into the Void.

120

The destruction of religion would constitute a serious loss of moral strength and mental hope to mankind. Its dogma of the existence of a higher power, its insistence that a virtuous life is rewarded and a vicious one punished, its periodical call to drop worldly thoughts and activities are values of which the multitudes cannot afford to be prematurely deprived without grave peril to their higher evolution. The philosophical student should be sympathetic to the genuine worth of religion as he should be hostile to the traditional abuses. He must not permit himself to be swept away on the emotional tide of extreme fanaticism, either by the materialistic atheists who would utterly destroy religion and persecute its priesthood in the name of science or by the blind pious dogmatists who would destroy scientific free thought in the name of God.

121

Popular religion, suited to rural peasants and city crowds, asks for simple faith, not reflective thought; questionless obedience and not critical inquiry. It is easier to follow. And besides, conformity in this matter means fewer troubles and freedom from harassment for those who have to live among others. A philosopher who pays outward deference to the religion of those around him because he wants a tranquil life is not necessarily a hypocrite. He knows what is true and what is superstitious in that religion. The truth he accepts, the other he ignores. He wants to worship God just as much as, more likely more, than the other people.

122

Religion must be regarded as a necessity for the masses, for whom it represents the best possible source of help; it is not right to disturb their faith. Nevertheless, for those who have begun to diverge from the herd

and who have developed an interest in mysticism, such facts as the forego-
ing should be pointed out and need to be discussed.

123

Many in the prewar period had so altered their outlooks as to be somewhat sceptical of the validity of religion. But scepticism is a negative
attitude which hides a real hunger, the hunger for some new truth to
replace the old belief which has been found lacking. It is for us to show
such minds that a rational mysticism, pruned of superstition, has much to
offer them. It is also for us to show the few among them who can ascend
so far that the hidden philosophy will satisfactorily fill their hunger and
provide an alternative to replace what they have renounced.

124

This clinging adhesion to the institutions and organizations of religions
and cults whether established or unorthodox, this lack of exploratory spirit
to search out little known but superior teaching, must be recognized by
the educator in philosophy. He must accept ruefully that what he has to
communicate will be welcomed only by a small minority.

125

But if we do not tell others that the truth exists, how will anyone ever
know about it? The answer is that telling is not a job for the incautious
beginner but for the seasoned proficient.

126

In meeting with religious advocates, the student should listen cour-
teously but not waste time arguing with them: he should keep his mental
reservations to himself.

127

He will carefully avoid disturbing the faith of others but, except in
special circumstances or for special motives—persecution, position, children, or mission—he will not go out of his way to encourage them. It is
not his business to encourage superstition.

128

The sage seeks to descend and meet a man at his own level, and then try
to lift him just a little higher. Thus he will try to give the remorselessly
cruel fanatical religionist a noble view of his own faith.

129

It is not that philosophy holds a different conception about man from
the religious one, but that it holds a deeper one.

130

The enlightened philosopher has no conflict with religion so long as it
retains its ethical force. When a religion is crumbling, when men reject its
moral restraining power, when they refuse to accept its historical incidents

and irrational dogmas as being vital to living, when in consequence they are becoming brutalized and uncontrolled, as our own epoch has painfully seen, then this religion is losing its raison d'être and the people among whom it held sway are in need of help. The mass of the common people now in the West mentally dwell outside any church, and are consequently outside its disciplinary moral influence. They cannot be left to perish unguided when religion becomes just a means of duping simple minds in the interests of ruling or wealthy classes, and is no longer an ethical force. This puts the whole of society in danger, and such a religion will inevitably fall, bringing down society with itself in the crash as it did in France and later in Russia. When the old faith fails then the new is needed. Thinking men refuse to bind their reason to the incredible articles of a dogmatic creed. They refuse to swear belief in queer concepts which they find impossible to reconcile with the rest of human life and certainly with modern knowledge. The philosopher finds that religion looms against a much larger background; it is the mere shadow cast by philosophy, but for the masses the shadow suffices.(P)

131

The pious man may keep his religious denomination when he adds philosophy, so long as he does not try to keep its conformism and dogmatism and smug monopolism. The one attitude is incompatible with the other. But the original living spirit behind its beginnings, the essential reverence of the higher power, the beautiful communion, the fervent devotion—these are perfectly philosophical.

132

Philosophy can never collide with religion. Indeed it includes a cult, a worship of the higher Power. But it may and does collide with superstition masquerading as religion, and with exploitation pretending to be religion.

133

Just as the confusion of planes of ethical reference between the monastic and householder's duties has introduced error into the whole subject of yoga, so the confusion of planes of intellectual understanding between the religious and the philosophic concepts has introduced error into the whole subject of truth. Philosophy has no quarrel with religion so long as it does not go beyond its legitimate frontiers.

134

If some men find help in the regular formal observance of established religions, philosophy does not object. But if they assert that these observances should be honoured and followed by all other men, as being indispensable to their spiritual welfare, then philosophy is forced to object. We must allow tolerance in spiritual and social matters to all except those whose doctrines would subvert tolerance itself or whose action would destroy it. If we regard it as wrong to impose our religious views on others, we also regard it as wrong to allow others to impose them on us.

135

They are not asked to give up their faith in God but to broaden their idea of God.

136

The gap between the religious approach and the philosophic approach cannot be closed except by time and development. Fools ignore it only to suffer disillusionment for their trouble.

137

Philosophy is forced to support existing religious bodies not because it conceives them to be the best, but because it can find no better ones. It is grieved by their faults and imperfections, their past history and present selfishness, but it believes that a world without them would be a worse one.

138

To the ignorant sceptic, the venerable institution of religion rests on the twin pillars of superstition and prejudice, but to the philosopher these are but the incrustations of time on the real pillars, which are understanding and reverence.

139

Philosophy is always sympathetic towards religion because the parent is always sympathetic towards its offspring.

140

Just as the worship of an anthropomorphic Deity is a proper prescription for the masses, so the worship of a personal saviour is a proper prescription for them too. Philosophy warmly endorses both kinds of worship. Let it not be thought that it would obliterate them. On the contrary, it rationally explains their necessity and defends their utility. They are valuable aids to millions of people. Moreover, they yield genuine and not illusory results. However, when ignorant or intolerant persons would set up these elementary goals as the highest possible ones for all men, or as the sole paths leading to divinity, then philosophy feels it necessary to refute the ignorance of the one and to denounce the intolerance of the other.

141

If personality is denied to Universal Being, this is only because of the littleness it imposes on that Being, because it lessens and minifies. But if children, adolescents, and many or most adults need the support of such a belief to maintain religious aspiration and provide personal comfort, why not let them have it? The others, who have been educated so highly as to regard it as an illusion, are entitled to their view too. Philosophy is able to point out what is correct and what is not in both views.

142

When one talks or writes in public about popular religion, one must be cautious and careful, for it is very easy to tread on the feet of those who take popular religion quite literally and most seriously. Just as the educated Greeks and Romans could not, because they dared not, tell the masses that the various cults they worshipped were really the laws of nature, so the philosopher must be very careful if he hints that popular religion is merely the first step on the way to God—a step too often mixed with confusions and superstitions.

143

Those who have reached its higher levels and stand at the portals of philosophy can get a point of view which will harmonize all old and new religions which now compete or even conflict with each other.

Intolerance toward philosophy

144

The sage of former centuries was prudent in the presence of established religious authority. He took care to avoid being persecuted for heresy, although he did not always succeed in protecting himself against its suspicions. Even on a lesser plane, a mystic like Miguel de Molinos could not be saved by the Pope, his friend, from the dungeons of the "Holy" Office, the Inquisition. Remember that the Jesuits were hostile to the work of Molinos and also Madame Guyon because of its success. They were also jealous of his intimacy with the Pope, who lodged him in the Vatican. Plots were laid, the Inquisition was brought into their opposition, he was denounced as a heretic and, further, falsely libelled. The Jesuits succeeded in winning the French king to their cause: he used all his influence with the Papacy to have Molinos arrested. The poor victim never regained his freedom but died in the dungeons of the Inquisition some twelve years later. His books were termed "dangerous" and destroyed.

145

The so-called normal condition of the human mentality is really an abnormal one. Sanity has not yet been stamped upon the human race. That is still a perfectionist ideal which is being approached slowly, haltingly, and with many side-wanderings. The narrow, unbalanced, and confused mentalities of most people naturally react indifferently, impatiently, or intolerantly to the broad straight truths of philosophy. Nothing can be done by anyone to assist them so long as they not only do not understand this teaching but do not even care to understand it. Only when they will have sufficiently awakened to regard it as being not too absurd or too idealistic to be considered will they have attained civilized maturity.

146

The narrow-minded and little-hearted among orthodox institutions will resent his independence and protest that to allow him freedom and equality is to allow anarchy and chaos to reign.

147

This word "religion" is very often and very glibly used. Yet the meaning given it by the seers is too frequently not the same meaning given it by the hearers. Consequently history has witnessed the curious spectacle of Spinoza, whose entire life was a contemplation of God and a practice of virtue, denounced as an atheist by the Jewish ecclesiasts, and as a scoundrel by the Christian ones, of his times.

Philosophic independence, universalism

148

The philosopher who would be completely loyal to Truth will also be non-denominational in religion. Among those who boast of their formal membership in a solidly organized or socially respected church he will be a churchless outsider. The very membership they are so proud of would be an oppressive limitation to him. Intellectually he is fully justified in refusing to affix to himself any label bearing the name of any sect. His detached impartial judgement allows him to see the errors and weaknesses of all sects no less than their truths and services. He can gladly share what is true in all beliefs but not what is false in them or limiting in their followers and organizers. Yet this true position will not be what it seems from the outside. It will paradoxically be both in and out of all religions—in by reason of his deeper understanding of them than their own believers possess, and out by reason of his knowledge that the inspired Word has been spoken in many lands, among different races, to the most varied individuals. He is in by reason of his sympathy with all groping for light and all giving Light, which a religion represents, but out by reason of his inability to narrow down his receptivity to that Light through adopting a dogmatic creed or through identifying himself completely with any particular faith. He cannot for the sake of partial truth endure the imitating error. He is out too because he sees each denomination locked in on itself, restricted in outlook and inadequate in tolerance. He feels the need of a larger liberty than any of them can give him, so as to express somewhat the infinite freedom of the Spirit itself. Nor will he, for the personal or social benefit of associating with a closed congenial group, yield to the temptation of losing interest in all other groups. His intellectual attitude is the only truly catholic one, and the neutrality of his feelings is the only really universal one. He stands at the frontier between every pair of religions, a foreigner but yet a friend, serene and immobile. In all this what else is he doing except expressing not only a stricter adherence to truth but also to love? For no man, whether believer or atheist, is shut out from his circle. All men are included in it.

149

No universal rule can be laid down for the illumined man to follow in the matter of relationship to the religion into which he was born. He may adhere to it, observe all its rites, and fulfil all its requirements quite faithfully or he may anarchically reject all allegiance to it. If he follows the first alternative it will most probably be because of the need to set an example to those who still need the support of such outward and visible institutionalism and such fixed forms and dogmas. If he follows the second alternative, it is most certainly because first, his inner voice tells him to do so, second, because the hour is at hand to recall religion itself to the great verities which have largely vanished from it, and third, simply because his own temperament and disposition prefer it. This is why in history we find the strangely paradoxical actuality of some mystics following orthodoxy with pious conformity but others standing aside with heretical stubbornness.

150

In the end man will find that no church can give him what he can give himself or do for him what he must do for himself. And that is, to go back to the source of his being and seek communion there within his own mind and his own heart where God is hidden.

151

Real religion is as universal as the wind. Cut and dried religions are mere local limitations; they were originally put up as temporary trellis-work for the young souls of man to climb and grow upward, but they have become imprisoning hatches and sometimes instruments of torture. Let us look only for that which is *salient* in a religion, and we shall find ourselves set free from its lassoing limitations. We shall not arrive at its meaning by muddled talk in its favour any more than by muddled talk in its despite, for the powers of calm judgement and reasoned reflection are then stupefied. The philosophical student's attitude is simply this, that he can *begin* no discussion with acceptance of the existence of any dogma; such acceptance is only proper as the *culmination* of a discussion. He must question and cross-question every inherited belief, every acquired doctrine until he can elicit what we really know out of the mass of pseudo-knowledge, until he becomes conscious of the ignorance which is so often veiled by the mask of supposed knowledge. Through such agitated unsettlement and such sharp doubt alone can we win our way to rocklike certitude ultimately.(P)

152

The outer forms and observances, the liturgies and rituals of religion may be dispensed with by the person who has successfully opened up an inner way of communication with the higher self, so far as his own personal needs are concerned. But, for the sake of others to whom these are still necessary, he may, by way of example, continue with them, as he deems best.

153

You can no more decipher the name of his denomination than you can put the sky into a container. For he does not belong to one inwardly although he may, occasionally, for social reasons, belong to one outwardly.

154

He does not have to enter a church or temple to stand in God's presence: he is continually there.

155

Religion is for the masses of men, mysticism for the few, but philosophy is for the individual.

156

The orthodox offering of myth will never satisfy the man who has had a glimpse of the star of truth.

157

Who is willing to sacrifice his worldly interests for the sake of coming closer to the intangible Overself? Who is willing to deviate from the conventional path of mere sensuality and narrow selfishness for the sake of a mysterious intuition which bids him obey and trust it implicitly? The answer to these questions is that only a scattered minority is willing to do so, and one small enough to show up humanity's actual state as being inwardly far from knowing why it is here on earth.

158

The shelter which religion offers the masses has its correspondence in the strength which philosophy offers the few.

159

Although the philosopher is not really tied to any dogmas or tethered to any cult but is friendly to all those which are not directly evil, this does not mean he is ready to agree deferentially with all the doctrines offered to the world. He may have to point out where acceptance must stop, but he qualifies this by showing up its relativity, its dependence on a particular level.

160

If others feel the need of a creedal, dogmatic teaching to support them, of a leader to take them along, of a group to give them gregarious comfort, it is right for them to accept these things. But the philosopher feels that he must remain uncommitted, must not put up fences and barriers behind which he is to shut himself in with a leader and a group. He remembers the experience of the spiritual glimpse, when he felt that God's love was for all, and not for any special sect or society, that God's truth was greater than any creed or dogma, and that he was set free from all man-made mental, social, and spiritual cages.

161

Too intelligent to accept the nonsense which is traditionally served in the name of religion, too intuitive not to feel the worshipful reverence for a higher Power demanded by religion, he is forced to follow an independent path.

162

In answer to the question which sometimes arises, whether the aspirant could continue to remain, without hypocrisy, in communion with an orthodoxy such as the Church of England, while holding the philosophic view of Jesus, the reply is that he could certainly do so. There is absolutely no need to break away from the Church nor to give up the services of institutional religion. Philosophy makes no pronouncements against these items but leaves it entirely to each individual to make his own decision in such matters. The decision must depend upon his circumstances, temperament, and so forth. Philosophy merely says that such services are not enough in themselves to ensure illumination in the case of the believer, while in the case of the sceptic they are useless. They may have their value to quite a number of people, and if one feels the need of them or of religious fellowship, it would be quite permissible for him to continue them. This need not at all be construed as hypocrisy or cowardice. However, no one should act hastily in so vital a matter. He has not only to consider the effect of such an act upon himself, but also upon the community around him. It might even be that, although the service no longer satisfied him personally, he might have to continue it for the sake of setting an example to other, less mature persons who still fully believe in it—since they think they are receiving help from it—and who are influenced by his decisions.

163

Philosophy sees that the problem of man's attitude to God is an individual problem, that organizations can at best only contribute towards its solution and at worst retard and delay its solution. No organization can ever solve it for him. Only he himself can do so.

164

The sceptic, who has no use for religious institutions and no belief in religious experience, is far removed from the philosopher, who criticizes these things but does not reject them.

165

The experience which carries him into the pure air of the Overself carries him also high above the limitations of creeds and dogmas, sects, rituals, and groups which so arbitrarily divide men.

166

Emerson overestimated the value of individualism because he tended to overlook the fact that all the fine things he said about it were true only of those rare individuals who had attained the zenith of noble character and inspirational wisdom.

167

He has freed himself from the biased creedal trap, from the fanatic sectarian exclusiveness, from the tight limits caused by non-existent or insufficient comparative knowledge. He has yet to free himself from himself, to become detached from the egoistic way of viewing ideas, to become detached and impartial and equilibrated.

168

It is not conversion from one religion into another that a philosopher seeks to effect, such as from Christianity to Hinduism, but conversion to the inner understanding of all religions.

169

The philosopher is inwardly a non-traditionalist. Why should he, who seeks or dwells in the fullest mental freedom, condition his mind by the opinions of others or conform his life according to the beliefs of others? Why should he, who knows that the Spirit bears no labels, attach himself to any particular system of thought, values, or rites? Do not therefore expect him to belong to any creed, religion, sect that you can name or to adore its symbols and submit to its clichés.

170

The Spirit which he has touched will not let him be confined to a single religious system but enables him to perceive what is true (and what is not) in all systems.

171

He is independent and neutral towards organized religions yet at the same time friendly and understanding of them. He is unable to commit himself to all their credos or join their institutions, yet he willingly studies those credos and recognizes the need of those institutions. He needs no formal authority to endorse his attainment for he needs no following, no publicity, no patronage.

172
Such a man will be highly advanced whatever religion or sect he follows outwardly, and not as the effect of that particular group to which he belongs. The credit is his own, not the group's.

173
He who acquires a thorough and correct understanding of philosophy acquires a property that will remain in his possession throughout life. He will never change it although he may broaden it.

174
If he chooses to remain within a particular denomination, it will not be at the price of regarding it as God's chosen one.

175
The sage is in himself a non-sectarian, yet his people's need or his personal destiny, or both, may make him active on behalf of religious sects. He is mentally nonpolitical, yet the same pressure may make him work for some political cause.

176
The philosopher has no general need to identify himself with any particular religion, with its bias and limitation, but he may have a special need to do so because of personal circumstances or of service to humanity.

177
He may attend his ancestral church, temple, mosque, or synagogue if he wishes but it will not be at all necessary for spiritual comfort to do so. His obedience to the obligation is merely a gesture, an outward symbol of acknowledgment that there *is* a Higher Power worthy of homage and worship. And he makes this acknowledgment to confirm the faith of the ignorant who are not able to do more than take their religion on external authority.

178
Traditional forms and organizations have little appeal to one who draws his inspirations from today's life, and not yesterday's: still less to one who holds to the superiority of the individual intuition above all organizations and prefers it to their tyranny and dogmatism.

179
With the fuller establishment of enlightenment he comes to understand

that if he is to transcend duality he must give up the idols he has worshipped—gods and gurus.

180

He needs no religious authority to interfere with or interrupt this glorious glimpse, no theologian to bring it down to the intellectual level and thus lose it for him.

181

Do not ask the name of his religion or the whereabouts of his church, for he does not know anything more than that it is a faith and worship which saturate his mind, penetrate his heart, and satisfy both, and that it goes with him regularly everywhere he himself goes.

182

The philosopher may recite no creed and observe no sacrament, or he may do both. He is free.

183

But if such an event as the formation of a new cult be in the destiny of things, then he is content to let it come in its own way by the activity of others, never by his own, and only after his death, for he will do all he can to prevent it during his lifetime.

184

All these minor stars of religious theology and intellectual theory pale before the bright constellation of final Truth.

185

Philosophy is profoundly religious, but it is not a religion. Men belonging to different folds may study and practise it.

186

If you regard it as a religion, then it is one which embraces all other religions.

187

Whenever the masses begin to question, they ask, "What are we to believe?" whereas whenever the intelligent few begin to question they ask, "What can we know?"

188

If he is to be at all understood, he must use the names and dogmas of the established religion, the ascendant faith, in his own declarations.

189

To accept an institution's usefulness to society generally without accepting the institution personally is his attitude.

190

A man who develops his own private approach to the spirit has as much right to hold independent views of it as others have to hold conventional ones. Societies rightly depend upon organized religions but they should learn to respect individuals who are unable to do so but who are not less appreciative of religious values in their loftiest sense.

191

Those who look for overnight miraculous uplifting and exalting changes in the minds of the masses are looking for rare happenings; this is for individuals only; all the others will be changed either by a long process of experience or by a shorter process of education, or, more usually, by a combination of both.

192

If ideas, truths, knowledge of enormous importance to the human race, as well as a way of life founded upon them, are not to vanish from the world altogether, a few men and women here and there must carefully preserve them and lovingly nurture them.

193

It is not a long step but rather an easy one from the universalizing of communications and transport which is such a feature of our times, to the universalizing of spiritual culture. The search for God, the quest of the Soul can now be carried on with the help of all the knowledge gleaned by all human beings everywhere. It can now be discussed in terms of basic human experiences and not mere sectarian ones.

194

This universal message is destined to flow all over the world. Its bearers will be none other than the writings of ancient and modern seers. It will bring people the opportunity to grow, to go forward. Those who will be mentally flexible enough to understand and emotionally courageous enough to accept the truth will break away from the effete tradition which holds them. The others will stubbornly prefer to remain as they are. It is not easy to desert one belief for another.

7

BEYOND RELIGION
AS WE KNOW IT

A better understanding of the religious instinct is replacing the old one. The elimination of fear and superstition as the accompaniments of this instinct are good signs of the spread of truer knowledge about it.

2

Humanity has to find a religious form to suit the coming era. It has to find something between the extreme of mere anarchy and the extreme of steel-trap institutionalism. In the first case, it becomes the victim of any and every phantasy which human imagination may throw up, which human ambition may put forth, or which human ignorance may blunder into. In the second case, it becomes the victim of a letter that kills the spirit or of a collective enslavement by outworn dogmas and selfish organizations and by mechanical worship. Humanity has to find a form which respects the individual's right to choose freely what will most help him and which to that extent leaves religion a personal matter. Yet it cannot afford to disdain the proffered hand of traditional experience, authoritative knowledge, and group association. The needed revelation must be relevant to external conditions and adequate to internal outlook. Those who are no longer attracted by church religion, who believe its claims are exaggerated and its dogmas untenable, can go forward towards higher religious truth only by going forward into a more mystical and more scientific cult. Instead of wasting time trying to resurrect the dead forms of an old faith, many people were moved up by the war closer to this point of view.

3

Religion must organize itself on a more intellectual basis to meet modern needs. It must present a fuller system, which will intelligibly explain the inner meaning of man, God, and the Universe. It must not contradict the verified knowledge of modern science. It ought no longer to attempt to outrage reason, but should go out of the way to convince it. It must be so timely and reasonable that it will give satisfying intelligent answers to the most disconcerting questions.

On the second point, it is a lesson of history that if religion is to be more rational it will have to be less ritualistic. The tendency of all external rites is to become empty and hollow. Nobody is worse off and everybody is better off when religious practices or rites which have become merely mechanical and utterly hypocritical are abandoned, whether in disbelief or in disgust. As a religion becomes less inspired, it becomes ritualistic. What it is no longer able to give men through inward power, it pretends to give them through outward forms. When the means of worship becomes an actual hindrance to communion with the Worshipped, when the worshipper is deceived by pretense of the act into belief that he has performed the act itself, it is time to call a halt. Nevertheless, ritual is useful if it helps the mind to think of diviner things and it therefore has a proper place in religion. If a religious ceremony acts as a springboard whence a man can enter more easily into a reverential mood, it has justified its value for him. This is usually the case with the peasant mentality among the lower classes and with the aesthetic temperament among the higher ones, although it is much less true of artisan town workers and city intellectuals who indeed may find it a hindrance to worship rather than a help. Religion will always be, by its nature, something of an allegory; but it need not always stick to the same set of symbols. Why should not this era find a new religious symbolism? In the end, religion will find its truer expression in the public acts and private thoughts of a man than in its own public rites. Those who would propagate it will best do so by their living example. It will then become less formal and more vital, less institutional and more free, less devoted to public parades in church, temple, or synagogue and more devoted to personal righteousness in home, factory, and field.

The practical question arises: What is to be done with orthodox religious institutions as they exist today? Much needs to be done with them. If mankind's religious leaders could broaden their vision, could recognize these truths, there would then be some hope for their institutions. If they cannot put themselves at the head of this movement, then they will have to become stragglers in its rear. The choice cannot be evaded. But first it may be said that unless the State dis-establishes religion, it will continue to get not religion in its purity but religion in its degeneration. To worship an institution merely because it is an established one, is to worship an idol. The new religious teaching must be a vocation, not a profession. Hence, teachers may receive voluntary contributions towards their expenses, but they must not be paid a prescribed salary.

If rites and ceremonies will be less needed, then the services of priests to perform them will also be less needed. The coming faith will not only be a rational and riteless one, but may also be a priestless one. It will tolerate no paid professionals to exploit it in their own interests, but will substitute direct, silent, inward communion instead. It will not mock at itself with ostentatious, theatrical ceremonies nor at truth with hollow clamour, but will substitute the remembrances of moral law in everyday conduct instead. The services of a professional priestly class were needed when the intellect of the race was still undeveloped and the masses still uneducated. But today, when men are becoming mentally individualized and when illiteracy is becoming rapidly eliminated, people can read and reflect over sacred scriptures for themselves and with their own understanding. Not only will there be no religious ceremonials, no paid clergy, but there will be no public prayers. For these, sooner or later, tend to degenerate into hollow, meaningless formalities. Here, indeed, "Familiarity breeds contempt."

Its very newness would be an attractive feature to many because it would not have had time to develop the maladies of stiffened arteries and congealed blood, but would possess an aura of hope and helpfulness, of enthusiasm and energy. The religion of the new era must be alive. It must be so radiant with inspiration that it will have something to give man, instead of weakly begging for its own support and sustenance from him. It must be effective because so long as young people are given an uninspired religion and a mistaken education, so long will they be badly equipped for the hard business of living. We say "uninspired" because not a few even of institutionalized religion's own ministers have raised their hands in helplessness as they watched the melancholy spectacle of a deserting flock and the inevitable results of an antiquated creed dwindling daily in its authority over the lives and hearts of men. In the early part of 1939, for example, it was noted that only 5 percent of the people of London thought it worthwhile to attend any place of worship. And we say "mistaken" because, to take a particularly glaring example, the German people were one of the best-educated in the whole world and yet the Nazi doctrines were able to impose successfully on the German mind.

On the third point, the postwar situation of society will depend, eventually, less upon its political arrangements and more upon its ethical decisions. If it fails to maintain enough of the idealism born during the war, then like a rudderless, propellerless ship it will be helplessly tossed about upon a stormy sea. The old values have miserably collapsed where they deserved to do so. And, unfortunately, in their fall they have dragged down some sound, ethical ones, which have not deserved to suffer in the same way but which selfish exploitation and stupid traditionalism have unfortunately associated with them. Consequently, many men have become morally perplexed and mentally hurt. Only so far as the religious faith into which he was born coincides with the reasoned faith which he has unconsciously worked out for himself, does anyone live practically by its ethics.

On the fourth requirement of the new faith, let it be noted that we need a technique which will be workable under twentieth-century conditions and understandable by the twentieth-century mind. Otherwise, we shall end up by becoming living anachronisms, human relics of an obsolete past, and consequently ineffectual dreamers. The mold into which the religious faith and mystical ideology of the postwar world will flow will not be shaped by the desires of the spiritual guides who cling closely to the half-moribund institutions and obsolete dogmas of the prewar world. If the representatives of dying and failing traditions have seen the writing on the wall, they will have seen that the future will not conform to their selfish hopes, much less obey their selfish dictates. New and different forces are inserting themselves into men's hearts. New and different ideas are rising vitally in their minds. And new guides and new institutions will perforce come into existence to assist this process where the old ones might merely suffocate it.

The universal religion, when it comes—as it will at an appropriately advanced stage of human evolution—will not be a melange of outgrown faiths which have already fulfilled their mission, but a perfectly new and timely one. That stage, however, is far off.

The fifth requirement is that a religious teaching, today, must contain these two elements: the spiritual and the social. It must develop the individual and yet regenerate society. It must kindle solitary, personal experience and promote general, public welfare. The postwar period, with all the moral confusion, economic disorders, and political complications legated to it, will open a period of great opportunity for starting a new faith which has the wisdom to combine mystical meditation with social renovation. This is evidenced by what happened in Japan, to take a single example, after the last war. In 1921, the Japanese government outlawed, in fear of its swift-rising influence, a new hybrid cult called *Omoto-Kyo*, which combined socialism, millenarianism and mysticism and which gathered a million followers in a few years and published its own daily newspaper and magazines.

There is a profound reason why the new faith must possess such an

188 / *The Religious Urge*

integral character. In ancient civilizations, the spiritual formulation preceded the social one. But in twentieth-century civilization, the social must precede the spiritual. For men and circumstances have so changed that today we can give a new significance to human life only by first giving it new economic and political creations.

It has elsewhere been explained that the evolution of the human ego is about to undergo its most momentous historic change. Hitherto, it has wandered farther and farther in its own thought from its divine source on an outgoing orbit, but henceforth it must return nearer and nearer on an ingoing one. Hitherto, it has followed an increasingly separative movement leading to selfishness, but henceforth it will have to follow an increasingly unitive one leading to balanced altruism. Therefore, the keynote of the coming age will not be individualistic competition but co-operation, not the brutal struggle of creatures with each other for mere existence but the nobler union of all for each, each for all. If the old idea was that man must struggle against man, class against class, nation against nation, race against race, the new idea will be that they must co-operate together for their common welfare. Thus, the immense significance of such a spiritual change is that it will first have a pathway cleared for it by social-economic changes. The creation of new structural forms in the social sphere will thus be part of a higher movement whose later unfoldment will operate in the religious, mystical, and philosophic spheres.

The evolution of each ego, of each entity conscious of a personal "I," passes through three stages through immense periods of time. In the first and earliest stage, it unfolds its distinct physical selfhood, acquires more and more consciousness of the personal "I," and hence divides and isolates itself from other egos. It seeks to differentiate itself from them. It feels the need to assert itself and its interests. This leads inevitably to antagonism towards them. Its movement is towards externality, a movement which must inevitably end in its taking the surface or appearance of things for reality, that is, in materialism. Here it is acquisitive. In its second and intermediate stage, it unfolds its mental selfhood and hence adds cunning to its separative and grasping tendencies, with intellect expanding to its extremest point. Here it is inquisitive. But midway in this stage, its descent comes to an end with a turning point where it halts, turns around, and begins to travel backward to its original source. In the third and last stage, the return towards its divine source continues. Its movement is now toward internality and—through meditation, investigation, and reflection—it ultimately achieves knowledge of its true being: its source, the Overself. And as all egos arise out of the Overself, the end of such a movement is one and the same for all—a common centre. Conflicts between them cease; mutual understanding, co-operation, and compassion spread. Hence, this stage is unitive.

The central point of the entire evolution is about where we now stand. Human attitudes and relations have reached their extreme degree of selfishness, separateness, struggle, and division, have experienced the resulting exhaustion of an unheard-of world crisis, but are beginning to reorientate themselves towards an acknowledgment of the fundamental unity of the whole race. Thus, war reaches its most violent and terrible phase in the second stage and then abruptly begins to vanish from human life altogether. The separatist outlook must cease. Most of our troubles have arisen because we have continued it beyond the point where it was either useful or needful.

The unequal state of evolution of all these egos, when thrown together into a conglomerate group on a single planet, is also responsible for the conflicts which have marked mankind's own history. They stand on different steps of the ladder all the way from savagery to maturity. The backward ego naturally attacks or preys on the advanced one. Thus, the purely self-regarding ego, which was once an essential pattern of the evolutionary scheme—a necessary goal in the movement of life—becomes with time a discordant ingredient of that scheme, an obstructive impediment to that movement. If humanity is to travel upward and fulfil its higher destiny, it can do so only by enlarging its area of interest and extending its field of consciousness. It must, in short, seek to realize the Overself on the one hand, to feel its oneness on the other.

We should preserve intact what is useful to us in the old systems, but at the same time we should create what is essential to our altered times. This is what present-day philosophy is trying to do. There are sincere religious prophets and teachers, ardent mystical swamis and monks eager to guide mankind in old dusty ways and well-trodden paths. But the special importance of the philosopher's work is that he is trying to hew out a new way, to cut a new path. For he perceives what these others fail to perceive—the vital necessity of re-adjustment to the unique evolutionary change which is now taking place. The philosophic seer knows how important to the race are the future purposes and distant goals hidden in the present confused tangle of events. He knows that the evolutionary twist, which is now appearing inside the human soul, is momentous in its ultimate significance. If the war did not change human nature generally, it did change a certain number of individual human beings. Everyone knows this. But not everyone knows that the war marked a moment of profound importance in human history—the change-over from a solely egoistic extroverted and materialistic basis to a deeper one.

At an earlier stage, the evolutionary path proceeded through an increased turning outward to the senses, a growing egotism, and a developing intellect. But now it is destined that human character and endeavour must strike out new paths for themselves—must reverse these trends. This evolutionary development represents what is virtually a new beginning in the history of the present race of mankind. Cosmic forces are communicating themselves to the human mind. The most tremendous changeover of its evolution is at hand. And the same forces which are working at it from within by prompting, are also compelling it to submit itself from without by events. The great inner evolutionary changeover will be responsible for increasing tension and conflict within the individual human being, his lower self beckoning one way and his higher self beckoning another way.

All the world-shaking events of our times are compelling men and women to rise out of their habitual thoughtlessness about life. Whoever thinks that these people will be permitted to relapse into torpor again with the conclusion of the war is mistaken. For the situation today is unique. New forces have entered the planet's atmosphere which will increasingly bring powerful inner and outer pressure to bear on its inhabitants, because the ego is destined to evolve in a different direction. Hitherto it has, in most human beings, travelled farther and farther away from its hidden centre, the Overself, as it expanded its own circumference. Henceforth it will, while holding whatever is of worth in its previous gains, return closer and closer to that centre. And it will do this partly because planetary evolution has reached a point where it will enforce it and partly because it is itself so constituted that it cannot escape time by a return to the source of its own life. With the subsidence of present turmoils, the human ego will resist the realization of its spiritual possibilities less fiercely, if more subtly, than in the past. This will be a distinct and definite advance. It will show in many different phases and aspects. There is a real basis for the hope that we have seen the worst in man's conduct and that he will begin to reflect some better qualities and nobler attitudes. In this faith, we may work for a more spiritual future, sure that our efforts will not be in vain or futile. It may sustain us amid present crises when personal misfortunes bid us despair. It may enlighten us during contemporary darknesses when world events bid us fall into helpless inertia.

It would be easy to misunderstand this tenet. The assertion of such a tremendous modification in the spiritual make-up of mankind as the disappearance of human egoism from human history is certainly not made here. Such an assertion is wildly fantastic and would be and could be made with any hope of acceptance only if made to wild enthusiasts. The clinging to the "I," or the aggressive assertion of it, is something which will yield only to the intermittent batterings of constant frustrations, repeated disappointments, and frequent misfortunes—that is to say, to the experience of hundreds, if not thousands, of earthly incarnations. What is really asserted here is that:

(a) The universal crisis is a sign that we have reached a point in the process of the ego's development where the more violent and hence more extreme aspects of its inevitable struggles with other egos must be curbed in its own interest or self-destruction will ensue.

(b) The very intensity and extensity of this struggle during the war have brought about a widespread recognition of this fact.

(c) We are only at the very beginning of it now, although in a half-dozen centuries this result will have been achieved to such an extent all over the world as to be quite unmistakable. The forces which are now beginning to release themselves in mankind's character will by then increase in intensity quite rapidly. And although this has been happening on all the continents, their quickest, strongest, and fullest manifestation will occur on the North American continent. Such a development will be closely connected with the birth of a new ethnological race, which is maturing out of the American melting pot.

(d) This spiritual overturn in the ego's evolutionary life refers not to all the egos here but to the largest wave of human egos travelling our planetary path, not to all entities but only to the human ones, and not to the entire history of this earth but only to its present evolutionary cycle.

(e) At any given time, this planet will not be inhabited by more than a small number of spiritually advanced persons. Nature maintains the balance between them and the unevolved masses by constant re-adjustment. This evolutionary overturn will not, however, directly involve the entire race, but only a part of it. Those who can accept such a higher world-view are and will be heavily outnumbered by those who cannot. Small groups and scattered individuals in every part of the world will continue to respond immediately, directly, and consciously to this urge; but the response of the masses will come mainly, vaguely, and indirectly through their leaders and rulers.

(f) It does not matter, at first, that this great change in human outlook is taking place without a parallel consciousness of the inner evolutionary development, which is its real motivator. Such a deeper understanding is sure to come later. The ideology may be imperfect, but the impulsion is being felt just the same.

The new spiritual impulse which inspires all these forward movements embodying this social principle is God-sent. The old interests may struggle fiercely against it, but they cannot win against it. Forces are today entering this planet's atmosphere and pouring themselves into the humanity it bears which, owing to our having reached this unique turning point in evolution, are themselves of a unique and special character. Shadows signify the presence of light, anti-Christ the presence of Christ, and the evil forces of materialistic Nazism signify the presence of sacred powers of spiritual regeneration. If we deplore the great darkness which has fallen over this planet, we should know that it speaks of a coming dawn, as the unparalleled destructive violence of this war speaks of an unparalleled constructive peace. In other words, tremendous unreckoned spiritual energies are now in our midst and only await the ripened opportunity to manifest themselves.

Such is the coming faith, a faith suited to the requirements of men of intelligence and goodwill, capable of bringing together those whom the old religions keep divided and even hostile. No sincere well-wisher of mankind can object to the introduction of a new, genuinely inspired faith. At the very worst, it cannot harm mankind, while at the very best it may save mankind. Only the selfish guardians of uninspired, unserviceable vested interests can object to such results. But it cannot come of itself—it must come through some Man. In short, the times require a new Prophet.

There are being put forward, as religions divinely preordained for and practically suited to our times, the Ramakrishna Mission form of Hinduism and the Iranian-born faith of Bahaism. Of the the first, it need only be said that Sri Ramakrishna himself warned his disciples against forming an organized cult and that none of the old religions, however polished up they may be, really suits us today. Of the second, it is needful only to examine a few of its leading tenets to show their insufficiency. The present-day version of Bahaism, which is markedly different from its original version, rejects mysticism. But we have already seen that the needed faith must have some mystical touch about it. This rejection is all the more curious and ironical because the founder of the Bahai faith was himself a mystic and a psychic. Next, divine claims are made on his behalf. The time when reason could receive such claims is vanishing. No one man can incarnate the ineffable, unbounded Absolute Spirit. Thirdly, the Bahai faith holds that there is a progressive revelation in time and that, because it is the latest one, it is consequently the best one. Against this claim, the informed observer may well smile and match the claim of Hinduism, which holds that the oldest and primal revelation is the best one and that time only brings deterioration. Incidentally, philosophy shares neither of these views and considers them both to be self-deceptions. Nor is the Bahai claim to be the latest religion tenable today. A hundred years have passed since the first Bahai prophet appeared. Several new religions and dozens of sects have been born during that time. That only a few achieved fame has nothing to do with the argument.

The totality of Bahai mystical, self-deification claims are equally irrational in their literal form. And the Bahai religious-unification predictions have psychological roots which are unsound. Its expectations of an imminent attainment of religious unity is as groundless as its claims to possess the only divine manifestation for our age.

When they descend from piety to practice, the Bahais embrace impracticable schemes. If a certain mystically advanced ashram could not live as a harmonious, peaceable united family, how will it be possible for a merely religious Bahai world to do so? It is useless to ask humanity to outrun its present capacity, to live in a visionary's dreams or a fool's paradise. If nowhere on earth, not even amongst the most religious, most mystical, and most spiritual assemblies, fraternities, societies, or hermitages, men can live as a loving, self-sacrificing family, how can they do so when still constrained by lower outlooks? The ideal of a single human family is not immediately realizable, for it cannot be formed out of the present defective human material. To demand its instant enforcement is to label oneself an impracticable dreamer.

Considering these predictions on the level of philosophy leads to quite a different result. In both cases, we find that they arise out of emotional complexes and unphilosophic outlooks.

Hence, mystics should not hesitate to invent new and better methods suited to our times and to combine them with the best of the old ones. We know more than well that in suggesting an innovation of this kind, we lay ourselves open to become a favourable target for the critical shots of the orthodox yogis. But the twentieth century is not called upon to subscribe slavishly to the methods, disciplines, and systems of the tenth. Intelligent persons know that we cannot limit ourselves entirely to the life of the past. They have to be synthetic and to mold such elements only as they can profitably use into a fusion with present ones. So the old Indian yogas, however admirably worked out they be, are to be regarded with critical yet appreciative eyes and not simply with mute acceptance. Men of today must build up their own methods out of the needs of their own natures.

4

If so many religious tenets are falling apart or even being let go altogether, let it be remembered that not a few deserve to go. They lacked truth and held only ungrounded but long-established opinions. But the pity of it is that the other parts of religion—solid, true, worthy—have also become suspect to the confused younger minds of today.

5

Inspiration did not stop in any particular year, nor with any particular man. If it was possible then, it is possible today, and to some other man.

6

This postwar period is the most morally dangerous in all mankind's history. The breakdown of religious sanctions is inevitably more widespread than ever before. For evolution has brought millions of people to the point where irrational dogmas and unscientific beliefs have become hopelessly outmoded. Such an intellectual displacement need not be deplored because sooner or later it had to happen. But unfortunately the loss of these sanctions is accompanied by the breakdown of that which depends on them. And the most important single item among the latter is the ethical standard. People have no cause to practise virtue and fear evil when they come to believe that the one will go unrewarded and the other unpunished. The whole world has witnessed, in the barbarous wrongdoing of Hitler and his young fanatic followers, how lost to all decent living, how utterly without a conscience, how unguided by any valid sense of right or wrong, men may become when they give up religious faith but are unable to replace it by right mystical practice or correct metaphysical reasoning. They exist thereafter in a moral "no-man's-land." It is this interregnum in moral evolution between the standards set by religions and those set by mysticism or metaphysics, an interregnum where morality lapses altogether, that must necessarily constitute a period of the gravest ethical crisis and danger to mankind. The depths to which the Nazis sank amply illustrate this truth.

7

Its originator left some power behind which was partly responsible for its wide and deep spread. This is the vivifying principle behind the spread of every historic religion, a principle whose results make us exclaim with Origen, "It is a work greater than any work of man." We should regard the great originators, the great religious saviours of the human race like Jesus and Buddha, as divinely used instruments. The individual centre of power which each left behind on our planet extended for long beyond his bodily death, continued to respond helpfully to those who trusted it, but then gradually waned and will eventually terminate after a historic period has ended. No organized religion ever endures in its original form for more than a limited period. All the great religions of the earliest antiquity have perished. The originators were admittedly not ordinary men. They belonged to higher planes of thought and being. They came from spheres of consciousness superior to that of average humanity. This was highly exceptional, but it does not turn them into gods. Nor does it justify us today in living in the past and leaning on what is vanishing. For despite all lapses and regressions, humanity is now coming of intellectual age. This is one reason why it must now furnish its own teachers, must recognize and appreciate its own wise men. For in the coming age, no further descents of these superior beings like the two just named may be expected. There will be no other Messiahs than those we can evolve from amongst ourselves.(P)

8

If we gaze into the soul of modern man as it has been during the present century, we shall discern therein a state of long-drawn crisis. For two opposed and conflicting world-views have been taught him during his youth: the one religious and the other scientific and both accusing each other of being untrue. The emotional consequences of this have manifested themselves in instability, immorality, cynicism, hypocrisy, and despair. The mental consequences have manifested themselves in frustration, uncertainty, and bewilderment. So long as these two forces cannot come to terms with each other within him, so long will they exhaust and not nourish him. Such a widespread and deep crisis, such a fateful and difficult situation cannot be left unresolved for long. It is driving men to sink in bewilderment and despair, where they fail to comprehend and master it, or to rise in clarity and strength where they do. It is inevitable that man should try to unify his thoughts into a coherent system and his experiences into a coherent pattern. All traditional concepts of religion will have to be reshaped to conform to this new knowledge. If, for example, his religion tells him that the world was created five thousand years ago whereas his science tells him that it was created very much more than five million years ago, a nervous tension is set up within him which harms his mental sight and hurts his physical health. Only when he can find a satisfactory synthesis which consolidates the claims of reason and feeling without sacrificing either can he find healing of his trouble. And such a synthesis exists only in philosophy.(P)

9

New religions will come, for the demands of the intellect and the needs of the young will have to be satisfied. Some will shape themselves as movements within the existing churches, but most will shape themselves outside the churches. But even the new ones will be taken over in time by men who will form a vested interest, for the tendencies of human nature at its present stage of evolution are too egoistic. History repeats this result again and again.

10

The emphasis upon mystical insight, the respect for spiritual illumination, the desire to be a personal witness for the presence of God—these are present-day signs of religious deepening.

11

It was enough for an ancient prophet to state the truth. Today he must do more that that: he must state the reasons why it is true.

12

The prudent way of quietly and little by little dropping beliefs found to be wrong has been practised by some Churches, notably Protestant ones, but never, or rarely, by others, notably Catholic and Oriental ones.

13

The need for precise knowledge to replace vague faith is as important today in religion as in any other sphere.

14

The message for this age must satisfy its primary needs, hence must contain three elements. First, the *doctrine* that there is a divine soul in man. Second the *gospel* that it is possible through prayer and meditation and study to commune with this soul. Third, the *fact* of the Law of Recompense and hence the necessity of good thoughts and righteous deeds.

15

The time has come when religion should depend upon the certainties of universal human experience rather than the uncertainties of questioned historical events.

16

More than anything, men need today to find some kind of contact with the Higher Power which is behind them, and behind the universe.

17

It may be that religion will have to be presented in non-religious language if we are to get away from dogma that has never been questioned, from terms that have become hollow and empty, from an approach which has a boring effect. It may be that the new and more appealing presentation will use art, music, the discoveries of science, and the offering of meditation to reach the consciousness of today.

18

A religion may be reformed from within by re-inspiring and regenerating it, or from without by critically re-examining its ideas and correcting its customs.

19

Too often have people been called upon by ecclesiastical organizations to repent their ways when it is the organizations themselves which should be called upon to do so. They should abandon false teachings, renounce worldly pomp, purify selfish motives, and return to genuine religion.

20

If institutional religion is to continue an active existence, and not a decaying one, it must accept the message of the times and adapt itself to the changed new conditions.

21

Will a new world-wide religion of the future come to birth in this century? The astrologers and clairvoyants—for what their personal interpretations of the signs are worth—believe so. The old religionists think their own creed will arise rejuvenated and purified. The mystics find it in their visions and meditations. The philosopher considers it will come because it must come. But only through one man's birth and mission can its birth come. Who, What, and Where is he?

22

The commonplace forms and moralities of conventional religion are not enough for this era, when tomorrow's existence is uncertain for the whole human species, and today's mind is fed with unprecedented knowledge.

23

Even the simple assurance that there is a higher power in the universe and a loftier meaning in human existence, which religion gives—come in what shape it may—helped in the past to support life and endure death. Instruction in science at first weakened or destroyed this faith but now, through opening of the mind by relativity, nuclear physics, and biological discoveries, is beginning to confirm it, as Bacon predicted.

24

Holiness must become a reality—something vividly felt and inwardly realized—if it is to become a sincere part of religion. The consequences will then be historically shown by constructive ennobling and deepening actions, changes, or events.

25

The thoughtful man today is beginning to perceive the futility of such a shallow penetration of his own being and such a childish idea of the divine being.

26

There are young people today who have strong religious feelings, but who do not find in the traditional forms of religion sufficient satisfaction, because they do not find that they can carry it fully into their activities in the world and because they have intellectual difficulties in reconciling it with the knowledge of science.

27

The possible evils and probable dangers of venturing to reform an ancient religion are certainly there and must be recognized; but there ought not to be a total concentration on these negative sides of reform alone. The positive ones should not be ignored, the beneficial consequences in the present and to the future should not be neglected. What actually happens, the good and the bad, can be seen historically in the case of all existing and dead religions. The proper approach would not deny reforms, but measure carefully how far they can and ought to be carried out. This not only applies to the mass religions but also to the metaphysical systems and devotional theologies.

28

The Age of Faith has been succeeded by sceptic psychology, but the cycle of development is not at an end yet. For we shall return anew to our starting point, but this time it will be an intellectual Faith. We have learned to question the universe and life; we have pushed thinking to its uttermost limits; we can go no farther and must perforce sink to our knees once more in humble prayer. Then we shall acquire an unshakeable faith that will survive every question, every doubt, and that will carry us through the struggles of existence with serenity and strength.

29

The fuller entry and further permeation of religion and mysticism by science will take a few hundred years more, but will inexorably lead to the displacement of old established churches appealing to blind faith by new religions appealing to reasoned intuition.

30

War shakes the belief of mankind in a benevolent Deity. They begin to revolt against the doctrine that its hideous suffering is compatible with God's omnipotence and all-mercifulness.

31

Churches are anachronisms while the heart of man turns sick at the cold comfort of meaningless monotonous words; while the body looks up at the sky of hope and sees it turn to grey lead and tarnished brass; while the mind is tortured by despairing queries during the night that surrounds it; while faith craves for saner religion, actual and living, and is handed instead the pious aspirins of a future after-death heaven.

32

War reveals agnostic rationalism to be but a reed that breaks in one's hand. This is why the aftermath of war brings scepticism, although the presence of war brings faith to the frightened. Such is the startling contrast which the trial of scepticism and its disappointing consequences must inevitably bring about.

33

The broad masses of the people must live by accepted faith and not by reasoned enquiry; they have neither leisure, mentality, nor inclination for the latter. Consequently they have to live by religion which is ultimately and immediately based on faith. Religion is and must remain the motivating force behind their moral outlook on life. From this standpoint we have always to ask ourselves whether a religionless world would not place mankind in great jeopardy. If the defects and degeneration of old religions have caused millions to desert them, still there are vastly more millions who cling to the old dogmas simply because they have nothing else to grasp. It would therefore be an unwise, even wicked, act to abolish all religion and it would be an act which must end in failure. Those who would exterminate religious thought and practice must pause to consider the ethical breakdown which might follow. Can they offer to replace that which is taken away? They are faced with the choice of quarrelling with this view or compromising with it. But this does not mean that twentieth-century intelligence is to be insulted by offering it obsolete dogmas and ridiculous assertions; that because the multitude must have a religion therefore any worn-out creed and senseless rite will suit them. They will not. The religion that is needed by our age is a rational one.

34

When comparing the relative appeals of Christian and Buddhistic thought, remember that the weight of tradition, the power of vested interests, and the difficulty of embracing ancient forms of approach would prevent any widespread flow of the Buddhistic system in the West. The present need seems to be more for a new form that would synthesize the two systems and also add something to satisfy the special requirements of modern humanity. But the truth of the need of three progressive presentations to suit the three types—religious mystical and philosophical—has not been antiquated but only modified by present conditions.

35

Jesus today would not ask you to rely only on belief, for we can now comprehend things which were beyond the comprehension of his day. People of his time did not have the comprehension that this electric age has given us. It is through scientific comprehension of nature that the doors will open to the Light and give us greater consciousness of the One Being within us.

36

The time is approaching when orthodox religions must yield to the demand of the modern mind for doctrines that are intellectually satisfying and inspiration which is actually livable. The age of dogmatic assertion has come to an end for intelligent people and the age of scientific demonstration has come upon them. Faith can no longer convince the modern mind, but reason may and must. Modern conditions are so different that the appeal of mere dogma and myth is dwindling rapidly, though mythical explanations of the universe were necessary in pre-scientific times because the human mentality could not then grasp a better one. There are signs that this hour is almost upon us, for religious doctrines have already begun to dress themselves in the clothes of modernist philosophy and to walk in the shoes of progressed science. Nothing but good can come from the collaboration of science, philosophy, and religion, provided these terms are not limited to narrow meanings.

37

What the Western nations need to comprehend is that a large proportion of those who have been drawn into socially destructive atheistic movements fail to find satisfaction in orthodox and established religions, and that this has happened because their capacity for faith has been reduced by the development that evolution, although limited, one-sided, and unbalanced, has been working on them. Abusing and denouncing these rebels will not meet this situation. The correct way is to restate spiritual truths and laws in a scientific manner and to show that they can be saved from avoidable suffering and disaster only by learning these truths and obeying these laws.

38

The established religions are too intent on helping themselves, too forgetful of their original mission to be able to serve man sufficiently in this staggering crisis, let alone save him from its worst effects. A new force must be introduced—fresh spontaneous and sincere, unhampered by trivial pomposities, uninhibited by traditional egoisms.

39

Let us readily admit the earlier usefulness of those aged forms, but let us not desist from the search after vital, timely, and inspiring forms suited to our present needs.

40

Not by kindling the cold grey ashes of outdated religions shall we succeed in saving them. Only by facing the fact that new religions and new prophets are needed shall we save what is more important—humanity's soul.

41

What is lacking from the modern heart is a feeling of reverence in the presence of inspired men and of awe at the thought of the Power behind the universe.

42

If the old texts are to be brought to a new life today, and made to serve us too, they must be expounded by inspired men and explained by perceptive ones.

43

The widespread stimulus given to intellectual development since the opening of this scientific epoch two and a half centuries ago, and, even earlier, since the Renaissance, will reflect itself in the coming religion of the new epoch for which the world will be prepared. It will be a religion of intellect vivified by intuitive feeling, of the head balanced by the heart, sane and not superstitious. The coming of a new faith will inevitably be contested by the old ones, by those forces which are evil or materialistic, and by the selfish vested interests which profit by human ignorance.

44

Not the least of the obstacles to a spiritual revival is that the mere appearance of religion has posed as its authentic reality. When it will be openly admitted that the truths of religion have faded from the modern man's psyche, leaving only their mere shadows behind, it will be possible to do what can and should be done to revivify them. The first step will be to cast out primitive superstitions, to correct functional abuses, to democratize authority, and to get rid of hollow formalism. Yet although religion clings so desperately to what is outworn and outmoded, the desire to revive decaying creeds, techniques, and attitudes is futile; the attempt to do so is predestined to eventual failure. There is also no future for obligatory beliefs, cultural absolutisms, or imposed ideas. We have lived to witness the last desperate effort in this direction, that of Nazism, and its failure. The religious world is too hampered by its past to produce easily the new faith which mankind must construct today, if it is to survive. It is too much caught in its own medieval creation to provide dynamic leadership. If spirituality, therefore, begins to make itself felt a little among us today, it is not because of organized religion but in spite of it.

45

If many men and women have lost interest in the futilities of institutional religion they have not lost any interest whatever in the wonderful words of those grand men whose mission these institutions have purported to represent. They honour their benign sayings more than most pious people but they detest the puerile creeds and intolerant actions which were perpetrated under the shelter of such hallowed names. They revere and love those teachers who give a higher ethic to man. Although they can take no interest in the dogmatic utterances of mitred clerics and professional priests, they ever raise their minds in homage before Jesus, Krishna, Buddha, and Muhammed. If they appreciate the missions of these messianic men and receive a deeper significance in their sacred glowing utterances, they remain indifferent to the foolishness of followers who take the name of these Masters in vain, and who have strayed far from the ethical precepts. If the rebels have left behind the public observances of established religion, it is because they regard them as having degenerated into meaningless mumbo-jumbo. "Repent and return" is an old maxim but a sound one. A church which has departed from the straight and narrow road of its master can always return if it wishes. A pontiff who holds a million minds in benighted thraldom can always set them free again. A temple-priest who has battened on the trust of numerous pilgrims can always cease to be an official charlatan and help them to a higher view of God. A clergyman who entered a pulpit as his profession and not as his inspired vocation can always resign. But these decisions demand immense sincerity to make and immense courage to implement. Why should not a religion go from strength to strength, instead of from weakness to weakness? Why should it not deserve increasing success? Will not its tangible and intangible profits be greater, grander, and more enduring if it fulfils its task of emotionally comforting and morally uplifting mankind? Has not history proved such profits to be fitful and fugitive when its followers are ignobly exploited and their minds forcibly enslaved?

46

Because there will be no paid sacerdotal class, there will be no public prayers in the ideal religion. Man's mental and emotional traffic with the higher power will be a private and personal one. Therefore there will be no empty show of religiosity for the benefit of his neighbours, no chance for hypocrisy to parade itself as devotion, no mechanical phonographic repetition of phrases which time or familiarity has divested of emotional significance and mental content. For although a congregation may gather in a public building, the prayers it will silently utter, the devotions it will silently perform, will not follow a set collective form but will be quite individual. Furthermore no separate order of clergy will be set apart from or be permitted to dominate over the laity, but a democratic basis of mutual consultation will support. Thus it was a sixteenth-century German, Sebastian Franck, who wrote in one of his books that a minister of the Gospel should resign his living when he finds that his sermons bear no spiritual fruit in changed lives. Franck himself soon demonstrated his sincerity by following his own advice. The old religious faith found itself at war with reason; the ideal faith will look to reason as an ally in its own camp. That is why the religious society which is to express such a faith will inevitably refuse to submit itself to any priesthood. But this is not to say that it is to submit itself to a completely democratic system. How could it, when the tenets which it holds speak plainly of the spiritual inequality of man, of the distinctions which show themselves in moral outlook and intellectual equipment? It will find an alternative way between these two extremes, the way of honorary, unpaid, inspired expositors. It will be the birth of a new priesthood, a priesthood that could give men the inner peace they hunger for, that could inspire them with the wisdom and courage to tackle personal problems rightly, and that could show them that there is something back of life worth living for; it would not need to mortgage its services to the State. It would get all its needs voluntarily satisfied by those whom it helped. But if it could not really help men, then its failure would eventually become its own scourge. People do not want empty puerile words alone; they want new hope and new faith that their problems will be solved and life's essential worth can be found.

47

If one dares to look forward, a new religion will arise with the decay of the old; a new prophet will bring the fresh wind of divine inspiration to a dulled humanity. But both religion and its prophet must be *new*, fresh, vital.

48

The need and demand today is for explicit statement, not for enigmatic ones. They are a survival from medieval periods when religious persecution was rife and intolerant. Or they are the unhealthy symptoms of mental disorder.

49

The existing orthodox religions both in the Orient and in the Occident have lost a great part of their inner vitality and exist largely as a collection of conventional mechanical forms. It is the duty of religions to guide mankind correctly and uplift them morally. When they can no longer fulfil this function sufficiently, they slowly die off or are destroyed by their own karma. In 600 years all the existing orthodox religions will have disappeared from this planet and new ones will have arisen to replace them. This means that new prophets will be appearing among mankind in different parts of the world, of whom there will be one who will be the greatest of all. From him there will start a new religion which will spread in all the continents side by side with the other religions of more limited influence. In this world religion, the prophet will appeal to the combined intellect, feelings, intuition, and will of human beings.

This new world religion will include some simple elementary meditation as well as prayer. It will state some of the laws which govern the universe as well as human life.

In the situation which now faces us and will continue to face us for several years, what is the best way in which we can help humanity and also help ourselves? It is to remember that we can help mankind only to the extent to which we develop ourselves. In that way only can we become a channel through which spiritual forces can flow to others and in that way only can we find the true protection against the dangers that menace the world. Therefore each student should work on himself, and especially on his character, harder than ever before.

Human life is like a river which must keep overflowing onwards and not become a stagnant pool. Our era needs and must find a new inspiration, a new hope, and a new life. There was a time when it could have done these things quite peaceably but because it did not understand its own situation it is being made to do them in pain and suffering. Those who will not wake up to the hard facts of the situation will be awakened later by the terrific crash of atomic bombs, and worse.

50

The Indian *sadhu* who marks his forehead with a bond of ashes, or smears his scalp with them, or covers his whole body under them, is symbolically reminding himself that everything is destroyed in the end. This is supposed to help him abandon desires and free himself from attachments. If the same mental attitude can be developed without using ashes, why give them more importance than they deserve? It is not clear enough that what really matters are the thoughts, and that by proper education they can be trained to understand, appreciate, and hold spiritual values without resort to ash-smearing—a messy affair anyway since they have first to be prepared and then mixed with butter and lime-juice. A further supposition for the existence of this religious custom is that God himself, being depicted with three lines of ash on his forehead, is brought to mind by the custom when followed, as recommended, by ordinary laymen, and thus they are better strengthened to bear their troubles. Why then is this custom fast vanishing from India along with several others which were inaugurated in the childhood of the race? There are several reasons for this disappearance. One of them is that the higher level of intellectual education is creating a habit of questioning what is old and anachronistic. If nuclear physics is leading more and more to the superior image of God as

Universal Mind and Power rather than as glorified Man, if knowledge of meditation as a help to calm the mind when suffering is present is rippling over into the masses, the latter will exchange more and more these indirect primitive helps for direct and more advanced ones. Even Emerson, a former clergyman, predicted well over a hundred years ago that the religion of the future would be, and have to be, more intellectual to keep pace with the growth of mankind.

51

The coming faiths will be wider than the old ones, for they cannot be deeper. They will explain more to more. They will not reject intellect, nor its modern product, science, but will put both in their own place, just where they belong. Their conception of God will be infinitely more godlike than so many familiar, limited, and anthropomorphic conceptions that have been babbled in the past.

52

When the spirit of impartial research for its own sake no longer prevails, when the aspiring mind is half-strangled by narrow traditions and absurd superstitions, it is time for a fresh religious impulse to be given.

53

It was an error in the past, whose consequences the whole world is suffering today, to believe that in order to conceal the truth from the unready, untruth should be taught to them. For with the growing capacities of men, growing rebellion against being misled was certain to come.

54

What is the religious ideology which is to reign over the coming age? It must be: first, rational in form; second, effective in inspiring faith; third, powerful in uplifting character and influencing conduct; fourth, quick in meeting the requirements of modern times; and fifth, attentive to social needs.

55

If orthodox religion would as vigorously denounce its own hypocrites as it does its heretics the believing world would be better served.

56

There are movements of thought and shifts of standpoint in religious circles today which could not have been entertained last century. Even the mere fact that there has been discussed—quite apart from whether or not there have been negotiations—reunion between the Orthodox and the Anglican Churches and Protestant Churches, is highly eloquent of the change of atmosphere. In England, for example, The Fellowship of Saint Alban and Saint Sergius has done useful work in bringing together the intellectuals of Orthodoxy and Anglicanism, so that there is better understanding of one another's beliefs, more correction of errors and knowledge of agreements, where they stop and why.

57

The history of even our own unfinished century has shown unprecedented changes in every department of human life, circumstance, and thought. How then can religion escape? There are grave weighty problems which it did not have to meet in the earlier periods.

58

A merely pious attitude whose basis is blind faith and whose technique is simple prayer makes a good beginning yet is only a beginning. For the conditions through which we have to pass, the experiences which life ordains, bring about in the course of reincarnations a questioning which only philosophy can satisfy in the end. The Jew whose piety is mocked by the slaughter of six million of his co-religionists, the Hindus and Muhammedans whose meditations or prayers are interrupted by riots which remove another million from earth's scene, must sooner or later come to realize that faith is not enough, and that knowledge must be acquired to supplement it, not to supplant it. A refined understanding of cosmic purposes and cosmic laws is also needed. They find that sentimentality does not save them in their hour of need.

59

The old established and traditional religions will crumble with time and events, as they are doing more quickly in Asia, but as they pass they will carry with them what is intrinsically good for, and helpful to, the masses. Their negative attributes and disservices are regrettable, but it is not fair to note the one side without the other. The cultivation of religious reverence is a basic need on any level of human existence and comprehension.

60

There is a feeling among many more than is realized, because it is often somewhat obscure, that the contemporary conditions of life in time, which may well be the last lap for most living people, have made the finding of a satisfactory spiritual relationship to God urgent and essential, if life is to be raised from confusion and redeemed from terror. There is a vital and urgent need in human minds today of relating personal experience to the universal experience in which it has been born. Put into religious terms, it is a need of finding God.

61

In these days of criticism and revision it would be prudent for any established religion to shed its accumulated superstitions so long as the process does not affect fundamental truths.

62

What is beautiful or useful or serviceable in tradition should be kept.

63

The disaster in which European humanity found itself did not indicate the failure of Christianity, as its enemies declare, but the failure of Churchianity. A nation without some genuine spiritual inspiration is a society without a spine. It will collapse when the big test comes.

64

Religion in its purity deserves reverence; in its decay, scepticism. When a noble tradition tails off into a mere travesty of itself, the end is near, and none ought then to complain when somebody attempts to hasten it. When honest men feel they no longer receive any spiritual help from a church, they stay away. And what help can come from those who are full of the letter but empty of the spirit?

65

Orthodox religious leaders rightly condemn the unsatisfactory nature of an education which leaves out the making of moral character, but the remedy which they offer is only a little better than the disease. For they would deform the growing rationality of the young and clip their intellectual wings by reverting to a narrow type of education based on outworn religious dogmas and unacceptable scriptural statements. The coming age will demand reason alongside its righteousness, a sharper intelligence rather than a drugged one, and a religious truth rather than religious distortion and debasement.

66

We need a bold and unconventional departure from ordinary methods of approach sanctified by time and usage.

67

Unless a religion renews itself constantly, like every living organism, and develops itself periodically in relation to the varying needs of new epochs, its doctrines will become dead, petrified formulae, its priests or ministers will become mere mechanical gramophones, and its followers will become hapless stumblers in the night.

68

Outwardly the religious situation may seem excellent, the religious institutions well-supported, but inwardly the real effectiveness may be little.

69

Those who believe that the spiritual awakening of mankind must express itself necessarily through the old faiths, the old organizations, believe that the way forwards leads backwards. The old forms may share some of the fruits of this awakening but it will be only until the new forms get strong enough to replace them more and more.

70

The religions of Europe are torpid; its cults are in a state of apathy. Those leaders who have conquered the small groups of occult and mystical students possess no influence with the people at large because they possess no spiritual power; they pour but a continuous cascade of *words*. The crowd who follows them confuses this windy rhetoric with spiritual reality.

71

Let us not be afraid of the truth: *new* bibles will appear in the history of man, his religion, and his culture. The end of revelation and inspiration is not in sight.

72

If popular institutional religion is to save itself and at the same time serve the people, then it must recognize that the time is at hand when it ought no longer stand between them and the higher truths.

73

At this late hour in cultural and educational history, men will not accept the view that they are not to look into these things, not to search for answers where knowledge seems impossible. It may well be so, but the right to search must be safeguarded.

Part 2:
THE REVERENTIAL LIFE

He who sits with humbled, bowed head and folded, clasped, or knees-rested hands, with mind and heart in awed reverence, in sincere, worshipful, and rapt absorption which is aware of nothing else than the divine presence—he is praying, is meditating, is worshipping, is in heaven already.

1

DEVOTION

All living forms everywhere embody this principle of being—the One Infinite Life-Power. It is not itself personal yet it is open to man's personal access and will respond to his invocation—provided he succeeds in establishing contact with it and provided his approach is right—but its response must come in its own way and time.

2

The devotional element belongs as much to this quest as to any other. *Adoration* of the divine soul and *humility* in the divine presence are two necessary qualities which the quester ought to develop. The first is expressed through meditation and the second through prayer.

3

Look how the smaller birds greet the sun, with so much merry chirruping and so much outpouring of song! It is their way of expressing worship for the only Light they can know, an outer one. But man can also know the inner Sun, the Light of the Overself. How much more reason has he to chirp and sing than the little birds! Yet how few men feel gratitude for such privilege.(P)

4

Why ought I to cultivate religious faith, feeling worship? Because it lifts up the feeling nature generally. Because it develops humility. Because it invites Grace. Because it is the duty of a human being in relation to its Source.

5

Krishna, in the *Bhagavad Gita*, is the individual's own higher self. He must keep his inner shrine within the heart reserved for the Ideal. He should worship there the Spirit that is birthless and deathless, indestructible and divine. Life in this world is like foam on the sea: it passes all too soon; but the moments given in adoration and obeisance to the Soul count for eternal gain. The most tremendous historic happenings on this earth are, after all, only pictures that pass through consciousness like a dream. Once the seeker awakens to the Real, he sees them for what they are. Then he will live in Its serenity, and it will no longer matter if the pictures themselves are stormy and agitated. It is the greatest good fortune to attain such serenity—to be lifted above passion and hatred, prejudice and fear, greed and discontent, and yet to be able to attend effectively and capably to one's worldly duties. It *is* possible to reach this state. The seeker may have had glimpses of it already. Someday, sometime, if he is patient, he will enter it to stay—and the unimaginably rewarding and perfect purpose of his life, of all his lifetimes, will be fulfilled.

6

He will come to perceive that his real strength lies in remembering the higher self, in remembering the quest of it, and, above all, in remembering the two with intense love, devotion, and faith.

7

If the aspirant will cultivate a feeling of reverence toward the higher power, whether it be directed toward God, the Overself, or his spiritual guide, he will profit much.

8

There is a sacred quality about one side of philosophy which ought not be underrated by those who are unattracted by anything religious.

9

When devotion, worship, and reverence are fortified by knowledge, they can one day reach a stage where notably less is desired or demanded and peace then naturally arises. Nor is a measure of peace the only gain. Virtue later follows after it, quietly and effortlessly growing.(P)

10

Metaphysical study will not weaken reverence but will rather put it on firmer ground. Metaphysical understanding will not weaken devotion but will rather more firmly establish it. What it will weaken, however, is the attachment to transient *forms* of reverence; what it will destroy is the error of giving devotion exclusively to the individual and refusing to include the Universal.(P)

11

Since true philosophy is also a way of life, and since no such way can become effectual unless the feelings are involved, it includes and cultivates the most refined and most devotional feelings possible to man.(P)

12

Nature displays her beauteous landscapes in vain if he who has wandered into her presence lacks the aesthetic reverent sensitivity to glance appreciatively at the grand vistas. Similarly, philosophy calls for a tuned-in, quieted, and reverent mentality if a man who wanders to its feet is to profit by it.

13

Our greatest strength comes from reliance on the Higher Self and faith in the Higher Laws.

14

The ancient pagan who greeted the sunrise by stretching out his arms to it and the simple Oriental who still does so obeyed true instincts of worship which civilized religions have not improved.

15

I will never tire of telling men that the Overself is as loving as any parent and that it does care for our real welfare. But we must return that love, must give our unconditional devotion, if we are to have a correct relationship with it.

16

A proneness to veneration is necessary in an aspirant: it helps him in different ways. But the sceptical and denigrating attitude which is so common in certain intellectual and social circles tends to make any manifestation of this quality quite impossible.

17

The need is for much more *bhakti*, especially during meditation, for intenser and warmer yearning to *feel* the sacred presence. It is really a need to descend from merely knowing in the head to knowing and feeling in the heart.

18

Intense devotional religious feeling is as much a part of the philosopher's character as quietly mystical intuitive feeling.

19

I have been astonished to meet Buddhists in the Orient and Theosophists in the Occident who deny the usefulness and scorn the need of devotion. How can there be any higher life without this very holy feeling, without the reverence, worship, communion, self-humbling, aspiration, and self-surrender that it embodies?

20

This deep, inner, and indescribable feeling which makes him yearn for closeness to the higher power is neither a misguided feeling nor a vain one.

21

It is a queer notion which regards a philosopher as a man without feeling, only because he has brought it under control. Not that it is altogether to his credit that he has been able to do so, for grace must share some credit too. There is plenty of feeling in his communion with the Higher Self.

22

This is the magic talisman which will strengthen and save you, even though you go down into Hades itself—this faith and love for the inner self.

23

It is a necessary moment in a man's life when he turns attention away from self to humbled recognition of the divine being which activates the planet on which he dwells. From such wondering thoughts he may be led to worshipful ones and thence to a still deeper self-forgetfulness. The climax, if it comes, will be the feeling of divine Presence.

24

Truth is not only to be known with all one's mind but also to be loved with all one's heart.

25

Reverence, awe, adoration—these are evoked by, and themselves evoke the feeling of, the Overself's presence.

26

In the French nineteenth-century Academy painter Jean-Léon Gérôme's picture *The Two Majesties*, a lion squats on a flat high rock in the desert fringe watching the setting sun. Its concentration of attention seems perfect, its interest in the golden orb is complete. The ordinary human, having no access to the precise state of animal consciousness, could even ask himself whether the lion is rapt in worship; it may have seen from a distance the desert Bedouins so engaged in their prescribed daily devotions. Certainly chimpanzees have been observed greeting the rising sun and thumping their chests in salute.

27

Reverence and homage are apparently not limited to animate beings, particularly not to human beings. We read in early Greek texts of inanimate ones, namely doors, which opened of themselves magically and uncannily on the approach of a divinity.

28

The message of philosophy in this matter may be summed up as this: Look beyond your tiny circle of awareness and forget the little "I" for a while in order to remember that greater and grander Being whence you have emanated.

29

His search for intellectual precision and scientific factuality need not and must not be allowed to dry up his heartfelt devotion and sensitive feeling.

30

Through associating reverence with knowledge both ways of spiritual self-recovery are enriched, while the man himself is equilibrated.

31

It is a mistake to believe that anyone could be a good practising philosopher if he is without warm feelings for the philosophic truth he professes to regard as important or to interpret with fidelity.

32

We need the turgid devotion of religion, the clearer devotion of mysticism, and the understanding devotion of philosophy. With each stage of ascent, there is more purity and less publicity, more real holiness and less lurking egoism.

33

To that self-existent untouched Reality, the heart in simple reverence must forever bow in homage, and the mind must make it the object of keenest meditation.

34

Devotion must be dovetailed in with knowledge, reverence must be locked together with understanding, if this inner work is not to be one-sided, unbalanced, and even, in some cases, unreliable.

35

The key word here is reverence. It ought to enter every remembrance and every meditation.

36

He has raised an altar to the unknown God in his heart. Henceforth he worships there in secret and in silence. His hours of solitude are reserved for it, his moments of privacy dedicated to it.

37

He has become conscious of the sacredness of existence.

38

If they do not come to this quest with enough reverence, they are led later to the reverence by the quest.

39

Memorable are those minutes when we sit in silent adoration of the Overself, knowing it to be none other than our own best self. It is as though we have returned to our true home and rest by its hallowed hearth with a contentment nowhere else to be known. No longer do we possess anything; we are ourselves ineffably possessed. The individual hopes and fears, sorrows and desires that have so plagued our days are adjourned for the while. How can we, how dare we hold them when our own personal being is tightly held within an all-satisfying embrace?

40

His devotion to the quest is something that he may not usually talk about to others, something that he finds himself forced to hide like a secret love. He dare not speak one word about it for fear that it will be received with utter incomprehension or open ridicule. This may be true of his family or his friends, his associates or his chance contacts. A shyness develops which may make him unable to seek help even from those who are more advanced on the same quest.

41

Without such faith or without some intuitive feeling, how can anyone rise to the true meaning of the Christian Gospels or the Hindu *Gita*?

42

We revere God best in silence, with lips struck dumb and thoughts hid deep.

43

This tender gentle and even beautiful feeling which moves him, holds him, and humbles him is worship, reverence, and holiness. He senses the higher power is closer than it normally is.

44

The word *bhakti* includes not only worship but also reverence.

45

Here we walk on holy ground, reverently adoring the Supreme.

46

Reverence is a beautiful quality when directed toward the higher power. The more it is developed the humbler a man must become in the Presence.

47

Humbly the ego bends in silent homage, held by the benign peace; and then this second self appears: it is the Overself. Gently the smiling Presence spreads around.

48

If men really wish to revere God, they may best do so by revering God's deputy in their hearts, the Overself.

49

Reverence, if it is to be true, authentic, and feelingful, will also be humble, self-abasing, and an act of the heart.

50

He is there all alone in a sanctuary no being can share with him, except Divine Being. This is the meaning of life for those who feel this loneliness as a form of suffering.

51

He is the best of worshippers who comes to Me in secret, who prays in silence, and who tells no one.

The greatest love

52

From the base to the apex of the philosophic pyramid, every stone should be chiselled with meticulous thought and ardent love.

53

Aspiration which is not just a vague and occasional wish but a steady settled and intense longing for the Overself is a primary requirement. Such aspiration means the hunger for awareness of the Overself, the thirst for experience of the Overself, the call for union to the Overself. It is a veritable power which lifts one upward, which helps one give up the ego more quickly, and which attracts Grace. It will have these desirable effects in proportion to how intensely it is felt and how unmixed it is with other personal desires.

54

Remember that no enterprise or move should be left to depend on the ego's own limited resources. The humble invocation of help from the Higher Self expands those resources and has a protective value. At the beginning of every day, of every enterprise, of every journey, and of every important piece of work, remember the Overself and, remembering, be obedient to its laws. Seek its inspiration, its power. To make it your silent partner is to double your effectiveness.(P)

55

If you want to know how to set about finding the Higher Self, Jesus has very clearly given the answer. Seek, knock, and ask; pray to it and for it— not just once but scores of times, if necessary, and always with your whole heart, lovingly, yearningly, reverently.

56

He must give himself up to the daily practice of devotional exercises in prayer and meditation. He must give up to this practice time that might otherwise be spent in pleasure or wasted in idleness.

57

What intellect cannot do because of its feebleness the aspirational feeling can do by its force.

58

The fourth state *is* attainable but his yearning for it must be whole-hearted and his efforts must be sustained ones.

59

To yearn only at times for this spiritual awakeness is not enough. He must yearn for it continually.

60

To remember the Overself devotedly, to think about it frequently and lovingly, is part of this practice.

61

The quest is not a thing to be played with; that is only for those who merely talk about it. To engage in it is of necessity to devote one's entire life to it.

62

Aspiration seeks its proper level. Rising waters are difficult to dam.

63

If at times he feels a kind of holiness welling up within him let him nourish it without delay. It can expand and give the fruit more sweetness.

64

Dwelling upon the beauty and tranquillity, the wisdom and the power of the Overself, he lets thoughts move towards it of their own accord.

65

If he is to achieve his purpose, it should be clearly pictured in his mind and strongly supported by his will. It should be desired with all his being, believed in with all his heart.

66

This feeling of reverence, awe, and inner attraction should be nurtured and developed so that it may grow into a great love, an aesthetic communion which is fully satisfying.

67

That which I address as "O Mind of the World!" and whom Kabbalists address as "Master of the Worlds!"—That which is without name or face or form, That alone I worship. That upon which all things depend but itself depends on nothing, That I revere. That which is unseen by all beings but which itself sees all, That I worship.

68

Each act becomes a holy remembrance: we speak on behalf of the Divine Being, we work for It, we do everything as if we were Its agent. A letter is written, or a book composed, in this reverential spirit. Hence, Shankara writes in *Saundaryalahari*: "Let all that I do thus become Thy worship."

69

Henceforth he lives on and for the quest, killing in his heart all other desires.

70

The presence of the Great Spirit can be recognized, approached, felt, and loved.

71

Life, history, experience—each gives us the same clear message. The temple of Solomon, once a pyramid in its vast area, is felled to the ground, and its thousands of worshippers gone with it. What, then, how, and where shall we worship? Let us seek the timeless Power which transcends the centuries, let us utter no word but fall into silence, for here the voice of the little ego's thoughts is an insult. Let us go where Jesus advised—deep inside the heart. For we carry the truth within ourselves—yet how few know it—and bear the closest of ties with that Power in consciousness itself.

72

Loving attention to the Overself should not be limited to moments spent in meditation or prayer, but should form the background for all one's other thoughts.

73

Hindu scriptures enjoin worship before taking any important step in life.

74

That Being from which all beings come forth and to which they finally return—that I worship!

75

To create faith is one thing; to sustain it another.

76

Why does not the Overself show its existence and display its power once and for all? Why does it let this long torment of man, left to dwell in ignorance and darkness, go on? All that the ego is to gain from undergoing its varied evolution is wrapped up in the answer. This we have considered in *The Wisdom of the Overself* and *The Spiritual Crisis of Man*. But there is something more to be added to that answer. The Overself waits with deepest patience for him—man—to prefer it completely to everything and everyone else. It waits for the time when longings for the soul will leave the true aspirant no rest, when love for the divine will outlast and outweigh all other loves. When he feels that he needs it more than he needs anything else in this world, the Overself will unfailingly reveal its presence to him. Therefore a yearning devotion is one of the most important qualifications he can possess.

77

By thought, the ego was made; by thought, the ego's power can be unmade. But the thought must be directed toward a higher entity, for the ego's willingness to attack itself is only a pretense. Direct it constantly to the Overself, be mentally devoted to the Overself, and emotionally love the Overself. Can it then refuse to help you?

78

The way to be admitted to the Overself's presence can be summed up in a single phrase: *love it.* Not by breathing in very hard nor by blowing out very slow, not by standing on the head nor by contorting like a frog can admission be gained. Not even by long study of things divine nor by acute analysis of them. But let the love come first, let it inspire the breathing, blowing, standing, or contorting, let it draw to the study and drive to the thinking, and then these methods will become really fruitful.(P)

79

Love the Overself with your whole heart if you would have it reveal the fullness of its receptive love for you.

80

When the divine has become the sole object of his love and the constant subject of his meditation, the descent of a gracious illumination cannot be far off.

81

Love is both sunshine for the seed and fruit from the tree. It is a part of the way to self-realization and also a result of reaching the goal itself.(P)

82

The love which he is to bring as sacrificial offering to the Overself must take precedence of all other loves. It must penetrate the heart's core to a depth where the best of them fails to reach.(P)

83

He needs to hold the sacred conviction that so long as he continues to cherish the Ideal his higher self will not abandon him.

84

Amid all his mental adventures and emotional misadventures, he should never lose sight of the goal, should never permit disappointment or frailty to cause desertion of the quest.

85

The reverence of confusion, when we kneel down to seek guidance out of it, is good; but the reverence of love, when we are attracted by the soul for its own sake, is better.

86

He who is possessed by this love of truth and who is so sincere that he is willing to subordinate all other desires to it will be repaid by truth herself.

87

Only when the Overself becomes the focus of all his thinking is it likely to become the inspirer of all his doing.

88

He will come, if he perseveres with sufficient patience, to look upon his practice not as a dry exercise to which he reluctantly goes at the call of duty but as a joyous return to which he is attracted by his heart's own desire.

89

If the quest calls him to sacrifice human love, will he have the strength to do so? Will he be able to crucify his ego?

90

How close he comes to the truth may depend on how deeply he cares for it.

91

Love will have to enter his quest at some point—love for the Overself. For it is through this uniting force that his transformation will at the end be effected.

92

Unless he loves the Overself with deep feeling and real devotion, he is unlikely to put forth the efforts needed to find it and the disciplines needed to push aside the obstacles in the way to it.

93

Love of the Overself is the swiftest horse that can bear us to the heavenly destination. For the more we love It, the less we love the ego and its ways.

94

The devotional attitude will not decrease with the growth of the mystical one. It too will grow, side by side with the other. But it will cast out of itself more and more egoistic selfish interest or grasping until it becomes the pure love of the Overself for the latter's sake alone.

95

Why do we come to God's presence only with our messy problems and our dark troubles? Why only as beggars, or when unhappy, miserable, unhealthy? Can we not come to Him joyously, for His own sake, for love of Him alone?

96

"Absolute truth is *the symbol of Eternity* and no *finite* mind can ever grasp the eternal; hence, no truth in its fullness can ever dawn upon it. To reach the state during which man sees and senses it, we have to paralyse the senses of the external man of clay. This is a difficult task, we may be told, and most people will, at this rate, prefer to remain satisfied with relative truths, no doubt. But to approach even terrestrial truths requires, first of all, *love of truth for its own sake*, for otherwise no recognition of it will follow. And who loves truth in this age for its own sake?"—H.P. Blavatsky

97

His longings after the Beloved's presence alternate with his despairs of ever attaining it. Indeed the higher self seems to play hide-and-seek with him.

98

Cling by love to the real.

99

This yearning for spiritual light will at some periods be accompanied by anguish but at others by pleasure.

100

The fierce loving constant devotion, even worship, which most mothers give to their only or favoured child would be enough to carry an aspirant through all the vicissitudes of the Long Path.

101

The love which really matters is love of the Highest. All other kinds are merely cheap substitutions.

102

When the idea that a Higher Power which always was, is, and shall be, becomes impregnated with faith so strongly as to have explosive force, he comes closer to Truth.

103

A man or woman to whom fate has denied the outer human love may find that it has also offered him or her the very real feeling of divine love. In that case, he or she cannot receive the gift *in its fullness* unless he or she accepts the denial with resignation.

104

Whereas he came first to the quest out of dire need for solace in suffering failure, tragedy, or despair, he comes now out of heartfelt love for the True, the Good, the Real.

105

If men offer worship at all, it is offered to a Power infinitely wiser and grander than any condition which they dare hope to attain.

106

Some feel this aspiration for a higher life so strongly that it becomes an ache.

107

Worship and thankfulness should be reserved for the Source alone. The right way to express these is to inculcate them into one's Being.

108

He is to find his highest satisfaction, his strongest attachment, in the divine Beloved.

109

You are no longer wanting God. You are now loving God. The former is only for beginners.

110

He reserves his worship for the infinite and ineffable Unseen Being alone. He will honour, and humble himself before, the human teachers who affirm its existence, but he cannot give them the same worship.

111

The more we are devoted to the diviner attractions, the less devoted or susceptible do we become to the earthly ones. Thus the mere exercise of the faculty of veneration for something beyond ourselves gradually lifts us nearer to the desireless state.

112

Only when he comes to love it deeply and understand it instinctively can he be said to have arrived at real discipleship.

Warnings and suggestions

113

The path of devoting oneself ardently to a religious love of God ought to be trod by all. But it need not be the only path; indeed that would be undesirable.

114

A worldly refusal to honour the sacred is as unbalanced as a monastic refusal to honour the secular. In a balance of both duties, in a common-sense union of their ordained roles in a man's life lies the way for present-day man. Each age has its own emphasis; ours should be equilibrium.(P)

115

The danger of the religio-mystic devotional path is the danger into which blind faith tends to fall. A facile credulity easily takes up with a harmful—because ego-satisfying—superstition.

116

It is unphilosophical to set up a cult, a system of worship with one person—the guru—as its object. He may be respected and admired, revered and loved, but he is still human and should not be worshipped.

117

Devotion to any historic or mythological deity must end, if grace is won and if advancement be experienced, in devotion to the Overself—to pure being. Precisely the same must happen with devotion to any human guru.

118

Too often this holy and beautiful feeling deteriorates under the ego's pressure and falters into mere sentimentality.

119

The notion that any human being has anything to give which God needs—be it love, adoration, or worship—is inadmissible, notwithstanding the dogmas of some popular theology and statements of some advanced mystics like Eckhart. It would make God less than what He must be.

120

The duty of worship, whether in a public temple or a private home, exists not because God needs our praise—for he is not in want of anything—but because we need to recollect him.

121

Is he thinking of the truth or is he thinking of himself? Is he interested enough in the higher self to forget this lower one? In short, is he worshipping God or the "*me*"?

122

He prostrates himself before his own ego several times daily: this is often the only worship modern man performs.

123

When we want the inner light at least as much for its own sake as for its effects, we shall begin to get it. But to seek the effects while calling on the kingdom is to deceive ourselves.

124

When this devotional path is overstressed and not balanced with any counterpoise, when the guru is made into the object of a hysterical love-game, then the imagination leads the mind into pseudo-illuminations that are worthless for Truth. The guru himself is involuntarily made into an accommodating substitute for the friendship or love, the companionship or drama or motherhood, which the world failed to offer. The august relationship of disciple and Master is turned into a love affair, with all the egoistic accompaniments of jealousy, intrigue, exaltation, or depression that go with one. Is it not understandable why atheistic sceptics sneered at the mystical raptures of cloistered nuns who saw erotic images in their visions of embracing the Lord? Admittedly the mystical eroticism of medieval nunneries may be explained, either in part or in particular cases, by this repression of sex. But it fails to explain the other part and the other cases.

125

What is prayer but a turning to the higher unseen power in the only way that simple, spiritually untutored people know? Why deprive them of it? What is wrong about its use in organized religion is that they are not taught the further facts. First, prayer is only a beginning, its continuing development being meditation. Second, it ought not be limited to material demands but always accompanied by moral and religious aspiration. Third, it is best performed, as Jesus taught, in private and secret.

126

Although the attainment is not possible without a devotional singleness of mind, this does not mean that other interests should be banned.

127

We must distinguish between a true sincere aspiration and one which is only wishful thinking.

128

Jalaluddin Rumi, the Sufi: "When men imagine they are adoring Allah it is Allah who is adoring himself."

129

There is danger to every man who denies this inner part of his being any share in daily life, any love, reverence, and worship. This danger may appear, fully realized, in his body or mind.

130

When religious devotion never rises above the physical details of the form of its object, it becomes materialistic. When it is centered in the human details alone, it becomes hysterical.

131

It is true that many of the gods worshipped by man are clothed in *forms* that are merely the products of his own imagination. But the basic *idea* behind those forms is not.

132

The feeling of religious reverence, the attitude of humble worship, must well up of themselves in the heart. It is not enough merely to go through the external and physical motions which accompany their inner presence.

133

Any image which a man forms of God, whether it be painted, mental, or human, has a place if its familiarity helps him to worship. But it still remains an image and must one day be transcended.

134

The symbols and ceremonies need to be clearly and simply interpreted to the layman so that he may not only follow intelligently what happens at a service and why it is so, but also more strongly share emotionally in it.

135

A rite may create a mood of reverence. It is active outside him yet helps the receptive mind within.

136

If the people are shown that going to church is not and ought not to be only a social habit, they can better draw from such attendance some uplift and moral strength.

137

The intellectual mystic often rejects all those liturgical, ritual, and hierarchical aspects which are so prominent in most institutional religions. For they lead human aspiration outward whereas true mysticism leads it inwards.

138

When you are fortunate enough to discover that there is both an ashram and a guru within you, just as there is also a church and a Presence within you, you may well ask, why go hither and thither for them?

139

The three little manuals of devotion, *The Bhagavad Gita*, *The Voice of the Silence*, and *Light on the Path*, used by so many, form a perfect and excellent trio and surely belong to the philosophical teaching.

140
Recommended reading list of books

Sri Aurobindo: *Lights on Yoga*

H.P. Blavatsky: *The Voice of the Silence*

Buddha: *Dhammapada*

John Bunyan: *The Pilgrim's Progress*

Sir Edwin Arnold: (1) *The Song Celestial*; (2) *The Light of Asia*

Annie Besant: (1) *In the Outer Court*; (2) *The Path of Discipleship*

William Q. Judge: translation of the *Bhagavad Gita*

Ralph Waldo Emerson: "The Over-Soul" (essay)

Evelyn Underhill: (1) *Mysticism*; (2) *Practical Mysticism*; (3) *The Essentials of Mysticism*; (4) *The Life of the Spirit and the Life of Today*

Swami Vivekananda: Works

Sri Ramakrishna: *Sayings* [Editors' note: Three selections are available. (1) F. Max Müller, *Ramakrishna; His Life and Sayings*; (2) N. Gupta, *Sayings of Parahansa Ramkrishna* (sic); (3) Sri Ramakrishna Math, *Sayings of Sri Ramakrishna*: the most exhaustive collection of them, their number being 1120]

Brother Lawrence: *The Practice of the Presence of God*

Sri Rabindranath Tagore: *Sadhana; the realisation of life*

Jacob Boehme: (1) *The Way to Christ*; (2) *Dialogues on the Supersensual Life*

Yogi Ramacharaka: *Advanced Course in Yogi Philosophy and Oriental Occultism*

Joseph Sieber Benner: *The Impersonal Life*
Ralph Waldo Trine: *In Tune with the Infinite*
Wisdom of the East Series
Smith: (1) *Persian Mystics;* (2) *Attar*
Sheldon Cheney: *Men Who Have Walked with God*
Kahlil Gibran: *The Prophet*
F.L. Woodward (trans.): *Some Sayings of the Buddha*
Plato: Works (especially "Apology of Socrates")
Seneca: Writings and other Roman Stoic writers
Gordon Shaw: *The Road to Reality*
Albert E. Cliffe: (1) *Lessons in Successful Living;* (2) *Let Go and Let God*
David Seabury: *Help Yourself to Happiness*
Mary Strong (editor): *Letters of the Scattered Brotherhood*

2

PRAYER

Prayer is one of the oldest of human acts and one of the first of human needs.

2

"Teach us how to pray," cried the disciples to Jesus. The modern man is just as bewildered as they were. He has to learn the answer afresh.

3

The quest begins with prayer and even ends with it too. No man, whether novice or proficient, can afford to throw away this valuable means of communion, adoration, worship, and request.

4

The call for prayer which, in most religions, is timed for once or twice a day and, in the Islamic religion, for five times a day, has at least two objectives in the mind of those sages who originally framed it. The first is to act as a reminder of what one is—a soul—and where one is going—ultimately to God. The second is to rescue us from the narrowing materializing routine of work or business.

5

Prayer is very necessary. It helps to clean or purge the feelings. Prayer later leads to intuition.

Do not pray for things to happen in the way you wish them to; this is not always the same as what is best for you. Even in your daily prayers you can do something to better your character.

Most people start their prayer asking for something. That is not right; prayer is an act of devotion and love to God. It is the manifestation of the feeling that there is something higher with which it is possible to come in contact. Prayer is not only asking, it is first and foremost an act of worship and love of God. Only after that is done may you ask for something for yourself—mainly, of course, for spiritual things and not material. You should pray in solitude, if possible. But you may pray with others if they are in harmony with you.

6

There is no man so advanced that he can afford to dispense with prayer. It occupies a most important place in the philosophic aspirant's life.

7

The sceptic who deems all prayer vain and useless, who regards the reasons for it as foolish, is too often justified. But when he ceases to search farther for the reasons behind prayer, he becomes unjustified. For if he did search, he might discover that true prayer is often answered because it is nothing less than making a connection—however loose, ill-fitting, and intermittent it be—with the life-force within the universe.(P)

8

There is no one so sinful or so degraded in character that he is denied this blessed privilege of a contrite yearning for communion with his own divine source. Even the failure to have ever prayed before, even a past life of shame and error, does not cancel but, on the contrary, merely enhances this right. This granted, it will be found that there are many different forms of such communion, different ways of such prayer.(P)

9

There are those who object to the introduction of prayer into the philosophic life. In a world governed by the law of cause and effect, of what avail is this whining petition for unearned boons, they ask. Is it not unreasonable to expect them? Would it not be unfair to others to grant them?

These objections are valid ones. But the subject is covered with clouds. To dispel two or three of them, it is worth noting two or three facts. The first is that whether a prayer is addressed to the Primordial Being, to the Overself, or to a spiritual leader, it is still addressed to a higher power, and it is therefore an abasement of the ego before that power. When we remember the smug self-complacency of man, and the need of disturbing it if he is to listen to a truer Voice than his own, what can be wrong with such self-humbling? He will not be exempted by his petitioning from the sway of the law of cause and effect. If he seems to get an answer to his prayer we may be sure it will be for reasons that are valid in themselves, even if he is ignorant of those reasons. But how many prayers get answered? Everyone knows how slight the proportion is.

The man who is earnestly seeking to advance spiritually will usually be ashamed to carry any worldly desire into his sacred prayer. He will be working hard upon himself to improve, purify, and correct himself, so he need have no hesitation to engage in prayer—for the right things. He will pray for better understanding of the higher laws, clearer sight as to what his individual spiritual obligation consists in, more and warmer love for the Overself.(P)

10

It is strange that most just persons usually acknowledge having no right to get something for nothing, yet in the matter of prayer they feel no shame in requesting liberation from their particular weaknesses or habitual sins. Are they entitled to ask—often in a mechanical, importunate, or whining manner—for a result for which other persons work all-too-hard? Is it not effrontery to ask for divine intervention which should favour them while the others toil earnestly at reshaping themselves?

How then should a man pray? Should he beg for the virtues to be given to him gratis and unearned for which other men have to strive and labour? Is it not more just to them and better in the end for himself if, instead of demanding something for nothing, he prays thus: "I turn to you, O Master, for inspiration to rise above and excel myself, but I create that inspiration by my own will. I kneel before you for guidance in the problems and decisions of life, but I receive that guidance by taking you as an example of moral perfection to be followed and copied. I call upon you for help in my weakness and difficulty, my darkness and tribulation, but I produce and shape that help by trying to absorb it telepathically from your inner being." This is a different kind of prayer from the whining petitions often passing under that name, and whereas they seldom show direct, traceable results, this always shows them.(P)

11

He should not fall into the error of believing that the transition to philosophical study has exempted him from the duty of mystical practice or that the transition to the latter has exempted him from the need of religious devotion. We do not drop what belongs to a lower stage but keep and preserve it in the higher one. Aspiration is a vital need. He should become as a child at the feet of his divine Soul, humbly begging for its grace, guidance, and enlightenment. If his ego is strong, prayer will weaken it. Let him do this every day, not mechanically but sincerely and feelingly until the tears come to his eyes. The quest is an integral one and includes prayer alongside of all the other elements.(P)

12

Prayer is the mood of the lower self when it turns towards the higher self.

13

We pray to confess sin or to humble self, to commune with the Divine or to invoke Grace, in joy as well as in despair.

14

Prayer does not mean bribery, flattery, or fright.

15

Those endowed with strong critical judgement may feel that it is useless to bow the head and bend the knees in prayer. It might be better for the personal balance if they did so, but their difficulty must be recognized.

16

Buddha labelled prayer as quite useless. Jesus, on the contrary, invited his followers to frequent prayer.

17

We are called to prayer because we can achieve no success, whether in human life or in the spiritual quest, without seeking and gaining divine help.

18

In those situations wherein it is totally helpless to save itself from danger and death, every creature sends forth an anguished cry from the heart. And this is as natural to animals as to human beings. The younger animals address it to their physical mother, the older ones to the Father-Mother of all beings, God.

19

Can anyone correctly say that he can put no feeling behind prayer for spiritual light, guidance, or help because he knows so little about it or has so little faith in it? At least he realizes the need of help from an outside source and can beseech or petition whatever powers there be to give whatever help they can. Telepathy being a fact and the mental world being no less real than this one, such concentrations cannot be without some kind of value.

20

The first value of prayer is that it is a confession of personal inadequacy and, by consequence, an aspiration to personal upliftment. It is a self-humbling of the ego and the beginning of a detachment from it. It is a first step in obedience to Jesus' paradoxical proclamation, "He that loseth his life shall find it."

21

Dionysius the Areopagite said that there were three kinds of prayer: the circular, the spiral, and the direct.

22

Those who believe prayer to be a remnant of primitive superstition, outmoded in a modern spiritual life or unheeded by a higher mystical one, are wrong. The twentieth-century man may as profitably give himself to it today as the second-century man did—perhaps more profitably because he requires more help from outside himself.

23

However, if prayer is an indispensable part of the spiritual life, lower conceptions of prayer are not indispensable to a higher grade of that life.

24

Within the conception of philosophy there is room for the humblest prayerfulness as well as the acutest intelligence.

25

The Christian grace before, the Hebrew thanksgiving before and after meals, were prescribed for the same reason that the Muhammedan's brief five-times-a-day prayer was prescribed. And this was to bring the remembrance of life's higher purpose into everyday living.

26

Many philosophic students do not realize the importance of prayer and are genuinely surprised when counsel is given to preface their meditations with a few minutes of humble worship. Some protest that they do not know to What or to Whom to pray; that God as the Absolute Principle is incapable of intercommunication, whilst God as the popular dispenser of boons and woes is a mere fiction of priests and clerics. They seem to think that those who have started practising mystical exercises—and certainly those who have commenced philosophic studies—have no further need for prayer. They could not be more mistaken.

The positive gains from each stage of the Quest are never lost. Those of religion are preserved in the mystical stage, and must not be rejected; those of mysticism are retained in the third and higher degree of philosophy. Naturally, the individual advances to higher conceptions of prayer, but that is not to say he advances beyond its practice altogether. Such an atheistic attitude could never be sanctioned. Sincere prayer is a necessity and a delight to the earnest student.

To return to those who are still wondering to What or Whom they should address their prayers: it is suggested they offer them in the direction of That in whose existence they presumably do believe—their own Higher "I."

27

Too many individuals—and some of them are followers of this Quest—fail to remember the importance of simple prayer. There is not enough humbling of intellectual pride at the feet of the Higher Power and there is an obvious neglect of reverent worship in their attitudes and daily lives.

28

One must not overlook the importance of prayer, particularly at a certain stage of development. This does not mean the mechanical formula of an orthodox church, but simple, spontaneous, fervent worship—a petition for communion—directed from the heart to the Higher Self.

29

The mystic has to pass through the earlier stage of regarding the Overself as an "other" before he can arrive at the later stage of regarding it as his own essential self. Hence the need of prayer for the first stage.

30

True prayer may be any of several things: humble opening of the whole heart so that the Divine may enter if it chooses to do so, allowing endeavour to achieve silent communion with the higher power, or a selfless seeking to understand the divine will in any particular situation.

31

The suggestion that the student devote more time to prayer is made and repeated because it is believed that prayer can be of great help to his progress.

Forms of prayer

32

The devotional nature of the student should be brought out by cherishing love for the Divine, nurturing aspirations toward the Divine, and cultivating earnestness in quest of the Divine. These qualities are best expressed through the habit of daily prayer. The love will be expressed by the eager feeling with which he turns his thoughts to prayer every day; the aspiration will be revealed by the height towards which the worship will reach during the prayer and by the depth towards which his self-abasement will fall during the same time. The earnestness will be shown by the fundamental mood of endeavour after self-betterment which should underlie his whole waking life.

33

Each morning the inner work is to be prefaced by a brief prayer and physical obeisance, the first asking to be used as a channel, and the second seeking a reorientation of contact.

34

A philosopher's prayer: "That which is the ever-living presence in man: to That I turn when in trouble; on That I meditate when at rest; may That bless with its grace my entry into the other side of death."

35

It is good to pray that the coming year may find in you a more aspiring and more determined person, a calmer and better balanced seeker after truth.

36

The power of thought is greatest when it is inspired by that which is beyond thought, and so, with the approach of the Christmas–New Year season, the mystic takes others with him into this mental remembrance which is to him a form of meditation and which he believes will not be without some inner value to them.

37

Kneeling, the Western bodily attitude of prayer, expresses the mental attitude of humility. Prostration, the Eastern attitude of prayer, with the forehead bent close to the floor, carries the same mental attitude to the extreme degree—abasement.

38

Thanks for Thy presence and existence here and now.
Praise for making life on earth more bearable and more endurable when it becomes oppressive.(P)

39

The Egyptian priest knelt on the floor on his haunches, heels supporting buttocks, both arms stretched out sideways to receive invisible powers from above, the palms upturned toward heaven.

40

Prayer is at its best, and consequently most effective, when it is done in humility and love.

41

He should make use of prayer. Every day he should go down on his knees and pray for grace, offer himself in self-surrender to the higher self, and express his yearning and love for it. Such readiness to go down on his knees for a minute or two, to abase the ego's pride in prayer, is extremely valuable. This is what Jesus meant by becoming "as a little child"; this humility is inspired childlikeness, not stupid childishness.

42

It was Origen, the early Church Father, who asserted that the true posture of prayer is the standing one, where the arms are stretched out in the shape of a cross.

43

O Thou Divinity within me, (and in whom I similarly am)—may I ever remember why this earthly life must be elevated and redeemed.

44

With hands upraised, the palms and fingers steepled in the gesture of prayer, a man expresses himself, with or without voice, to the Infinite instinctively and physically.

45

"May He guide our minds," prays the Hindu every day. This is a good humbling thought.

46

At some point during your prayer surrender your personal self to God, and your personal will to His Will.

47

If you want a workable and faultless prayer, what is better than the one which Socrates habitually used, "Give me that which is best for me," or the one which some older pagan used, "May I love, seek, and attain only that which is good"?

48

In all times hands have been lifted—whether in supplication or in aspiration—before God. This is an instinctive natural gesture.

49

Hymn: "Praise God from Whom all blessings flow,
Praise Him, all creatures here below;
Praise Him above, Angelic Host,
Praise Father, Son, and Holy Ghost!"

50

Buddhist form of showing homage: Place both hands together with palms touching. Raise up the arms and then bring them backward until the thumbs rest on the forehead.

51

What a privilege to carry
Everything to God in prayer!
Oh, what peace we often forfeit,
Oh, what needless pain we bear—
All because we do not carry
Everything to God in prayer!
—nineteenth-century hymn

52

It is advisable to bring your prayer or healing treatment to an end with a silent or spoken expression of thanks to the higher power. It should be uttered with strong fervour and deep humility.

53

The Jain saint Amitagati: a) "Pray my mind, O Lord, be always at equilibrium, at home and abroad." b) "By self-analysis, self-censure, and repentance, I destroy sin."

54

Thou!
Unseen, untouched and unknown,
The only grace I beg for
Is the grace of loving Thee!
—My prayer

55

The Seven Sacred Physical Postures and Mental Attitudes of Philosophic Worship (Essay also printed in volume 4)

The function of these postures is suggestive and helpful. They are symbolic of seven emotional attitudes. Each physical posture is to some extent an index to the feelings which actuate it. Because man dwells in a body of flesh, his bodily posture is as significant during prayer and worship as during any other activity: it becomes a sacred gesticulation.

Some mystically minded people, either because they reject all ceremonial observance or because they can see no utility in them whatever, object to using these postures. On the first ground, we answer that in philosophy such practices are not hollow rites, but valuable techniques, if performed with consciousness and with intelligent understanding. On the second ground, we answer that the exercises depolarize the physical body's earthward gravitation and render it more amenable to the entrance of spiritual currents. They clear the aura of undesirable magnetism. If anyone feels that he has no need of them, he may dispense with them.

Three remarks by Avicenna serve as an excellent introduction to the use of these postures.

"The act of prayer should further be accompanied by those attitudes and rules of conduct usually observed in the presence of kings: humility, quietness, lowering the eyes, keeping the hands and feet withdrawn, not turning about and fidgeting."

"These postures of prayer, composed of recitation, genuflection, and prostration and occurring in regular and definite numbers, are visible evidence of that real prayer which is connected with, and adherent to, the rational soul. In this manner the body is made to imitate that attitude, proper to the soul, of submission to the Higher Self, so that through this act man may be distinguished from the beasts."

"And now we would observe that the outward, disciplinary part of prayer, which is connected with personal motions according to certain numbered postures and confined elements, is an act of abasement, and of passionate yearning on the part of this lower, partial, compound, and limited body towards the lunary sphere."

—from *Avicenna on Theology*,
by A.J. Arberry

1. *Standing and remembrance.*

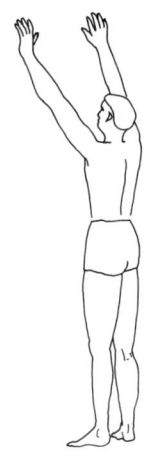

(a) Stand comfortably, facing towards the east or the sun. (b) Plant the feet ten inches apart, raise arms forward and upward until they are about halfway between vertical and horizontal levels, at forty-five degrees above the horizontal, and fully extended. (c) The palms of both hands should be turned away and upward. (d) The head is slightly raised and the eyes are uplifted.

Bring the mind's attention abruptly away from all other activities and concentrate only on the Higher Power, whether as God, the Overself, or the Master. The act of uplifting the arms should synchronize with decisively uplifting the thoughts. The mere fact of abruptly abandoning all activities and of practising the lifting of hands for a certain time will help to bring about the uplift of the mind.

2. *Stretching and worship.*

(a) Assume the same position of feet and arms as in the previous posture. (b) Bend in lower part of arms at elbows and bring palms of both hands flatly together, at the same time inhaling deeply. Hold the breath a few seconds. Exhale while letting arms fall.

The attitude should be one of loving, reverential, adoring worship of the Overself.

3. *Bowing and aspiration.*

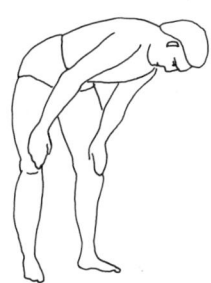

(a) With feet still apart, place both hands lightly on front of the thighs. (b) Bend the trunk forward at the waistline until it is nearing a horizontal level. Take care to keep both knees rigidly straight and unbent. (c) Let the palms slide downward until they touch the knees. Relax the fingers. (d) The head should be in line with the backbone, with the eyes looking down to the floor.

By pouring the devotion and love towards the Higher Power, the feeling of a personal relation to It should be nurtured.

4. *Kneeling and confessions.*

(a) Drop down to the floor and rest the knees upon it. (b) Lift the trunk away from the heels, keeping it in a straight erect line with the thighs. (c) Flatten the palms of both hands together and bring them in front of, as well as close to, the breast. (d) Close the eyes. This, of course, is the traditional Christian prayer posture.

Remorsefully acknowledge weaknesses in character and confess sins in conduct in a repentant, self-humbling attitude. Be quite specific in naming them. Also confess the limitations, deficiencies, and imperfections one is aware of. Second, ask for strength from the Higher Power to overcome those weaknesses, for light to find Truth, and for Grace. The qualities needed to counteract them should be formulated in definite terms. This confession is an indispensable part of the philosophic devotions. When it is sincere and spontaneous, it makes a proud man humble and thus opens the first gate in the wall of Grace. It compels him to become acutely conscious of his ignorance and ashamedly aware of his weakness. The praying person humbles the ego and breaks up his vanity; therefore he must not hide his mistakes or look for excuses. Only through such frankness can the time come when he will get the strength to overcome that mistake. This confession forces the praying person down to the ground and his self-respect with him, like a humiliated beggar. In his anguish, he constantly rediscovers his insufficiency and need of help from God or God's man.

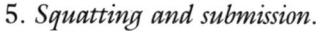

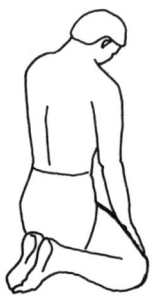

5. *Squatting and submission.*

(a) Remaining on the knees, sink down until both heels support the trunk's weight, spine and head erect, hands on thighs. (b) Lower the chin until it touches the chest. (c) The eyes should be kept half-closed.

This posture is to be done with the mind and heart together completely emptied and surrendered to the Higher Power in utter resignation of the self-will. Humbly surrender the ego and discard its pride. Pray for Grace and ask to be taken up into the Overself completely. It is a sound instinct which causes a man to bend his head when the feeling of reverence becomes strong within him.

6. *Prostrating and union.*

(a) Without rising, and keeping legs folded at the knees, bend the torso forward and incline the face as low as possible. (b) Bring the hands to rest upon the floor-rug, with palms outstretched, taut, and touching. (c) Place the forehead upon the hands. The knees should then be crouched up toward the chest. All ten toes must touch the floor. (d) Shut the eyes. The ancient Egyptian religion made *hetbu* or "bowing to the ground" an important part of its worship. The Muhammedans make bowings of the body during prayer equally important. This posture is practised widely in the Orient, but it is inconvenient to most Western people and is therefore usually withdrawn from them. If anyone, however, is much attracted to it, he may practise it.

During this posture, one should empty the mind of all thoughts and still it. Relax the emotions, open the heart, and be completely passive, trying to feel the inflow of heavenly love, peace, and blessing.

7. *Gesturing* (with thoughts concentrated on service and self-improvement).

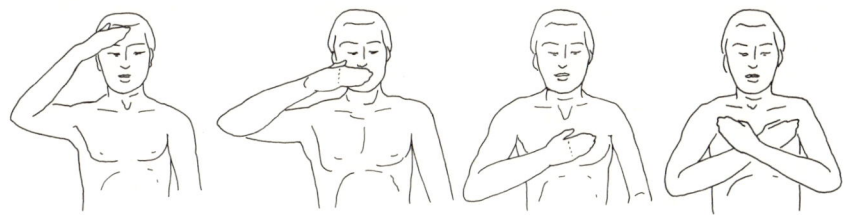

(a) So as not to lose this high mood, rise from the floor slowly and smoothly to resume ordinary activities in the world. At the same time, turn attention away from self towards others, if inclined. Intercede for them, draw blessings down upon them, and hold them up to the divine light, power, and peace. (b) Press the right hand to brow, mouth, and heart by turns, pausing at each gesture. Resolve to follow firmly the ideal qualities mentioned during the confession of posture 4. When touching the brow, resolve to do so in thoughts; when touching the mouth, resolve to do so in speech; and when touching the heart, resolve to do so in feelings.

Epilogue.

Cross and fold the arms diagonally while standing. The hands will then rest upon the chest, the fingers will point upwards toward the shoulders. In this last stage, you are to be sincerely thankful, joyously grateful, and constantly recognizant for the fact that God *is*, for your own point of contact with God, and for the good—spiritual and material—that has come your way.

56

The first part of his prayer should be spoken aloud. His lips must give his thought a physical embodiment. This is because he lives in a physical world and the prayer should start on the same level. But the second part should be silent and mental, introverted and absorbed. Yet he should not arbitrarily fix the moment of passage from the first to the second part. The change from speech to silence ought to come about of its own accord and by his own inner prompting.

57

Prayer, if it is petitionary, is best formulated just before and just after entering the stillness. In the first case, the heart is then purer and will ask more wisely. In the second case, if the silent communion has been established, and the afterglow of peace is there, the heart will then understand that the whole problem is then best left with the higher power and anxiety dismissed, that demands made from ignorance merely limit or thwart the power.

58

Prayer ought to be a reaching out to the spiritual presence of the higher power. It ought to satisfy itself with obtaining a certain intuitive feeling, above and beyond all its ordinary everyday personal feelings. Then, if it seeks something specific, it ought to ask for more light of understanding, more power of self-mastery, more goodness of heart—not for more dollars in the bank, more furniture in the home, more horsepower in the car.

59

He should not hesitate to pray humbly, kneeling in the secrecy of his private room, to the Overself. First his prayer should acknowledge the sins of his more distant past having led to sufferings in the later past or his immediate present, and he should accept this as just punishment without any rebellious feeling. Then he may throw himself on the Grace as being the only deliverance left outside his own proper and requisite efforts to amend the causes. Finally let him remember the living master to whom he has given allegiance and draw strength from the memory.(P)

60

To enter this stillness is the best way to pray.(P)

61

It is not to be, as it is with so many unenlightened religionists, nothing more than a request to be given something for nothing, a petition for unearned and undeserved personal benefit. It is to be first, a confession of the ego's difficulty or even failure to find its own way correctly through the dark forest of life; second, a confession of the ego's weakness or even helplessness in coping with the moral and mental obstacles in its path; third, an asking for help in the *ego's own strivings* after self-enlightenment and self-betterment; fourth, a resolve to struggle to the end to forsake the lower desires and overcome the lower emotions which raise dust-storms between the aspirant and his higher self; and fifth, a deliberate self-humbling of the ego in the admission that its need of a higher power is imperative.(P)

62

Do not make your request until you have first made the highest grade of your devotional worship or scaled the peak of your mystical meditation. Then only should you formulate it, and hold it before the Power whose presence you then feel.

63

He should believe that he is at that moment receiving that which he is praying for. But he should do so only if he feels no contrary indication of coldness or doubt, and only after he has made contact with the power through pure worship or meditation.

64

Whenever an emergency arises wherein you require help, guidance, protection, or inspiration, turn the thought away from self-power and bring it humbly to the feet of the higher power in prayer.

65

Prayers really begin when their words end. They are most active not when the lips are active but when they are still.

66

Many people turn to prayer through weakness in desperation and pain. Others turn through strength in the desire to establish communication or attend holy communion.

67

That which is prayed for in the turbulent desire of the ego may be wrong. But that which is prayed for in the deepest stillness of the Overself's presence will be right and, therefore, received.

68

A public place is an unnatural environment in which to place oneself mentally or physically in the attitude of true prayer. It is far too intimate, emotional, and personal to be satisfactorily tried anywhere except in solitude. What passes for prayer in temples, churches, and synagogues is therefore a compromise dictated by the physical necessity of an institution. It may be quite good but too often alas! it is only the dressed-up double of true prayer.

69

Perhaps the best solution of this problem is to combine the two: to perform private prayers in a public building as the Catholics do. But those individuals who have gone some way ahead of the mass will usually prefer to follow Jesus' advice and pray in the secrecy of their own chambers.

70

Too often prayer is mere soliloquy, a man talking to his own ego about his own ego, and heard only by his own ego. It would be far better for him to learn how to keep his thoughts silent, to put himself into a receptive listening attitude; what he may then hear may convince him that "the Father knoweth what ye need."

71

Oh, Lord, if I have any prayer at all it is, "Make the 'me' absolutely quiescent and lead me into thy utter stillness where nothing else matters but the stillness itself."

72

Prayer is of course only one part of the Quest. Prayer should be the expression of his reverence and love for the Higher Power, God, or the Soul, or whatever he likes to call it. It can be silent or not. In his prayers he should follow this worship with a confession of those defects and weaknesses which hinder his full communion with God, and, only at the end of the prayer should he ask for help in overcoming them and for light to guide him.

73

What shall he pray for? Let him aspire more intensely than ever to the Overself and ask to become united in consciousness with it, surrendered in will to it, and purified in ego.

74

If the presence of divinity is felt, no name need be uttered in invocation and no prayer need be made in petition.

75

It is wiser not to talk excessively in prayer, better to remain silent a while and thus give God a chance to speak to us.

76

Prayer and meditation are private acts for they do not concern a man's relations with other men, but with God. Therefore they should be practised privately.

77

Pray by listening inwardly for intuitive feeling, light, strength, not by memorized form or pauperized begging.(P)

78

When we are actually in the vivid presence of this holier self, we may utter our petitionary prayers, but not before.

79

The step from public worship to private communion is a step forward.

80

The Russian Staretz Silouan wrote, in the notes which he left behind when he died in monastic Mount Athos, that prayer should be so highly concentrated that each word comes forth slowly.

81

He may always rightly close his prayer by soliciting guidance and sometimes by asking for forgiveness. Such a request can find justification, however, only if it is not a request for interfering with karma, only if it comes after recognition of wrong done, perception of personal weakness, confession leading to contrition, and a real effort to atone penitently and improve morally. The eternal laws of karma will not cease operating merely for the asking and cannot violate their own integrity. They are impersonal and cannot be cajoled into granting special privileges or arbitrary favours to anyone. There is no cheap and easy escape from them. If a sinner wants to avoid hurtful consequences of his own sins, he must use those very laws to help him do so, and not attempt to insult them. He must set going a series of new causes which shall produce new and pleasanter consequences that may act as an antidote to the older ones.

Misunderstandings and misuses

82

If the world's business were to be at the mercy of every uttered petition that rises from the lips of man, then it would tumble into chaos, and life would become a bewildering maze. No!—before we talk glibly about prayer being answered, we should first distinguish between pseudo-prayers and genuine prayer.

83

The belief that the Supreme Principle of the universe can be drawn away from Its work by every call from every person, or induced to obey every request of every kind, or persuaded to cancel the operation of cosmic laws to suit one creature who dislikes its effect upon himself, is not only naïve but also insulting. For it would lessen God and dwindle him down to the status of a mere man. Ascribing more power to his own prayer really implies that there is so much less power in God.

84

Men and women who find themselves in situations of great need, or confronted by problems which render them desperate, or oppressed by sickness, loss of employment, in debt, or involved in circumstances of grave peril, are not to be blamed if they turn for help to the Source of all love. Their prayers are as legitimate as the outcries for help from every child to its mother or father. Their call for relief is pardonable and not improper. But what is unreasonable is the refusal to enquire how far they have themselves contributed to their situation and how much they must themselves do to amend it. The immature child cannot be expected to make such enquiry and its parent may have to do alone everything that is required to help it, but the grown adult has also grown into responsibilities and duties. What I am trying to say is that he must share with the higher power the work of saving himself, a work which begins with examining the past causes of his calamity, goes on to taking present steps off the beaten path on required action, and ends only in resolving on a future character or capacity which will throw out the seeds of such causes. Call this rational prayer, if you like. The act of praying is here neither wildly denounced as being quite useless, a kind of childish talking to oneself, nor foolishly praised as being the right way out of all troubles.

85

If men knew, as the seers know, how wide a gulf lies between established, organized religions and true religion itself, they would understand why the prayers of such religions, whether for national or individual objects, so often fail to reach God and get no response. On May 26, 1940, there was a mass appeal to God from every house of worship throughout England and the British Empire. The British Government declared it a National Day of Prayer for this purpose. But within a few days Belgium surrendered, and within a month France collapsed. Britain was left to fight alone. Was this the answer to her prayer? Religious prayer, when neglected at other times and resorted to only when material benefit is sought, is the greatest example of wishful thinking the world has ever known. If the response of the Almighty Deity is to be in direct ratio to the volume of the prayers He receives, if He is to be amenable only when these incantations reach a certain figure, then the Tibetan prayer-wheel deserves to be manufactured in the West by mass-production methods!

86

To regard—as W. Tudor Pole regards—the successful withdrawal from Dunkirk or the successful air battle of Britain as being the result of the Church's intercession or of the National Day of Prayer is merely to fall into superstition. Why not say that the capitulation of Belgium and the collapse of France were also due to the same cause because they also occurred about the same time? Why did not all the clergy's prayers save the thousands of British churches which were destroyed by German bombs? No—karma is more powerful than the Church, evolution more fateful than intercession; Britain was saved because both the British karma and the world's evolutionary needs demanded its saving.

87

The idea that because of national days of prayer the war took a different course than it might otherwise have taken is one that must be questioned. Since the most ancient times, nations have had such days whenever they found themselves in trouble and usually they consisted of nationwide requests that the trouble be taken from them. Merely making such a request cannot of itself alter the course of Destiny, nor influence God. True prayer should be something more, something deeper than that. There must be true repentance and not merely an attempt to escape a situation toward which one has contributed by one's own wrong thinking and wrong actions. How few are the nations who have genuinely re-pented; once out of trouble they have quickly resumed the same old course. One may have the greatest faith in the value and power of prayer, but in order for it to be effectual, it must be genuine and it must be practised correctly.

88

The emotional worship and wishful thinking of popular religion have not saved the millions who practise it from following leaders who led them into war and destruction, or from customs which caused sickness and spread disease. Prayer will not prove a substitute for intelligence nor pre-vent man experiencing the effects of his own failure to restrain his lower nature.

89

So many believe that if only they keep on begging, God will magically put into them the good qualities which they lack. Is such a great result to be achieved as simply as that? The hundreds of thousands of disappointed persons who find themselves the same as they were before, despite months and years of pouring out their emotional petitions to a crudely and child-ishly imagined God, show that this naïve belief is either a misuse and misunderstanding of true prayer or a mere superstition.

90

When we consider the tremendous number of public prayers which have been spoken, chanted, read, or muttered in public gatherings for so many centuries, the human race seems to have derived disproportionate profit from the practice. May it not be because the utterance has become too formal, a matter of mental repetition without the supporting inward loving devotion needed to make it real?

91

Considering that all is known to God, and that therefore all our needs must be known to him too, what is the use of offering this information to God in our prayers?

92

How useful are prayers which are set, formal, and prepared? All too often they lack individual appeal and fail to stir any feeling. Nevertheless, it would be wrong to say that they are quite useless.

93

Who has kept count of the number of ministers who prayed for sick patients, only to witness the latter get worse and die! How many relatives have gone to the bedside of their ailing one, there to pray earnestly for recovery, but the ebbing underflow of life trickled away despite their request? Nobody knows the ratio of answered prayers to unanswered ones, but everybody knows that it is a small one.

94

To utter routine prayers whose words have never received sufficient thought, or even any thought at all, is a waste of time.

95

It is a great and grave fallacy to believe that it is necessary to pray in order to be taken care of by God. The truth is that there is no moment when God is not taking care of us or, indeed, of everyone else. God is in every atom of the Universe and consequently in full operation of the Universe. This activity does not stop because we stop praying.

96

When these three signs of the most elementary stage are brought to-gether and united—the public rite, the spoken utterance, and the set wording—there is danger of the whole prayer itself becoming a mere gabble unless the individual safeguards it by the utmost humility and sincerity.

97

Many more people than is usually admitted fall into the posture or utter the petitions of prayer without much hope that it will be effectual.

98

For so many thousands of years in the historic epoch, and for unknown thousands of years in the prehistoric epoch, men have propitiated God, and prayed for boons or relief; yet the world today is more miserable and more engulfed in suffering than ever before.

99

Father John of Kronstadt was called to the Imperial Palace to pray for the Empress, who had had only girls born to her, whereas the Tsar urgently wanted a son and heir. The holy man's prayers failed to produce the desired result. Yet at other times and with other persons, they had been granted.

100

Dogmatic or mechanical prayer is really valueless. The only effective prayer comes straight from the heart. It should be fervent, reverent, and spontaneous, expressing both idealistic aspirations and spiritual needs.

101

Offering prayers to the kind of God whom most people talk about is almost as useful, as helpful, and as rational as offering chocolates to the law of gravitation.

102

How foolish are those men who try to make their prayers heard on earth, as if God were also a man!

103

With the departure of superstitions from religion, waste of time in meaningless religious activities will also depart. What is the use of praying to the Source for those things which man himself, by using his natural capacities, can supply? He should turn to prayer only when his own efforts are in vain, an indication that it is time to turn the problem over to the Source, the Overself. How many of his illnesses, for example, come from wrong ways of living, eating, drinking, or thinking? The body has its own laws of hygiene, and the learning of them is as much part of his development during his lives on earth as the learning of spiritual laws.

104

True prayer is first fellowship, then communion, and ultimately merger. That is, it is a drawing closer and closer to the Overself. Asking for things is not even to attain the first step. Such things are merely the secondary results of prayer. They will surely come, for the Overself knows your needs, your *true* needs, and will surely take care of them.

105

The man who prays for material goods is performing a questionable act, but the man who prays for spiritual goods is performing a wiser one. The man who asks to have his troubles taken away is also acting questionably, but the man who asks for the strength and guidance to deal wisely with his troubles is more likely to get them.

106

The hour of prayer is a time not to beg but to ascend, not to be filled with thoughts of yourself but with thoughts of God. It is not to be concerned with this world but to lift the mind above it.

107

The more we use prayer for communion and worship, the less we use it for begging and petition, the more will our prayers be answered. God has given us both intelligence and will: we have the business of using as well as developing them. Prayer is not to be used as an alibi to save us from these duties.

108

Too many people do not know how to pray, or try to use meditation to satisfy their selfishness. The first group comes to prayer with the attitude "My will be done." The second group comes to meditation with worldly desires as the object of their worship. Both are doing wrong.

109

The belief many people have that they can call out in prayer to the higher power for their needs without fulfilling their obligations to that power is illogical. They ought not to be so naïve. They ought to enquire first how far, through ignorance, they are disobeying the higher laws and how far, through negligence, they are departing from the hygienic laws. The first concerns their fortunes, the second their health.

110

True prayer is not a devotional act which is done only when we happen to be frightened. It is not a temporary reaction to fear but a constant expression of faith.

111

If people pray only when they have something to ask for, if they think of God only in crises, they have only themselves to blame for their infantile spiritual growth.

112

Before you venture into the prayer of petition ask yourself first, is it really as wise to get what you seek as it seems to be; second, are you deserving of it; and third, what will you do to justify its bestowal.

113

Just as the animal cries out when in fear and the child when in need, so the adult man when in grave stress silently calls out to God for help—unless a one-sided education has stupefied his deeper instincts or a brutalized life has crushed them.

114

What usually passes for prayer seldom gets near the divine presence, remains ego-encircled and useless.

115

If an attempt is made to inform God what is required from Him by and for us, that would be wrong.

116

To pray, asking that an exception be made in their favour, is a common enough act with many people.

117

In return for the favour which they confer on the Higher Power by believing in it, they demand the satisfaction of their personal desires.

118

The true purpose of prayer is not to keep asking for some benefit each time we engage in it, but rather to express the yearning of the underself for the Overself, the attraction felt by the ego living in darkness for its parent source dwelling in light.

119

Whimpering is not praying. It is another form of the self's long littleness.

120

We will begin to get some fruit from prayer and hear less of its many failures when we begin to regard it less as a petition than as a transaction. We have to pay over our arrogant self-reliance and receive in exchange what the infinite wisdom deems best for us.

121

He may, if he wishes, add a prayer for material help but this should be done only under critical or urgent circumstances. The highest, and therefore most philosophic, use of prayer is not to beseech satisfaction of worldly desires but to beseech light into the darkness spread by those desires and to implore the soul for its strength to enter into him for the fight against animal passions.

122

The internal ego does them more harm than anything or anyone else, yet how few appeal to the Divine for protection against themselves, how many for protection against merely external evils?

123

Prayer has value to the extent that it inevitably makes man think of the higher power, but he detracts from that value to the extent that he joins that to the thought of his world by needs, desires, or problems.

124

It is better not to beg nor to demand in prayer, not even for spiritual things or help. It is more fitting to render homage to the higher power, to think of it worshipfully and reverently and humbly and, above all, lovingly.

125

When men pray it is mostly the ego praying, and for itself. If this attitude is maintained until the end of the session, God gets very little chance to say anything to the devotee.

126

Many prayers are dictated not by reverence, but by fear. This is as true of those emanating from the clergy as of those from the lay people.

127

The farther the aspirant is advanced in this Quest, the less he is likely to ask for worldly things in his prayer. In any case, all such petitioning should be strictly limited. Whoever enters a sanctuary to ask for worldly things should beware how far he goes in this direction, and how often he goes there.

128

When prayer is not selfish commerce but holy communion, when it is not worldly minded but spiritually minded, when it seeks the inner Ideal rather than the outer Actual, it has the chance of becoming effectually realized.

129

"If thou canst do what He enjoins on thee, He will do what thou dost ask assuredly," said Awhadi, a medieval Persian mystic. This is the key to prayer. Failure results from ignorance of this key.

130

It is a human and pardonable urge of the devout believer to bring forward specific requests, however trivial, as the main thought in prayer, and to do so repeatedly. This is the little ego petitioning God as a big Ego. It shows faith; it is a part of religion at that level, which is a low one. Personal prayers ought to be the exception, not the rule, and limited to graver matters. Later they may be limited to spiritual matters, and, in the end, left out altogether.

131

It is a great temptation to pray for named persons or for particular things.

132

This begging for personal favours through religious prayer may be a waste of time, especially where it demands divine intervention to escape the consequences of its own acts. But it may also be a prompting to acknowledge the existence of a higher power, a humbling of the ego.

133

Immeasurably better than begging God for things is to beg him for himself.

Human petition, divine response

134

Self-purification is the best prayer, self-correction is the most effectual one.(P)

135

It is good and necessary to practise confession in one's prayer at all times but especially so in distressful times. If one is praying for deliverance, it is not enough merely to ask for it—indeed, that would be egocentric, childish, and useless. One should also ask in what way one is responsible for, or has contributed toward, the making of the trouble from which escape is sought. Nothing should be hidden that can help to bare this guilt. The natural inclination to blame others or protect one's self-esteem should be resisted. Nor should one confess only moral sins; it may be that the cause lies in intellectual incapacity, poor discrimination, or lack of balance.

136

It is common to pray for help to overcome our shortcomings, and this is right; it is even more common to pray to escape the painful results of our shortcomings, but this is not right. Their results are needed for our development and if God took them away from us we would be robbed of a chance to make this development.

137

Man does not always know what is good for him, let alone what is best for him. Moreover, his mistakes may involve others and bring them suffering too.

138

When faced with problems which seem beyond adequate solution by reason or experience or counsel, take it as an indication that you are to put them to divine intervention. Ask during the time of prayer or meditation for the illuminating idea.

139

Too many believe in their own weakness, and in prayer implore or request a higher being to bestow upon them a personal power, virtue, or capacity felt to be lacking in themselves. Yet they, too, have latent inner resources, untapped and awaiting exploitation.

140

The stresses and strains have been increasing in intensity. In our time, life is like climbing a steep rocky path. It does not permit us to rest. It calls us to overcome internal struggle and external opposition. One of the Indian Emperor Akbar's spiritual guides was the Jain master Myoe Syonin. When a friend asked him to offer a prayer on his behalf, Syonin answered: "I pray every morning and every evening for the sake of all beings, and I am sure that you are also included among them."

141

He who can kneel down in utter humility and spontaneously pray to his higher self out of a genuine desire to elevate his character, will not pray in vain.

142

If the confession of sins and faults is an indispensable part of philosophic prayer, striving to forsake those sins and faults must be made an active part of the daily life after prayer.

143

Beware what you pray for. Do not ask for the truth unless you know what it means and all that it implies and nevertheless are still willing to accept it. For if it is granted to you, it will not only purge the evil out of you but later purify the egoism from your mind. Will you be able to endure this loss, which is unlikely to be a painless one?

144

It is better to pray to be led into truth, for then, as Jesus knew and remarked, "All these [other] things shall be added unto you."

145

If anyone claims to have enough faith to pray, let him have a little more faith and act out his prayer in conduct. This is the way to get an answer!

146

Everyone seeks in prayer forgiveness of the consequences of sin, but few seek freedom from the sin itself. That entails hard personal effort, but success in it could bring forgiveness also.

147

The aspirant who finds himself separated, either by force of circumstances or by deliberate desertion, from someone he cares for, may follow the conventional way of praying that the other person should come back to him, or he may follow the philosophic way of praying that he shall come to truth and peace and strength.

148

The kind of prayer which tries to coax God into bestowing something which he wants but cannot get by his own effort presupposes that the thing is for his benefit.

149

A particular problem should be carried into prayer again and again until the solution is found.

150

Why always importune God to answer your prayers? Try sometimes to answer them yourself.

151

It is one sign of progress when we stop informing the higher power of our need, which It must already know. It is another sign of progress when we stop expecting from It some boon which we ought to set about getting for ourselves.

152

If a man will not contribute towards his own welfare by at least attempting to improve himself, what is the use of his constant prayers to God for it?

153

To ask God to do for us what we should be capable or willing to do for ourselves is to show laziness and express dishonesty. We have no right to do this and such prayers consequently are futile.

154

Meditation in a solitary place remote from the world may help others who are still in the world, but only under certain conditions. It must, for example, be deliberately directed towards named individuals. If it floats away into the general atmosphere without any thought of others, it is only a self-absorption, barren to others if profitable to oneself. It can be turned toward the spiritual assistance of anyone the practiser loves or wishes to befriend. But it should not be so turned prematurely. Before he can render real service, he must first acquire the power to do so. Before he can fruitfully pray for persons, he must first be able to draw strength from that which is above all persons. The capacity to serve must first be got before the attempt to serve is made. Therefore he should resist the temptation to plunge straightaway into prayer or meditation on behalf of others. Instead he should wait until his worship or communion attains its highest level of being. Then—and then only—should he begin to draw from it the power and help and light to be directed altruistically towards others. Once he has developed the capacity to enter easily into the deeply absorbed state, he may then use it to help others also. Let him take the names and images of these people with him after he has passed into the state and let him hold them there for a while in the divine atmosphere.(P)

155

It is a commonly used religious formula to say "God will take care of him," or "May God bless him," or "May God forgive him." To utter such words, even mechanically and automatically, is better than to utter words burning with resentment and antagonism against someone who has injured us, or tingling with nervousness and fear for someone who is meeting with trouble. But most often they have no positive value, especially where they have become almost meaningless and empty through excessive familiarity and frequent repetition.

That would not be the case if immediately after speaking these words the person sat down and considered deeply, earnestly, and adequately their full semantic meaning and connections. There would then be a creative building up of the correct mental attitude towards the other man, which would keep away negative thoughts about him, generate a happier feeling about the situation concerning him, or assist to bring about a better relationship with him.

Such a procedure is excellent. But it is mainly an intellectual operation. For those who are travellers upon the Quest of the Overself there is a still higher one available which would use spiritual forces and which is much more effective in making the blessing come literally true.

This they can do by temporarily dismissing from the mind the problem connected with the other person and then calmly taking as a subject of meditation the metaphysical nature of the Overself, how impersonal it is, and how glorious are its attributes. Then they should bring ardent aspiration into the meditation and try to lift themselves into that pure, beautiful atmosphere. When they feel that, to some extent anyway, they have succeeded in doing so, they should stay there for a while and let themselves be thoroughly bathed in its large impersonal peace. Finally, it is at this point only, and not earlier, that, before descending and returning to ordinary life, they may take up afresh the thought of the other person and of the situation connected with him. They should commend him to the care and ministration of this beneficent Spirit. Here is the real way to make the words of these all-too-familiar blessings come true.

156

The best kind of prayer which we can make for another person is uttered without words—that is, by leading him to the stillness; the lesser kind is to beg for him by voiced sound.

157

He is neither to pity nor to despise those whose weaknesses are very pronounced, but he is to wish to help them. If actual aid seems beyond his capacity, he can at least turn them over during the peak period of his meditation hour to the care of the higher power. In this way he makes some kind of a mental link for them with this power.

158

If he will mentally release the relative or friend from his personal fears and anxieties concerning her, she will benefit. She will be helped by his telepathic and auric radiation mentally supporting her by this positive thinking. Mental possessiveness must be abandoned and the girl turned over to God's care in his mind.

159

If you seek to invoke the divine grace to meet a genuine and desperate physical need or human result, seek first to find the sacred presence within yourself and only after you have found it, or at least only after you have attained the deepest point of contemplation possible to you, should you name the thing or result sought. For then you will not only be guided whether it be right to continue the request or not, but you will also put yourself in the most favourable position for securing grace.(P)

160

The highest help we can give another person is not physical but spiritual. And in giving it we benefit ourselves too. For the lofty mood, the loving thought, the peaceful feeling, the full confidence in higher power that we seek to transmit in prayer or meditation to him, must be first created within ourselves. From that creation, we benefit as well as he. Yes, we may introduce the remembrance of other persons, toward the close of our meditation, and pray silently on their behalf. The wonder is that this remembrance, this prayer, this meditation for another may have some effect, although we may be in Canada and the other in Africa. Like a radio broadcast, it reaches out to him.

161

He has no right to bring other persons into his meditation or prayer unless they are aware and willing that he should do so or unless his own motives are absolutely pure and his own knowledge of what he is doing is absolutely true. Much less does he have the right to draw them to the performance of his desires at the expense of their own integrity as individuals.

162

In the exercise of intercessory prayer, first seek to make contact with the higher power by aspiring to it and dwelling upon its nature and attributes. Then, when you feel the presence of this power—and it is ineffectual to do so before—think of it as protective. Next, think of the person whose protection you seek and place him in the presence and hold him there.

163

All those who remember instances of successful prayer bringing large sums of money, as George Miller's and Saint Francis' prayers for the institutions they founded, ought also remember that these were ego-free prayers for the welfare of others: they were not for personal benefit.

164

A person who has not yet found the peace and power of the Overself is in no position to give blessings to other persons.

165

If the attempt at intercession—be it healing, helping, or blessing—is successful, he will feel exultant as the sensation of power flows through him.

166

If petitionary prayer, whether for self or others, is possible at a certain stage of meditation, it is impossible at a deeper stage.

167

He cannot be aware of any individual human while he is deeply enfolded by that state, but shortly before entering it, or shortly after emerging from it, he may be. This makes intercessory prayer and meditation a real possibility.

168

When he is able to bring himself to practise this bestowal of silent blessing upon all others, and to practise it both lovingly and universally, he will find it a quick cure for the trouble of nervous self-consciousness. Instead of feeling uneasy in the presence of certain persons or of a crowd, he will feel poised. Why is this so? Because he is drawing Grace down to himself. This secret was seen by Oscar Wilde when he said: "One cannot search for love. It comes to us unbidden, when we give love to others."

169

The counsel that you are not promiscuously to interfere with other persons in order to improve them, or unwisely to involve yourself in their lives in order to help them spiritually, does not mean that you are to do nothing at all for them. You may, if you wish, take them beneficently into your prayer or meditation to bestow blessing.

170

Those who write a blessing at the end of a letter but who lack the spiritual power to make it real, waste their time. Those who read the feeble words may feel pleasantly hopeful but are the victims of their own imaginations.

171

He feels infinity with others and that is enough reason to include them in the circle embraced by his meditation. He needs no other reason.

172

He who is a follower of this Path may help another by holding a mental picture of him in his own thought at the end of meditation, and by invoking the protective blessing of the Overself upon his name in prayer.

173

The quick recovery of a loved one prayed for in the silence is a remarkable illustration of the power of the spirit. Before such a circumstance he must indeed humble himself. While he was going through great agony, all the time his Higher Self was present in him. It gave him the chance to react in a higher way than the conventionally egoistic one. By rising to the occasion, he too could benefit as well as the one whom he loved.

174

There was the case of a man who lost his leg in the war. What could a student do for his friend? The thing he could do would be to hold him, when finishing a prayer or a meditation, in the thought of the Infinite Power—to hold the belief that he is completely taken care of by that Power and that all is well with him because it enfolds him. He should not attempt to work out any details such as wishing that his friend's second leg should be saved. He should leave all the results to the Power, and not introduce his personal ideas about the matter.

175

He should hold the person, the friend, or relative about whom he is troubled in this helpful and healing presence that he has found in the stillness. In this way he may employ the mystical art of intercession for another's benefit.

176

Do not give any "suggestion." All that is necessary is to pray to be used in whatever way best for the other person's spiritual benefit.

177

Intercessory meditation may be practised for the benefit of others, the illumination of others, and the healing of others. But these intercessions should never precede communion with the source; they should always follow it. All petitions are best presented at the end of a prayer, never at its beginning.

178

Both prayer and receptivity are needed. First we pray fervently and feelingly to the Overself to draw us closer to it, then we lapse into emotional quietness and patiently wait to let the inner self unfold to us. There is no need to discard prayer because we take up meditation. The one makes a fit prelude to the other. The real need is to purify prayer and uplift its objectives.(P)

179

Whereas prayer is a one-way conversation with the higher power, you being the talker, meditation is a reversal of this situation, for you become the listener. The praying devotee expresses what is in his own mind but the silent meditator is impressed by ideas from a diviner mind. In prayer man brings himself to the attention of God but in meditation God brings himself to the attention of man.

180

It is true that I have written almost nothing about prayer in my published books. This is because I thought that such an enormous amount of literature on the subject already existed. The philosophical approach to prayer, and conception of it, is somewhat different from the traditional one. It should act as a preface to meditation and as a help to prepare one to enter meditation.

181

In prayer we are trying to speak to God. In meditation we are trying to let God speak to us. There lies one difference.

182

A further difference between prayer and meditation is that in prayer, when successful, there is felt an intimacy with the Holy but not an identity with it, as is the case in the latter.

183

When prayer reaches its highest manifestation, it closely resembles meditation.

184

Every philosophic aspirant should devote a little time to prefacing meditations or studies with a worshipful, devoted, and reverent supplication of the higher self for enlightenment.

185

The praying devotee regards the object of his worship as being outside himself, whereas the meditating one regards it as being inside himself.

186

The correct order is to follow prayer with the declaration and to follow them in turn with meditation.

187

More than four hundred years ago a Dominican monk, Louis of Granada, affirmed: "Contemplation—is the most perfect prayer."

188

Prayer not only must be used as a suitable preface to meditation, but may also be effectively used as a help to meditation. Where an aspirant is unable to calm his restless thoughts, in addition to the constant daily regular effort to do so—for perseverance is part of the secret of success— he may pray to the higher self to take possession of his mind. Such prayer must be deeply heartfelt, constantly repeated, and animated by a longing to get away from the peaceless ego.

189

If there is response to prayer, who or what is it that responds? The orthodox religionist believes that it is a personal and interested God with whom he establishes contact in prayer. The philosophical religionist knows that it is his own higher self, his divine soul, that he reaches. All that the first expects in the way of consolation strength and help from his personal God, the second also expects from his own soul. Thus the results in practice are somewhat the same; it is the interpretation of their origin that differs.

190

Prayer begins to make itself heard and get itself answered when the praying one begins to penetrate his own within-ness, to experience his own spiritual selfhood. For the only God he can reach, and the only one who will help him, is the God in him, the Overself.

191

From the moment that a man looks for God in himself, his prayers begin to have a chance of being heard. When, before that moment, he looked for God as far off, outside of and unconnected with himself, the prayers were unable to make themselves heard and consequently unable to get answered.

192

It seems to be a law of the inner life that we have to ask for the inner help that is needed long long before it begins to manifest.(P)

193

Whether this effective power be deep within the inner self or out beyond in the universe is more of theoretical concern than practical; what matters is that it really does exist and we really can at times enter into active relation with it by an inner act. And that act is expressed through prayer in some cases or meditation in others. If all the conditions created by us are right, the response of the medium of power will be reciprocal and effectual, thus augmenting our own power in connection with our need.

194

His prayers and longing, his aspirations and yearnings are not in vain. They are all heard, let him be assured of that. But their fulfilment must necessarily come in the Overself's time, not his own. A seed cannot shoot up all at once into a tree. The processes of growth in nature satisfy the criterions of soundness, although they dismay the criterions of sentimentality.

195

The answer to prayer may come in a wholly unexpected way that we neither desire nor like. It may come as an apparent misfortune, for that may be the real "good" for us just then.

196

If the response to prayer could set aside universal laws for the sake of those who pray, then the universe would become a chaos.

197

Even where prayer is correct in form and spirit, it may be followed up by an incorrect attitude. Many are the cases I have observed where this has happened, where half the answer has already come in internal guidance or external contact with some man or book or circumstance but, because the mind had been made up beforehand to a preconceived solution, it was not recognized for what it was, and was either ignored or rejected.

198

He may carry such problems into his prayers. The answers do not necessarily come at the time of the prayer itself, but may only come some time later, maybe days or even weeks later.

199

Such is the untouched depth of the human being that when a man prays to God he really prays to himself, his Overself.

200

The praying ego will have its prayer answered if it gets taken up momentarily by the Overself, and swallowed by it. But although the answer will be the right one, it may not be the desired one.

201

The Power to whom prayer should be addressed—for Its Grace, Its Self-Revelation and Guidance—is one's own higher self, the Overself.

202

In praying, the aspirant should direct his prayer to the only God he can *know*, that is, the God-Principle within himself—his own Divine Soul.

203

The man who finds God within himself feels no need to pray to a God who is to be sought and addressed outside himself.

204

Where the response to prayer is so direct definite and unmistakable, it is mostly because the devotee has touched this infinite power through and in his Overself. This does not mean that the Deity has intervened to set laws, decrees, or circumstances aside for this one man's personal benefit. It means rather that he has himself drawn on his own latent godlike capacity. This can happen only when the attitude of prayer becomes so intense and so concentrated that it is really a form of meditation.

205

If the sincere desire of his heart is echoed by a prayer that expresses humility and requests guidance, it will be heard. Although he may receive no answer for quite a time, sooner or later it will come.

3

HUMILITY

The need

We complain that there is no response to our prayer for uplift or light. But that is because there is no propriety in our approach. The intellectually gifted comes with his arrogance and the artistically gifted with his vanity, while each man comes with his pride. The correct approach was described by Jesus: "Become as a little child"; for then we become humble, feel dependent, and begin to lay the ego aside. With that the door to the Overself opens and its grace begins to shine through.

2

The need of self-humbling before the Overself (which is not the same as self-humbling before other men) is greatest of all with the aspirant of an intellectual type. The veil of egotism must be lifted, and with his own hand pride must be humbled to the dust. So long as he believes he is wise and meritorious for entertaining spiritual aspiration, so long will the higher self withhold the final means for realizing that aspiration. As soon as he believes he is foolish and sinful the higher self will begin by its Grace to help him overcome these faults. Then, when his humility extends until it becomes a realization of utter helplessness, the moment has come to couple it with intense prayer and ardent yearning for Divine Grace. And this humility towards the higher self must become as abiding an attitude as firmness towards the lower one. It must persist partly because he must continually realize that he needs and will forever need its Grace, and partly because he must continuously acknowledge his ignorance, folly, and sinfulness. Thus the ego becomes convinced of its own unwisdom, and when it bends penitently before the feet of the Overself it begins to manifest the wisdom which hitherto it lacked. Instead of wasting its time criticizing others, it capitalizes its time in criticizing itself. In old-fashioned theological language, he must consider himself an unworthy sinner and then only does he become able to receive Grace. He should measure his spiritual stature not by the lower standards of the conventional multitude, but by the loftier standards of the Ideal. The one may make him feel smug, but the other will make him feel small.

3

Concentration is often a passport to spiritual attainment, but it needs the visa of Humility to make it an impeccable document.

4

We must be humble enough to recognize how imperfect we are, but instructed enough to recognize that the ego-covered part of us is shiningly divine. Thus both humility and dignity must be brought together in our make-up and reconciled and balanced.

5

Undue humility can be a fault, although not so repugnant a fault as undue arrogance. The first trait underestimates itself and thus refrains from what it clearly ought to attempt. The second overestimates itself and tries to do what it lacks the fitness for. Moreover, the first is too apt to depend on others until it becomes incapable of leading an independent life, while the second is too slow to seek expert advice which might save it from falling into failure or error.

6

What the ego's pride cannot do, the Overself's humility may. It is always worth trying this better way, even if it be a self-mortifying way.

7

Rare is the person who can witness his ego crushed to the ground and yet never forget his divine parentage, so that his mental equilibrium is not broken—who can be lifted up to the glorious heights of the Overself and yet remain humbly human.

8

Let us have enough courage to face life yet let us not forget the need of enough humility to face our creator.

9

"Thou standest not by thine own strength—from the invisible art thou sustained each moment."—*Bustan* of Saadi

10

If the need to communicate either in prayer or in meditation with that higher power is not felt by a man, his intellect may be too powerful or his pride too strong.

11

The last lesson to learn is an ancient one: be willing to be humble. For it was refined in pitiless fire and shaped by a holy communion.

12

There is no entry here for the proud, the conceited, the self-pedestalled. They must first be humbled, shorn, and shamed. They must drop to the ground on their knees, must become weeping beggars and wounded mendicants.

13

If he presents a firm assured face to the world, to protect his place in it, he presents a far humbler one to the Overself.

14

The proud heart of man must be humbled before the Overself will reveal itself to him.

15

There are certain times and certain experiences which a man must approach humbly and uncritically if he is to benefit by them.

16

Somewhere along this Quest humility and modesty become necessary acquisitions.

17

What is all our knowledge but trivial scratches in the sand?

18

When we come to know more fully and more really what we are, we have to bow, humbled, in heartfelt adoration of the Mind of the World.

19

Humility is needed, yes, but it should not be misplaced. It is not in self-effacement before other men nor in abasing oneself before them that we advance spiritually, as so many ignorantly think, but in self-effacement and self-abasement before the Divine.

20

The humility needed must be immensely deeper than what ordinarily passes for it. He must begin with the axiom that the ego is *ceaselessly* deceiving him, misleading him, ruling him. He must be prepared to find its sway just as powerful amid his spiritual interests as his worldly ones. He must realize that he has been going from illusion to illusion even when he seemed to progress.(P)

21

The Long Path seeks humility in order to abase and thin down the ego. But although pride is full of ego, even humility implies you are still thinking about it.

22

Let him not mistake mere timidity for true humility.

23

Do not confuse true humility with the false modesty which deprecates its own status.

24

Yet this repentance, this remorseful conviction of our personal unworthiness, ought not to paralyse our hopes for the future by stamping us with an inferiority complex.

25

It is so difficult to make a success of success. When the head is turned by it or swelled with it, danger appears and failure may follow.

26

He should not imagine that he is being humble when he is merely being servile.

27

There is a difference between the morbid and exaggerated self-abasement often found in ascetic circles and this true humbleness.

28

He will bow to nothing that is visible.

29

There are a number of people who call themselves "advanced" but the truth is that they have merely advanced into a cul-de-sac, whence they will one day have to return.

30

Let us be humble where it is right to be so but let us not forget that when humility becomes personal cowardice and disloyalty to truth, then its virtue is transformed into vice.

31

If he is over-sensitive to other persons to the point of always yielding to their wishes, always saying only what will please them, and that without emotional conflict or mental indecision, then his self-damaging condition is a false and futile egolessness.

32

No man need take himself so seriously that he thinks the world's happiness or understanding depends on him. The world found these things before he was born and can find them again.

33

If the spiritual preferment which grace seems to indicate inflates his vanity, then one day it will desert him.

34

It is an ironic truth that on every level of development, from the most primitive to the most cultivated, from the most materialistic to the most spiritual, every man says, "I know!" He says this either quite openly in discussion or quite unconsciously in attitude. Real humility is a rare quality. This amazing arrogance is generally self-justified by supporting experiences or vindicating feelings of the individual himself.

35

It is good to enrich intelligence but not at the cost of increasing spiritual pride. It is well to enjoy the glad uplifts of mystical presence but the afterglow ought to make him humbler still.

36

With the personal arrogance that credits all its powers to itself, he will surely lose them. With the personal humility that refers them to their true source, he will not.

37

"Convict our pride of its offense in all things, even penitence."—W.H. Auden

38

Too often the quester, after a certain number of years, wants to be admired for his magnificent spirituality. But too often, in another mood, he enters the confessional to be humiliated for his great egoism.

39

Spiritual pride has rightly been listed by the Christian saints as a source of deception, and as the last of the traps into which the would-be saint can fall. A man may be quite holy and well self-controlled, but if he notices these two attainments with self-complacency, or rather self-congratulation, he at once strengthens the ego—although he transfers his excellence from worldly to spiritual matters.

40

The simple recognition of one's own stature need not become a matter for pride or conceit.

41

It is a false humility and moral cowardice that lead a man to pretend he does not know how tall he is.

42

There are mystics who have developed a considerable depth of meditation. They come back from their session of practice feeling the peace they have touched, but at the same time they come back smugly satisfied with the experience and especially with the attainment it seems to point towards. This is not enough. Even if they go apparently to the apex of the stillness, the ego has travelled with them. They may be aware of where they have been, but they were aware that they were aware. Thus there was duality in what *they* thought was unity. Do not praise the ego for having found God. It was Grace which brought about the discovery. It was not the ego. It is true that the beginner needs humility but it is even more true that the advanced man needs even more humility.

The practice

43

Humility, sensitivity, and emotional refinement are essential qualities which must be developed. Even more necessary is the daily practice of humble worship, devotion, and prayer.

44

The cultivation of reverential, prayerful, humble worship is needed to attract Grace. The putting aside of pride, self-conceit, and complacency is indispensable in order to assume the correct attitude during such worship. At such a time the saying of Jesus "Except ye be as a little child . . ." is directly applicable. The shy reticence of the Overself cannot be overcome without utter humility on the practitioner's part. Of course, this is the attitude to be adopted during devotions, not during worldly activity.

45

Man naturally shrinks from acknowledging frankly his defects and mistakes, his weaknesses and vanities. Yet such acknowledgment is the beginning of his salvation.

46

What are the attributes of a little child? A child has a flexible mind. It has not become mentally set or prejudiced by a collection of conceptions about life. It is fresh. Its head is not stuffed with a lot of so-called education. It is ready to learn—in fact, it is learning all the time. And the child has also a simplicity of spirit. It does not become complicated, tied up with all sorts of conjectures imposed by societies or families or newspapers. It has not become prejudiced by caste or environment. Moreover the child has not yet developed the strong sense of personality which adults have. Above all, the child is humble, it is teachable, it is willing to learn. This is what we need too. Humility is the first step on this path. We should realize how little we really know when confronted by the great mysteries of life. And even what we believe we do know, we cannot be too sure of in an age when the doctrine of relativity has undermined our bases. We must understand that what seems true today may seem false tomorrow. Many of the most widespread truths of last century have now been thrown overboard. Don't hold any doctrine too tightly.

47

Some seekers seize the goddess Truth by the throat and would fain strangle her in their efforts to embrace; I would suggest to them that to yield the hand to her like a child and to be led may compass their designs more quickly and surely.

48

To be humble is to be willing to admit the galling fact that one's own shortcomings of character or intelligence (and not other people's) were mostly responsible for most of one's troubles.

49

The higher he climbs, the humbler he becomes. Only he will not make an exhibition of his humility to the world, for it is not needed there and might even harm him and others. He will be humble deep down in his heart where it is needed, in that sacred place where he faces the Over-self.(P)

50

The practice of humility, especially in the form of obedience in monastic systems, is intended to subjugate the personal will and lessen self-love.

51

He has to kneel before his higher self and confess how weak, how ignorant, and how foolish a being he is. And then he has to pray for grace, to ask like a beggar for a little strength light and peace. Such daily recurring prayer is only a beginning of what he has to do but it is a necessary part of that beginning.

52

These great truths require great humility in a man to receive them. The bigoted and the prejudiced lack it.

53

He must be humble enough to admit errors in thought and conduct, never hesitating to retrace his steps when on the wrong road.

54

Let him not cover his weaknesses nor pretend to be what he is not.

55

Only so far as he is willing to confess his failings and shortcomings is there hope to remedy them. Herein lies the true esoteric importance and value of the exoteric practice of "confession of sins." (But this is no justification of the particular forms and historical abuses which such a practice has assumed in certain religions.)

56

The chief value of such confession lies in the ego giving up its habitual self-justification, the everlasting alibi-finding, its complacent and smug acceptance of itself. Such confession gives a jolt to the ego's vanity and self-righteousness by exposing its own weakness.

57

Such confession of sinfulness, wrong thinking, bad character, and mistaken deeds is valuable not only because it brings these defects to the surface and exposes them to the full light of conscious attention, but also because its effects upon the penitent himself are so humbling.

58

The days when he could speak glibly and assuredly on the most recondite phases of spirituality gradually go. A new humility comes to him.

59

It is safer to plead guilty than to give ourself the benefit of the doubt about our weaknesses. Let us confess them and tread on the ego's pride, even if they are not clear or strong.

60

Humility: See all men and women according to the Holy Ghost that is within them; always remember that the outer picture is still being worked on.

61

By maintaining the humility of the learner and the questing spirit of a seeker, he improves his own usefulness as a channel to help other people.

62

At first this humbling sense of his own sorry insufficiency will overwhelm him. He sees himself at his worst. Remorse for the past, anguish over the present, hopelessness for the future will momentarily blacken his outlook. This is a necessary step in the purificatory movement of his quest.

63

We must first acknowledge our guilt, we must have the courage to confess our errors and cast out our self-righteousness, before we can hope to start the new life aright.

64

With the onset of this overpowering sense of sin and in the hypercritical examination of conscience which it induces, he will react gloomily against, and condemn severely, his whole past.

65

His attitude need not be utterly pessimistic. He may say to himself, "If I have made a mistake, very well; I am undergoing a process of spiritual trial and error. Some errors are inevitable, but I shall catch up with them, study them, understand their results, and wring their meaning and their lessons out of them. In that way they will become steps which I shall mount towards Truth. If I suffer calamities of my own making, I will stand aside, calm, impersonal, and detached, and take the sting out of them by this ego-free attitude. In the long-range point of view it is not what I want but what I need that matters; and if I need the correction of adversity or calamity it is better that I have it."

66

The nearer his understanding comes to this higher Self, the humbler he becomes and the less likely is he to boast about this uncommon condition.

67

He needs to cultivate some degree of inward humility. There may be a tendency in his disposition to be somewhat strongly self-centered, proud, and overconfident. The best way and the quickest way in which he could begin to cultivate such humility would be through becoming a child again in the act of prayer.

68

There is much that we must let stand as inexplicable, must accept as a mystery, and thus avoid falling into the trap of smooth intellectual theories. We ought not demand what the human mind, because it is finite, has no right to demand.

69

For the man who has a strong ego, the religious approach with its cultivation of humility, its confession of sinfulness, and its redirection of emotion away from personality is the best to be recommended, if accompanied by some of the Philosophical Discipline's restrictions of the ego. However, such a person usually refuses to drink the medicines he most needs and therefore continues to remain involved in troubles of his own creation.

70

He must accept the chagrin of humbled pride, the bitter taste of self-accusing truth.

71

At such a time he feels that his entire past was a horrible series of self-deceptions.

72

To confess sins of conduct and shortcomings of character as a part of regular devotional practice possesses a psychological value quite apart from any other that may be claimed for it. It develops humility, exposes self-deceit, and increases self-knowledge. It decreases vanity every time it forces the penitent to face his faults. It opens a pathway first for the mercy and ultimately for the Grace of the higher Self.

73

He has emotionally to crawl on hands and knees before the higher power in the deepest humility. This kills pride, that terrible obstacle between man and the Soul's presence.

74

The ego must acknowledge its own transiency, confess its own instability, and thus become truly humble.

75

Humbly to accept our limitations, after long experience and repeated test, is also a form of wisdom. The innate tendencies that make us what we are from birth may prove too strong for our will to oppose successfully. Yet even if the leopard cannot change his spots, time may mellow their hard black to soft grey.

76

The Abbé Saint-Cyran's advice to a nun may be pertinent here: "It is against humility to want to do extraordinary things. We are not saints to do as the saints have done. One must hold oneself humbly in mediocrity and live in a certain disguise, so that people will see only ordinary things in you."

77

They are still frail and fallible mortals even though they are seeking and sometimes even glimpsing a state beyond all weakness and error.

78

He must come to see that his own strength is too limited, his capacity to help himself too small for a total self-reliance to be able to bring him through this quest successfully. Association with someone more advanced or, failing that, constant petition for the Soul's grace, will then be seen as indispensable.

79

Only when his ego's pride has been shattered, only when he has become depressed by future prospects and humiliated by present failure, is a man more likely to listen to the truth about himself.

80

Most of us are on the lowest slopes of the mountain; some of us have climbed to the middle slopes; very, very few have reached the peak.

81

It is not abject cringing humility but utter dependence which is called for by the Higher Power.

82

When affliction seems too hard to be borne any longer, when man has come to the end of his endurance, what other recourse has he than to fall on his knees or to cry out in humility?

83

The poignant feeling of hopeless aridity and helpless dependence on Grace brings one's ego very low.

84

When, with the arrogance beaten out of him by events which are stronger than himself, a man turns in humility to the higher power, he obeys a natural instinct.

85

When he sees how feeble are his resources and how formidable are his problems, he may see also the need of receiving help from outside or beyond himself.

86

To call himself a philosopher might be presumptuous when he is really a would-be philosopher, a student of the theory and the practice, a candidate trying for the philosophic goal.

87

To the wandering Indian *sadhu* or the cloistered Christian recluse of medieval times, Machiavelli's scorn for the person who has no social position in life is meaningless. For the holy man help must come from the higher power, not from other men.

88

Too often man has to have his ego crushed, has to be pushed into sorrow and even despair, before he is willing to turn his head upward or to bend his knees in prayer to the unseen power.

89

The more he is humbled by his failures, the more is he likely to find a way out of them.

90

A sharply critical, dryly intellectual aspirant who has had many troubles in his worldly life and physical health has had the opportunity of working out a lot of hard destiny. But it will not be without compensation if out of his suffering he develops a more religious attitude towards life, a fuller acceptance of the insufficiency of earthly things and human intellect, a greater throwing of himself into self-humbling prayer and upon the Grace. He is the type and temperament which must emphasize the religious, devotional approach to Truth and confess his helplessness. In this way he will begin to rely less on his own ego, which is his real enemy and hindrance to his true welfare.

91

When life seems to lose its meaning, when action seems in vain and ambition futile, when depression besets one like a dark cloud, the ego begins to feel its helplessness, its dependence on forces outside itself.

4

SURRENDER

In the end we have no choice. The head must bend, consentingly, to the higher power. Acceptance must be made. Some kind of communion must be established.

2

When we can fully accept the truth that God is the governor and manager of the universe, that the World-Mind is behind and controlling the World-Idea, then we begin to accept the parallel truths that all things and creatures are being taken due care of and that all events are happening under the divine will. This leads in time to the understanding that the ego is not the actual doer, although it has the illusion of doing, working, and acting. The practical application of this metaphysical understanding is to put down our burdens of personal living on the floor and let Providence carry them for us: this is a surrender of the ego to the divine.

3

If you identify with the little ego *alone*, you may believe and feel that you have to solve your problems *alone*. In that case, the burden will be heavier than it need be. But if you recognize that this planet has its own governor, the World-Mind, you need not feel forlorn, since you are included in the world.

4

Every problem that worldly men solve in a strictly worldly way leads to new ones. On this plane it has always been so. There is only one way to gain a final solution—transfer the problem to the celestial plane.

5

The ego does not give itself up without undergoing extreme pain and extreme suffering. It is placed upon a cross whence it can never be resurrected again, if it is truly to be merged in the Overself. Inner crucifixion is therefore a terrible and tremendous actuality in the life of every attained mystic. His destiny may not call for outer martyrdom but it cannot prevent his inner martyrdom. Hence the Christ-self speaking through Jesus told his disciples, "If any man will come after me let him deny himself and take up his cross daily and follow me."

6

Are we to wander with all our burdens from a hapless birth to a hopeless death? Or shall we surrender them?

7

It is when a man breaks down and finally admits that he cannot go on, that both he and his life must change—it is at such a moment that he is close to the guidance and help of the Overself, if only he can recognize them and is willing to accept them.

8

When life in the world becomes so formidable or so frightening that in desperation or bewilderment, panic or mental unbalance, the idea of suicide seems the only way out, then the time has come for a man to cast his burden on the Higher Power.

9

There is a panacea for all troubles. It is to turn them over to the Overself. This is a daring act; it will demand all your faith and all your understanding, but its results are proven. They are not available, however, for the lazy drifters and idle dreamers, for the insincere would-be cheaters of the Overself, and for the superstitious seekers of something-for-nothing.

10

Blessed are those who can find or keep this faith that, in spite of all unpleasant contradictory appearances, the course of human life will in the end be upward and the goal of human life will be spiritual self-fulfilment.

11

To try solving his problems by himself, without resort to a higher power, is to bring to bear upon them all his ignorance and unwisdom, all his faults and deficiencies, all his incapacities and maladjustments. How, using such imperfect tools, can he bring about a perfect result? How, for instance, can a muddled confused mind bring about any other than a muddled confused result of the efforts to solve his problems? How can his own unaided efforts be other than antagonistic to a correct solution?

12

He will come to the point where he will give up the burden of always trying to *do* something for his spiritual development, the burden of believing that it rests entirely upon his own shoulders.

13

The higher guidance may not be recognized or felt until after all efforts end in frustration, until the intellect retreats and obeys, until planning ends and surrender begins.

14

If you cannot see the proper way to deal with your problem, if making a right decision or coping with a difficult situation seems too much for you, if all the usual guides to action prove insufficient or unhelpful, then it is time to hand the trouble over to the Superior Power.

15

When a sensitive man loses faith in his own goodness, and even his own capacities, to the point of despairing hopelessness, he is really ready to pray properly and practise utter dependence upon the Higher Power's grace. When he realizes that the evil in himself and in other men is so deep and so strong that there is nothing below the surface of things he can do, he is forced to turn to this Power. When he abandons further trust in his own nature and clings to no more personal hopes, he really lets go of the ego. This gives him the possibility of being open to grace.

16

When a person is converted from one religion to another which is more ancient, more grandiose, or when a sceptic turns religious before dying, it is because he has reached a point when he feels helpless and his defenses have broken down. He must depend on other men, on other powers than his own, for now he has none. He is like a man lost in the desert, eager to accept anyone, any living thing, as a rescuer. What has happened? The profounder answer is that his ego has been completely crushed and he is ready to surrender.

17

The surrender of every problem as it arises to the higher self, the renouncing of personal will in the matter, and the readiness to accept intuitive guidance as and when it comes provide a superior technique and yield better results than the old ways of intellectual handling and personal planning alone.

18

So long as he is more afraid of giving up the ego than he is desirous of gaining the consciousness beyond it, so long will he dwell in its gloom.

19

He who has not learned to lower his head before the higher power, to surrender his personal aims to the World-Idea, to submit his desires to the need for self-governance, will suffer in the end.

20

Having worked to the utmost upon himself, but finding that a stable spiritual consciousness still eludes him, he has no recourse except to submit his further development to a higher power than his own will and then wait and let it work upon him.

21
Submit to the World-Idea—or suffer. Resign yourself to the higher course of things: go along with it—and be at peace!

22
When the ship on which the Muhammedan mystic Ibrahim ibn Adham was travelling was endangered by a storm, his companions begged him to pray for help. He retorted: "This is not the time to pray, it is the moment to surrender."

23
What the Hindus call detachment and what the Muhammedans call submission to God's will are really one and the same.

24
If we concentrate attention only on the miseries and distresses which afflict us, then we have to depend on our own intellect to find a way out of them. If, however, we turn concentration in the opposite direction, that of the Overself, and deposit our troubles there, we gain a fresh source of possible help in dealing with them.

25
When it seems humanly impossible to do more in a difficult situation, surrender yourself to the inner silence and thereafter wait for a sign of obvious guidance or for a renewal of inner strength.

26
In the end, after many a rebellion, he learns to trust God and accept his lot, like a tired old man.

27
To surrender is to know one's own incompetence and to put one's life in wiser hands.

28
No one finds that the pattern of his experience of life conforms to what he wished for in the past or wishes for now, so everyone in the end must learn acceptance.

29
The passage from black despair to healing peace begins with learning to "let go." This can refer to the past's crippling pictures, the present's harsh conditions, or the future's grim anticipations. To what then can the sufferer turn? To the Overself and its divine power.

30
The resignation which is advisable when circumstances are unalterable need not be a grim and hopeless one.

31

He has tried to manage his life by himself through all these years, but the results have been too deplorable too frequently. Is it not time to let the Overself take over?

32

When he has exhausted every means of finding a right and reasonable solution to his problem, it is time to hand it over to the higher self. Let him not indulge in self-pity under the delusion that he is indulging in self-abasement. There is a total difference between the two emotional attitudes, for the first will only weaken his capacity for the spiritual quest whereas the second will only strengthen it.

Avoid self-deception

33

There are great dangers in falling into a supine attitude of *supposed* submission of our will, an attitude into which so many mystics and religionists often fall. There is a profound difference between the pseudo-surrendered life and the genuine surrendered life. It is easy enough to misinterpret the saying "Thy will be done." Jesus, by his own example, gave this phrase a firm and positive meaning. Hence this is better understood as meaning "Thy will be done *by me*." A wide experience has revealed how many are those who have degenerated into a degrading fatalism under the illusion that they were thereby co-operating with the will of God; how many are those who have, through their own stupidity, negligence, weakness, and wrong-doing, made no effort to remedy the consequences of their own acts and thus have had to bear the suffering involved to the full; how many are those who have failed to seize the opportunity presented by these sufferings to recognize that they arose out of their own defects or faults and to examine themselves in time to become aware of them and thus avoid making the same mistake twice. The importance of heeding this counsel is immense. For example, many an aspirant has felt that fate has compelled him to work at useless tasks amid uncongenial surroundings, but when his philosophic understanding matures, he begins to see what was before invisible—the inner karmic significance of these tasks, the ultimate educative or punitive meaning of those environments. Once this is done he may rightly, and should for his own self-respect, set to work to free himself from them. Every time he patiently crushes a wrong or foolish thought, he adds to his inner strength. Every time he bravely faces up to a misfortune with calm impersonal appraisal of its lesson, he adds to his inner wisdom. The man who has thus wisely and self-critically surrendered himself may then go forward with a sense of outward security and inward assurance, hopeful and unafraid, because he is now aware of the benign protection of his Overself. If he has taken the trouble to understand intelligently the educative or punitive lessons they hold for him, he may then—and only then—conquer the evils of life, if at the same time of their onset, he turns inward at once and persistently realizes that the divinity within offers him refuge and harmony. This twofold process is always needful and the failures of Christian Science are partially the consequence of its failure to comprehend this.(P)

34

Most people who state that they have submitted their financial affairs to a higher power find things going from bad to worse. This point must be clarified. There is not actual surrender, but only self-deception, if it is made before reason, will, and self-reliance have been exhausted. There is no such easy escape out of difficulties, financial or otherwise, as mere verbal assertion of surrender. Education comes by negotiating difficulties, not by running away from them in the name of surrender. True surrender can only be made when one is mature enough. Life is a struggle for all; only the wise struggle ego-lessly, but they struggle all the same. They have to because the adverse element in Nature is forever at war, tearing down where they build, stimulating strife where they give peace, and enslaving minds where they lead to freedom.

35

There are those who believe that the mystical surrender to God's will means that they are to sit with folded hands, inert and lethargic. They believe also that to co-operate with Nature, to alter or to interfere with it, is blasphemous. It is not for them to try to make other men better, although they do try to make themselves better. Because they see that they can do little in every direction, they decide to do nothing. The humility behind this view must be appreciated, but the lack of rationality may not.

36

Giving up the ego does not require us to give in always to other people. That would be weakness.

37

This surrender of the future does not imply idleness and lethargy. It does imply the giving up of useless worry, the abandonment of needless anxiety.

38

If anyone refrains from using his own initiative and depends on the Overself for answers to his questions, for solutions to his practical problems before he is psychologically ready for such dependence, then he invites trouble.

39

The intuitive sensitivity of the artist and the discriminating intellect of a scientist are needed to keep that delicate balance which knows when to assume responsibility for one's own decision, action, and life and when to shift this responsibility to a higher power. The novice's statement that he commits his life into God's hands is not enough, for obviously if he continues to repeat the same foolish judgements and the same guilty conduct as before this commitment, his life still remains in the personal ego's hands. If his commitment is to be effective, it must be accompanied by the duty of self-improvement. Surrender to a higher power does not relieve him of this duty; on the contrary, it compels him more than ever before to its carrying out. The shifting of personal responsibility is achieved only when the awakening of consciousness to the higher self is itself achieved. The mere desire and consequent say-so of the aspirant does not and cannot become factual until then. He may seek to relieve himself of the pressure of obligation and the irritation of obstacles by this device, but the relief will be merely fictional and not factual.(P)

40

Such a prudent aspirant will surrender himself to no exterior organization but only to the interior Overself. He will permit no human group to annex his will and direct his thought, for they are to serve the Divine alone.

41

Surrender to the Higher Self is one thing; apathetic resignation to life is another. The one act gives birth to, or is the consequence of, mystical intuition. The other merely shuts out or prevents the arisal of such intuitions.

42

All talk of doing God's will becomes meaningful only if we are ourselves aware of God's existence. All talk of trust in God is meaningless if we are ourselves unaware of God's presence.

43

This practice must not be abused. It is premature and wrong to try to hand over a problem to the higher power before it has been thoroughly analysed and impersonally related to the causative factors within oneself.

44

We render much lip service to the theme of doing God's will; hundreds of writers, speakers, and clergymen utter its praise; but how few take a practical opportunity of giving it real expression by giving up the ego.

45

It is correct that we may trust absolutely to the higher power. But mystics should first be sure that they have found it and are not merely trusting some subconscious aspect of their ego. Otherwise they will be abusing the principle of inner guidance, falsifying the doctrine of inner light, even though they feel they are acting correctly in their own judgement.

46

It is a bias of certain religious persons to attribute to the will of God what is plainly the work of ego, or weather, or circumstances.

47

We must look within ourselves for the deliverance of ourselves. Nowhere else can we find it and no one else can effect it.

48

If the problem is really handed over to the Higher Power he is released from it. This lifts the feeling of being burdened with it. But if the feeling still remains, then he has deceived himself, has not truly committed it except outwardly in mumbled words.

49

If he is to surrender the conscious will, it should be only to the divine will.

50

The surrender to the Overself must not be misinterpreted as surrender to lethargy, to lack of initiative, or to absence of effort. It means that before initiative rises and before effort is made, a man will first look to the Overself for inspiration. When such inner guidance and rational thinking speak with united voice, then he can go forward with a plan, a faith, or a deed, sure and unafraid and confident.

51

To cast our ultimate reliance on the universal mind which, supporting all things as it does, can well support us, is a rule that works unfailingly. Only it must not be practised prematurely, for then the man will have the mere show of the thing instead of the real thing itself. He must first prepare for such a relation by developing himself sufficiently.

52

Such resignation does not mean that he shall let himself be always put upon, that he shall uphold truth, principle, justice, and goodness for others but deny them to himself.

53

This turning of a problem or a situation over to God may be real humility but it may also be a cowardly evasion of an unpleasant decision or difficult act.

54

Why do these religio-mystics worry about anything happening against

God's will? Do they not believe that, regardless of what they or others may do, everything will happen in conformity with that will anyway?

55

This blind abject apathy of many fatalistic Orientals is based, not on real spirituality, but on fallacious thinking. "Because the whole universe is an expression of God's will, and because every event happens within the universe, therefore every calamity must be accepted as expressing God's will." So runs the logic. The best way to expose the fallacy lurking in it is to place it by the side of a countersyllogism: "Because the whole universe is an expression of God's will, and because every individual resistance of calamity happens within the universe, therefore such resistance is the expression of God's will!"

56

There is a right and a wrong way of surrendering the outer life. To surrender it to one's own sorry foolishnesses or hallucinations, and call them God, leads to disaster. Yet this is precisely what many beginners in mysticism do.

57

Self-surrender does not mean surrender to someone else's ego, but rather to the Overself. Merely giving up one's own will to perform the will of somebody else is personal weakness and not spiritual strength; it is to serve the fault and negative qualities of other persons rather than to serve their spiritual life.

58

He is to turn it over to the higher power. He may do this for wrong motives to evade harsh facts and escape unpleasant consequences. In this case there will be no contact and no success.

59

Self-surrender should not signify merely letting others do what they wish with him or to him, but rather letting the higher nature work within and through him.

60

It is easy to ignore the fact that the cause of one's failure is one's own shortcoming, to cover incompetence in the management of earthly life by loud reiteration of trust in Providence—in short, to deceive oneself.

61

When dependence upon grace becomes total, when all effort is believed to be useless, when personal striving is renounced entirely, then the very belief which should have been fortifying becomes paralysing.

62

"It never consists in a sluggish kind of doing nothing so that God might do all," dryly wrote John Smith, seventeenth-century English philosophical mystic, about this struggle for truth and goodness within men's souls.

63

It is not a slavish and sentimental putting up with all that happens which is required.

64

Let no one confuse the calm delightful irresponsibility of such a planless life with the vague indolent irresponsibility of selfish or unbalanced men. There is a wide chasm between them.

65

"Trust your life to God" is an excellent maxim. But it does not mean, as some seem to believe, "Think foolishly or behave wickedly and trust to God to enable you to escape the painful karmic consequences of your wrong thought or action." If that were true the educative value of experience would be lost and we would go on repeating the same sins, the same errors. If that were true we would not grow up morally or mentally.

Accept responsibility

66

The ordinary mystic who has surrendered his will to the Overself is like a man floating downstream in a boat with his eyes turned up to the sky and his hands folded in his lap. The philosophic mystic who has surrendered his will to the Divine is like a man floating downstream with his eyes gazing ahead, on the look-out, and his hands keeping firm hold of the rudder to steer the boat. The first man's boat may crash into another one or even into the riverbank at any moment. The second man's boat will safely and successfully navigate its way through these dangers. Yet both men are being supported and propelled by the same waters, both mystic and philosopher have given their self and life to the Divine. Nevertheless, the consequences are not and cannot be the same. For the first despises and refuses to use his God-given intelligence.

67

To be truly resigned to the will of God—a demand made on the Muhammedan, the Hindu, and the Christian alike—does not necessarily mean blindly accepting all that happens as perfect, unquestionable, or best. According to the occasion, it may mean one or another of these things. But it may also mean looking with open eyes and intelligent mind at the course of events in order to understand them impersonally and then, this achieved, comprehending that given the factors and persons involved, only this could have happened.

68

It is for him to do whatever practical wisdom calls for in each situation but, having done that, to relinquish the results to the higher power for better or for worse.

69

It is true that every happening in the outer life can be accepted as being good for the inner life, that the most calamitous situation can be taken as God's will for us. But it is also true that unless we ask—and correctly answer—in what sense it is good and why it is God's will, we may fail to seek out and strive to correct the fault in us which makes it good and providential. For each situation presents not only the need and opportunity of recognizing a higher power at work in our life, but also a problem in self-examination and self-improvement.

70

The indispensable prerequisite to mystical illumination is self-surrender. No man can receive it without paying this price. Any man in any degree of development may pay it—he has to turn around, change his attitude, and accept the Christ, the higher self, as his sovereign. But once this happens and the Grace of illumination descends, it can affect the self only as it finds the self. An unbalanced ego will not suddenly become balanced. An unintellectual one will not suddenly become learned. His imperfections remain though the light shines through them.(P)

71

There is surely room for both surrender and self-reliance in a healthy life.

72

Where is the evidence that this trial, this suffering, was really the divine intention towards him, and not the consequences of his own stupidity or his own weakness?

73

If a man can give up his fears and anxieties to the higher self, because he is convinced that it is better able to manage his problems than the egoistic self, because he believes in trusting to its wisdom rather than to his own foolishness, yet does not evade the lessons implicit in those problems, his surrender becomes an act of strength, not of weakness.

74

It is right to say resignedly that it is God's will when we find ourselves in misfortune. But to content ourselves with such a half-truth is dangerous. It blinds our present perceptivity and bars our future advancement. Without perceptivity, we cannot accurately read the situation. Without advancement, we repeat mistakes and duplicate sufferings. A wiser statement would add the second half-truth, whose absence imperils us: that we ourselves often are largely the cause of our misfortune, that God's will is only the universal law of consequences bringing us the results of our own thinking or doing, our own tendencies or nature. Yes, let us submit to the divine will, let us surrender in acquiescence to what it sends us. But what will it profit us if we do so blindly, dumbly, and without comprehension? Is it not better to remember that it sends us what we have earned or what we need, either for self-perfection or self-purification? And, remembering, should we not seek out the lesson behind what is sent us and thus be able to co-operate intelligently with it? Then the Overself's will truly becomes our own. Are we not as aspirants to be distinguished from the multitude in several ways and not least in this, that we must try to learn from our experiences instead of letting them be useless and futile?

75

Swami Ramdas states in his autobiography: "It is beyond Thy humble slave to know the reason. Every move Thou givest to the situation of Thy servant is considered by him to be for the best." There are two statements here which are questionable and arguable. *Every* move? For how many of them arise as a direct result of his own character or capacities or tendencies or of those he associates with? How many situations are of his own direct personal making? If any particular situation in which he finds himself is caused by karma out of a previous birth, it is an inevitable one, not necessarily the best one from a practical viewpoint. It just *had* to happen. Of course, he could turn it to good by adopting the philosophical attitude toward it, but then that is true of every possible situation without exception. Where all of them may be regarded as the best, none is. The word then loses its meaning.

What are the correct facts behind Ramdas' claim? Because he surrendered his life to God, and sincerely renounced the world in doing so, God certainly guided or helped him in return at certain times, and brought about situations on other occasions. To this extent Ramdas' faith was fully justified. But because Ramdas' human self was still the channel through which he had to express himself, the individual temperament, characteristics, and intellect contributed also to giving a shape to the other situations or developments. His unfamiliarity with Western civilization led quite directly to certain results of his world tour. Had he been more familiar with it, these results would have been markedly different. Yet Ramdas told me personally that God had arranged every step of his way on this tour! This is not, of course, a personal criticism of Ramdas, who is one of my beloved friends, but a brotherly discussion of a topic on which he has often written or spoken and always in this manner. His conclusions seem to me, in the light of both the philosophic instruction I have received and the observations of mystical circles I have made, to be confused. It is *not* beyond us to know the reason for some situations; indeed, it is part of our development to learn the reason. And it is *not* God who intervenes in every petty incident or trivial circumstance of His devotee's life.

Those who refuse to exercise the reasoning faculty with which the divine World-Idea has endowed them will certainly believe that it is "God's will" for mishaps, disappointments, frustrations, or ill health to happen to them which, by proper thought or care, could have been avoided or diverted. They have been confused about the fact that outside of limited free will, God's will is inescapably and compulsively acting upon them, but within that limited freedom their own will may reign as it chooses.

76

"Trust in God but keep your powder dry" was as useful a maxim in a recent century as "Trust in God but keep your arrows sharp" might well have been in an earlier one.

77

We ought not to expect man to give what he is not yet ready to give. Only in the measure that he recognizes a higher purpose to be fulfilled will he renounce the ego which hinders that fulfilment.

78

Insofar as the whole of his future must be surrendered to his Higher Self, the planning of it through his ego-mind cannot be allowed. He resigns himself to God's will in this matter because he realizes that it will bring him only what is best for him or only what is needed by him or only what has been earned by him. He believes that God's will is a just will. Yet within the frame of reference of the intuition which may come to him as a result of this self-surrender, he may allow the intellect to plan his course and to chalk out his path. The intellect may function in the arrangement of his personal life, but it must function in full obedience to the intuition, not to the ego. Hence if he makes any plans for the future, he does so only at the Higher Self's bidding.

79

Where he depends on things events or persons too excessively, they may take an unfavourable turn and he will be thrown back on himself again and again. This kind of experience, taken to heart rightly, may quicken his spiritual progress; but taken wrongly, it may only arouse personal bitterness. If he intelligently accepts the suffering that the Overself, under the law of recompense, brings him, the evil will be transmuted into good. If he blindly clings to a completely egoistic attitude, he fails to show his discipleship.

80

Before we can do God's will we have to find out what it is.

81

Where, despite his best efforts, he finds that he cannot control the course of events, he should accept it as being the higher will, the ordained destiny. Where he can control it, he should seek to learn from and obey the inner voice in what he does.

82

That is true willpower which acts from the deepest part of our being, which sets the ego aside instead of expressing it. Not only can it thrust heredity aside and master surroundings, but then only is "Thy will" done by us.

83

Both ordinary mysticism and philosophic mysticism teach surrender to God's will, in any situation. But whereas the first is content to do so blindly, the second adds clear sight to its surrender. The first is satisfied with ignorance because it is so happy, so peaceful as a direct result of surrendering the ego's will. The second likewise enjoys the happiness and peace but uses its intelligence to understand the situation.

84

Having handed his life over to the higher power, he has handed his future over, too. But although much that will happen to him will not be of his own planning, he need not paralyse his will and negate his reason. They have their place and may be used, especially to work out the details of what he is led to do by intuition, or by inner guidance.

The process

85

His destination is also his origin. But if you say that he was born in the eternal Spirit, the question arises how can time, which is placed outside eternity, bring him to eternity. The answer is that it does not bring him there, it only educates him to look for, and prepares him to pass through, the opening through which he can escape. Need it be said that this lies at the point where ego surrenders wholly to Overself?

86

So few seem to know that surrender of the ego—what Jesus called denying self and also losing life—must be absolute. It does not stop with the more obvious and grosser weaknesses, the so-called sins. It must include surrendering the clinging to religious organizations and beliefs, religious dogmas, and groups. The attachments which hold us to the self are not only concerned with material possessions and material things. They are also concerned with social conventions and prejudices, with inherited habits and traditions. We remain deluded by the self until we are denuded of the self.

87

He is to sacrifice all the lower emotions on the altar of this quest. He is to place upon it anger, greed, lust, and aggressive egoism as and when each situation arises when one or another of them shows its ugly self. All are to be burnt up steadily, if little by little, at such opportunities. This is the first meaning of surrender to the higher self.(P)

88

No candidate could enter the King's Chamber and be initiated therein into the Greater Mysteries without stooping in emblematic submission beneath the low doorway at its entrance. For no man may attain adeptship without surrender of his personal egoism and his animal nature.

89

From the day that he abandons the egoistic attitude, he seeks no credit, assumes no merit. Hence Lao Tzu says: "Those most advanced in Tao are the least conspicuous of men."

90

Attempt to use no personal power. Rather get into meditation and quiet the person more and more until you can get away from yourself altogether. Turn the matter over to the Overself in the perfect faith that it has all the power needed to handle the situation in the best way. Having done that, do nothing further yourself, refrain from the slightest interference. Simply be the quiet spectator of the Overself's activity, which you will know to be occurring by its visible results, for its processes are mysterious and beyond all human sight.

91

Do not let the ego try to manage your worldly life. Do not let it even manage your search for truth! It is faulty and fallible. Better to cast the burden on the higher self and walk by faith, not knowing where you are going, not seeing what the future is.

92

Release your problems. Work in the Silence—until the Silence rules. The Infinite Intelligence will then take over your problems—to the extent that you release them to it.

93

When the ego is truly given up, the old calculating life will go with it. He will keep nothing back but will trust everything to the Overself. A higher power will arrange his days and plan his years.

94

But before he can even attempt to surrender the underself, he must first begin to feel, however feebly and however intermittently, that there *is* an Overself and that it is living there deep within his own heart. Such a feeling, however, must arise spontaneously and cannot be manufactured by any effort of his own. It does not depend on his personal choice whether he experience it or not. It is therefore an unpredictable factor; he cannot know when it is likely to come to him. This indeed is what makes this quest so mysterious. For such a feeling is nothing else than a manifestation of grace. Hence an old Sanskrit text, the *Tripura*, says: "Of all requisites Divine Grace is the most important. He who has entirely surrendered to his larger self is sure to attain readily. This is the best method." Without the divine grace (Faiz Ullah), the Sufis say, man cannot attain spiritual union with Him, but they add that this grace is not withheld from those who fervently yearn for it.

95

The more he becomes conscious of that thing in himself which links him with the World-Mind, the more he becomes conscious of a higher power back of the world's life, a supreme intelligence back of the world's destiny. It is consequently back of his personal destiny, too, and bringing him what he really needs to fulfil the true purpose of his earthly existence. With this realization he becomes content to surrender it to God's will, to abandon all anxiety for the future, all brooding over the past, all agitation over the present.

96

No man can penetrate into the being of the Overself and remain an ego-centered individual. On the threshold he must lay down the ego in full surrender.

97

The moth which throws itself into the candle's flame has practised self-annihilation. The man who lets himself be used by the Overself does the same, but only to the extent that he lets go.

98

You will have turned over the matter or problem if certain signs appear: first, no more anxiety or fretting about it; second, no more stress or tension over it; third, no more deliberating and thinking concerning it.

99

The extraordinary thing is that when, putting aside the ego-desires, we selflessly seek to know the divine will for us in any given circumstances, the answer brings with it the strength necessary to obey it.

100

If he wants the full Grace he must make the full surrender. He should ask for nothing else than to be taken up wholly into, and by, the Overself. To ask for occult powers of any kind, even the kind which are called spiritual healing powers, is to ask for something less than this.

101

Whatever happens in the world around him, he will so train his thoughts and feelings as to keep his knowledge of the World-Idea, and his vision of its harmony, ever with him.

102

The student should not habitually think that the problems with which he believes himself beset are really as grave as they appear. If he can let go, relax, and surrender his entire life with all its circumstances, and even all its aspirations, to the Higher Power, he should then patiently await the outcome of this surrender, in whatever form it manifests itself.

103

If he really surrenders his life to the Higher Power and turns over his sense of responsibility to It, he will be unable to act selfishly in his relationship with others, but will consider their welfare along with his own.

104

If he turns his problem over to the Overself in unreserved trust, he must admit no thoughts thereafter of doubt or fear. If they still knock at his door he must respond by remembering his surrender.

105

He will learn to live by faith where he cannot live by sight, to accept happenings against which the ego rebels and to endure situations which reason denounces.

106

Jesus said, "Take no thought of the morrow." What did Jesus mean? If we know to whom Jesus was speaking and the path along which he was trying to lead his hearers, we shall know also what he meant. It was certainly not that they should do nothing at all for the morrow; it was not that they should give no attention to it. It was that they should not fret and worry over the morrow; they should accept the duty imposed upon them to take care of the morrow, but reject all anxiety as to its outcome. They should not think that their little egos must manage everything, but they should have some faith also that the higher power can operate in their lives.

107

The real meaning of the injunction, so often delivered by spiritual prophets, to give up self is not a humanitarian one and does not concern social relations with other men. It is rather a psychological one, a counsel to transfer attention from the surface self to the deeper one, to give up the personal ego so as to step into the impersonal Overself.

108

"I tell you that the very holiest man in outward conduct and inward life I ever saw had never heard more than five sermons in all his days," was the testimony of old Dr. John Tauler. "When he saw how the matter stood he thought that was enough, and set to work to die to that to which he ought to die, and live to that to which he ought to live."

109

The real meaning of these constant injunctions to practise selflessness is not moral but metaphysical and mystical. It is to give up the lower order of living and thinking so as to be able to climb to a higher one.

110

Humbly recognizing our dependence on it, we must open our minds and offer our hearts to God.

111

He renounces the possession of his own thoughts and the performance of his own deeds. Henceforth they belong to the higher self.

112

It is the poor ego which worries and struggles to come closer to perfection. But how can the imperfect ever transform itself into the perfect? Let it cease its worry and simply surrender itself to the ever-perfect Overself.

113

The shoulders of the aspirant must be strong enough to bear the bitter blows of destiny without getting bowed down. He has placed his life utterly in the hands of the gods, and he must be ready to suffer with a sublime fortitude.

114

Whether in the artist's adoration of beauty or the mystic's aspiration toward the Glimpse, there must be willingness to turn from the present state to a fresh one. This is behind that denial of the ego, to which Jesus referred.

115

If the ego is led into surrender to the Overself, must it also be led to the guillotine? Can it not continue to live upon this earth, purified and humbled as it now must be, sharing a new inner life with the Overself?

116

All that he seems to be must dissolve to let the new self arise.

117

We achieve a total surrender of the ego only when we cease to identify ourselves with it. In this aspiration is the key to a practical method of achievement.

118

We may know God only by losing self, we may not lose self without experiencing pain. This is the inner meaning of the crucifixion.

119

If a problem or a life is to be handed over to the Higher Power for management or guidance, this can only be done if the faith is there to force a real turning-around from ego to counter-ego, from intellect or passion to inner quiet.

120

He is to receive passively what Grace bestows positively. Hence the need of a surrendered attitude.

121

Practise referral of doubts, questions, needs, requests to the Higher Power. Do not depend on the ego alone.

122

To surrender life to TRUTH is to desert the baser standards of conduct which have hitherto held us. It means that henceforth we will no longer consult our own comfort and convenience, but will accept the leading of the inner Master, no matter into how hard a path he may direct us.

123

"There is a principle which is the basis of things, which all speech aims to say, and all action to evolve, a simple, quiet, undescribed, undescribable presence, dwelling very peacefully in us, our rightful lord; we are not to do, but to let do; not to work, but to be worked upon; and to this homage there is a consent of all thoughtful and just men in all ages and conditions."—Emerson

124

To turn to the Higher Power and to wait patiently for its direction or support is a good practice but it must be remembered that one can only turn to a Higher Power by turning away from the ego.

125

He begins with turning his problems over to the higher unseen Power: he ends by turning himself over to it. This is what is also called "surrendering to God" and "taking refuge in Him alone."

126

The finite mind of man can not take possession of the Infinite Power any more than the little circle can contain the large one. At the point where the two come into contact there must be surrender, self-surrender, a willingness to let go of its own self-centre, its own instinct of self-preservation.

127

To die to one's self is to let go of all attachments, including the attachment to one's own personal ego. In some ways it is like the act of passing away from the fleshly body.

128

It happens by itself, this mysterious point where his own activity stops, when he surrenders to the feeling of the grace which suddenly comes within the glimpse of his horizon, when its presence is unmistakable surrender, offered of its own accord at the bidding of thinking, but gently and peacefully.

129

What it is necessary for him to do is really to surrender his fears and anxieties, whether concerning himself or those near and dear to him, or those who, he thinks, want to hurt him. He should surrender all these to God and be himself rid of them. For this is what giving up the ego truly means. He would then have no need to entertain such negative thoughts. They would be replaced by a strong faith that all would be well with him. To the extent that he can give up the little ego with its desires and fears, to that extent he invites and attracts divine help in his life.

130

It may be helpful for him to try a new angle on his spiritual problems. This is to stop striving and to wait with surrendered will for the higher power. This power is there within him and without him and knows his need. Let him stop being tense, stop working and striving. Let him even stop studying for realization of this presence, but let him just ask prayerfully for it to take hold of him.

131

The surrendering of his life to the Overself does not depend wholly upon his own efforts. He cannot bring it about as and when he wills. He can bring about the prerequisite conditions for this manifestation. He can fervently yearn for it, but the last word depends upon the Overself, upon

Grace. The Grace comes in time if it is wanted strongly enough, and then he steps out of the shadows into the sunshine and a benign assurance is born in the heart. Of course this can never be the result of metaphysical striving alone but only of a coordinated, integral effort of thought, feeling, and action. But whoever can arrive at it will surely be able to endure life's problems as well as, and perhaps much better than, he who has to endure and struggle without it.

132

We struggle to find God, we long after what seems unattainable, and we must hold nothing back, must yield all, surrender all, until the ego melts with every fetter that belongs to it.

133

This humble self-surrender is not the same as the supine resignation of the coward. On the contrary, it is an attitude of the brave.

134

To believe in the powers of the Overself is to believe rightly, but to suppose that those powers can be attained without complete self-suppression is to believe superstitiously. Few are ever able to exercise them because few are ever willing to pay the requisite price.

135

If we turn ourselves over to the higher power, surrendering our personal spiritual future to it, we must also turn over the personal physical future, with all its problems, at the same time.

136

"Whatever you do, offer it to Me," said Krishna. This implies constant remembrance of the Higher Power, which in turn saves those who obey this injunction from getting lost in their worldly life.

137

He who surrenders his future to the Higher Power surrenders along with it the anxieties and cares which might otherwise have infested the thought of his future. This is a pleasant result, but it can only be got by surrendering at the same time the pleasurable anticipations and neatly made plans which might also have accompanied this thought. "Everything has to be paid for" is a saying which holds as true in the realm of the inner life as it does in the marketplace. The surrender of his life to the Higher Power involves the surrender of his ego. This is an almost impossible achievement if thought of in terms of a complete and instant act, but not if thought of in terms of a partial and gradual one. There are parts of the ego, such as the passions for instance, which he may attempt to deny even before he has succeeded in denying the ego itself. Anyway, he has to make clear to himself the fact that glib talk of surrender to God is cancelled if he does not at the same time attempt to surrender the obstructions to it.(P)

138

When a man consciously asks for union with the Overself, he unconsciously accepts the condition that goes along with it, and that is to give himself wholly up to the Overself. He should not complain therefore when, looking forward to living happily ever after with a desired object, that object is suddenly removed from him and his desire frustrated. He has been taken at his word. Because another love stood between him and the Overself, the obstruction had to be removed if the union were to be perfected; he had to sacrifice the one in order to possess the other. The degree of his attachment to the lesser love was shown by the measure of his suffering at its being taken away; but if he accepts this suffering as an educator and does not resent it, it will lead the way to true joy.

139

The Inner Being will rise and reveal Himself just as soon as the ego becomes sufficiently humbled, subdued, surrendered. The assurance of this is certain because we live forever within the Love of God.

140

Within his heart, he may call or keep nothing as his own, not even his spirituality. If he really does not want to cling to the ego, he must cling to nothing else. He is to have no sense of inner greatness, no distinct feeling of having attained some high degree of holiness.(P)

141

Once he grasps that the higher part of his being not only knows immeasurably more than he what is good for him, but also possesses infinitely more power than he does to bring it about, he is ready to enter upon the surrendered life. He will no longer complacently assume that his imperfect mentality is wise enough to guide him or his faltering ego strong enough to support him. He will no longer predetermine his decisions or his doings. He realizes that other forces are now beginning to enter his life and mind, and his part is not to obstruct them but to let them do *their* work. The more his own passivity meets their activity, the better will this work be done.

Its effect

142

From the time when the Overself holds this ego in its enfolding embrace, he sees how its divine power brings great changes in his life, renders great service to others, and effects great workings in their outlook without his own effort in such directions. Therefore he cannot help concluding that it is competent to do all that is required to be done, that the ego may remain utterly quiescent, the body utterly still, and the whole man unemployed, and yet every need can be safely left to the Overself for attention. Thus, without an attempt to render service, nevertheless service is mysteriously rendered. It suffices if he leaves all activity to It, does nothing himself, and plays the role of an unaffected spectator of life.

143

He who has the courage to put first things first, to seek the inner reality which is changeless and enduring, finds with it an ever-satisfying happiness from which nothing can dislodge him. This got, it will not prevent him seeking and finding the lesser earthly happinesses. Only he will put them in a subordinate and secondary place because they are necessarily imperfect, liable to change and even to go altogether. And then if he fails to find them or if he loses them after having found them, he will still remain inwardly unaffected because he will still remain in his peace-fraught Overself. This is as true of the love of man for fame as it is true of the love of man for woman. The more he looks in things and to persons for his happiness, the less he is likely to find it. The more he looks in Mind for it, the more he is likely to find it. But as man needs things and persons to make his existence tolerable, the mystery is that when he has found his happiness in Mind they both have a way of coming to him of their own accord to complete it.

144

He who puts himself at the Overself's disposal will find that the Overself will in turn put him where he may best fulfil his own divine possibilities.

145

The unfulfilled future is not to be made an object of anxious thought or joyous planning. The fact that he has taken the tremendous step of offering his life in surrender to the Overself precludes it. He must now and henceforth let that future take care of itself, and await the higher will as it comes to him bit by bit. This is not to be confounded with the idle drifting, the apathetic inertia of shiftless, weak people who lack the qualities, the strength, and the ambition to cope with life successfully. The two attitudes are in opposition.

The true aspirant who has made a positive turning-over of his personal and worldly life to the care of the impersonal and higher power in whose existence he fully believes, has done so out of intelligent purpose, self-denying strength of will, and correct appraisal of what constitutes happiness. What this intuitive guidance of taking or rejecting from the circumstances themselves means in lifting loads of anxiety from his mind only the actual experience can tell. It will mean also journeying through life by single degrees, not trying to carry the future in addition to the present. It will be like crossing a river on a series of stepping-stones, being content to reach one at a time in safety and to think of the others only when they are progressively reached, and not before. It will mean freedom from false anticipations and useless planning, from vainly trying to force a path different from that ordained by God. It will mean freedom from the torment of not knowing what to do, for every needed decision, every needed choice, will become plain and obvious to the mind just as the time for it nears. For the intuition will have its chance at last to supplant the ego in such matters. He will no longer be at the mercy of the latter's bad qualities and foolish conceit.(P)

146
He is fortunate who hears the summons from within and obeys it. For despite its demands, it brings him ever closer to peace of mind.

147
Johanna Brandt came with little money and no friends to a strange land with a work of service to humanity's physical and spiritual health. She said that within a short time, "When it became necessary to have a secretary, a woman with great executive ability stepped forward and offered her services. Her rooms were placed at my disposal for the reception of visitors." This is an illustration of the truth that whoever is animated by the quest ideal will find that whatever and whoever becomes necessary to this true and best life will come into it at the right time.

148
When Jesus declared: "Whosoever shall say unto this mountain be thou removed, it will be," he did not mean the word *mountain* to be taken literally—surely that is perfectly obvious—but symbolically or poetically. Here it signifies problems. Whoever adopts the right attitude to them, the attitude explained in the heart-lifting words of this wondrous message, will find them removed from troubling his mind.

149
Five hundred years before Jesus said, "Seek ye first the kingdom of heaven and all these things shall be added unto you," Lao Tzu, a Chinese sage, said: "If you have really attained wholeness, everything will flock to you."

150
Emotional worry, whether it be worry about worldly and personal affairs or even about the spiritual quest, will vanish if one surrenders one's life to the Overself entirely. That is the only way to enjoy real freedom from worry; that is inner peace.

151

The total acceptance of this higher will changes life for us. It affects our relations with other people and brings some measure of serenity into ourselves.

152

Once this direction from within, this reception of the Overself's voice, is accepted, whatever comes to us from without falls into intelligible pattern. It is for our good even when its face is forbidding: it is helpful even when it is painful. For we no longer judge it egoistically and therefore wrongly. We seek its true meaning, its hidden message, and its place in the divine orderliness.

153

Anxieties subside and worries fall away when this surrender to the Overself grows and develops in his heart. And such a care-free attitude is not unjustified. For the measure of this surrender is also the measure of active interference in his affairs by the Divine Power.

154

When he has made this surrender, done what he could as a human being about it and turned the results over completely to the higher self, analysed its lessons repeatedly and taken them deeply to heart, the problem is no longer his own. He is set free from it, mentally released from its karma, whatever the situation may be physically. He knows now that whatever happens will happen for the best.

155

His confidence in the reality and beneficence of the higher power will increase as his experience of its inner working and outer manifestation grows.

156

There is a strikingly parallel thought in the *Bhagavad Gita* which confirms the New Testament's injunction, "Seek ye first the kingdom of heaven and all these things shall be added unto you." In the Indian scripture, Krishna, the Indian Christ, enjoins his disciple Arjuna: "Whoever worships Me and Me alone with no other thought than the worship of Me, the care of his welfare I shall take upon myself."

157

We become free from aims and ambitions: we are able to forgo all plans and projects.

158

He will feel all personal pride and claims ebb out of his being as the higher self takes possession of him. An utter humility will be the result. But this is not the same as a sense of inferiority; it will be too serene, too noble, and too satisfying for that.

159

Such a surrender to the higher self brings with it release from negative tendencies, liberation from personal weaknesses.

160

If he attains and maintains a harmony with the Overself (for which he must pay the price of submission to it) then the Overself will help him for it is being allowed to do so.

161

Courage in the face of a risky situation, an uncertain future, a harassing present, comes easily and spontaneously to the man who surrenders his self-will and submits to God's will.

162

The Overself—when you are fortunate enough to find it—will provide for and protect you, comfort and support you.

163

He who places his mind in Me enjoys Joy!

164

Once we accept the soul's existence, faith in its power and worship of its presence follow by deduction.

165

By escaping this common dependence on the ego, he enters into a dependence on the Overself. This, in one way, is utterly blind, because it may or may not show him even one centimetre of the path ahead; for he is led, like a little child, by the mysterious No-thing that is the higher power. But in another way, it confers greater freedom, openness, and flexibility.

166

So long as he has entrusted his life to the Overself wholeheartedly, on the practical as well as on the theoretical level, why should he entertain anxious thoughts about it? Rather should he let the Overself do whatever thinking about his welfare is needed, since he has handed over responsibility.

167

He who is faithful to his inner call at all times, whether in ideals, ego-sacrifice, meditation practice, or the like, loses nothing of worldly advantage in the end—except what ought to be let go. Providence is rightly named.

168

Saint John of the Cross: "If you fail not to pray, God will take care of your affairs, for they belong to no other master than God, nor can they do so . . . . God takes care of the affairs of those who love Him truly without their being anxious concerning them."

169

The Higher Power has given us the intelligence with which to solve these matters of practical daily life. When the human will has been truly surrendered, this Power may be counted on to guide—and guide aright.

170

The serenity of the Overself never varies and consequently the man who accomplishes the complete surrender to it is unvaryingly serene and unshakeably tranquil.

171

To the degree that he can surrender his mind to the higher self, to that degree does he surrender the worries and fears that go along with it.

172

Men love their egos more than anything else, or those extensions of their egos which are their families. But if and when the lesser self submits to the higher self, which is Egohood, this love is harmonized with love for the Overself.

173

If he has really turned his life over to the higher power, then he need not crease his brow trying to work out his own plans. He can wait either for the inner urge to direct him or for new circumstances to guide his actions.

174

The same power which has brought him so far will surely carry him through the next phase of his life. He must trust it and abandon anxieties, as a passenger in a railroad train should abandon his bag by putting it down on the floor and letting the train carry it for him. The bag represents personal attempts to plan, arrange, and mold the future in a spirit of desire and attachment. This is like insisting on bearing the bag's weight himself. The train represents the Higher Self to which the aspirant should surrender that future. He should live in inner Peace, free from anticipations, desires, cares, and worries.

175

He need no longer seek things essential to his life or needful to his service; they themselves will come seeking him.

176

He has nothing more to do, at this stage, than to give up the ego and give in to the Overself. This done, all that matters will be done, for from that time his farther way will be shown to him, and his subsequent acts guided, by the Overself.

177

The notion of making up an itinerary well in advance appeals to the time-bound calculating intellect but not to the spirit-led intuition.

178

He wastes no time on recovering the past or looking into the future.

179

Only when a man has reached this harmony with Nature's intent for himself can he unfailingly trust events as truly being what God wills for him.

180

Now that Grace is at work within him in response to his self-surrender, he may cease his struggles at self-improvement in the sense that he need no longer feel fully responsible for it. This does not mean at all that he is to become so careless as to throw away all the fruits of previous efforts. If this were to happen it would be evidence of a weakening setback rather than of a true surrender.

181

His life is no longer planned out meticulously in advance; he begins to live by the day, and cannot say what he will do within a month or a year, until the time actually nears or finally arrives.

182

A time comes when there is no longer any feeling of control and resistance, and discipline and opposition, simply because there is no longer any striving for an ideal to be attained. Having handed himself over to the higher power, he has handed both struggle and ideal over too.

183

At this stage he will tend more and more to stop counting on fixed, pre-thought plans for future movement, actions, or arrangements, to let the guidance of the moment take over, through the silent voice of intuition.

184

He finds that having attained this liberation of his will from the ego's domination, his freedom has travelled so far that it loses itself and ceases to be free. For it vanishes into the rule of his higher self, which takes possession of him with a completeness and a fullness that utterly hoop him around. Henceforth, its truth is his truth, its goodness is his goodness, and its guidance his obedience.

185

He who has turned all problems over to the Overself is no longer faced with the problem of solving each new problem that arises. He is free.

186

Jesus had no where to lay his head. He wandered from place to place, teaching without price as he wandered. Wherever he went he was at home in the complete confidence that Providence was taking care of him.

187

With this serene acceptance of Life, this glad co-operation with it and willing obedience to its laws, he begins to find that henceforth Life is for him. Events begin to happen, circumstances so arrange themselves, and contacts so develop themselves that what he really needs for his further development or expression appears of its own accord.

188

When a man has reached this stage, where his will and life are surrendered and his mind and heart are aware of divine presences, he learns that it is practical wisdom not to decide his future in advance but rather to let it grow out of itself like corn out of seed.

189

His struggle for survival has ended. Henceforth his life has been entrusted to a higher power.

190

He knows, having aligned himself harmoniously with the higher power that supports the universe, that it surely can and will support the little fragment of the universe that is himself. A sublime confidence that he will be taken care of in the proper way pervades him in consequence.

191

Few know the quiet security of having this inner anchorage, the secret power generated by this surrender of flesh to spirit.

192

Those who sincerely and intelligently live according to the philosophical ideal as best they can, surrendering the ego to the Overself continually, receive visible proof and wonderful demonstration of a higher presence and power in their lives. They can afford to trust God, for it is no blind trust.

193

He will be shown some way of dealing with his problem whether it leads to overcoming or to submission, to amendment or to sidestepping.

194

Either he will be inwardly directed to a certain move with successful results, or without any effort of his own something will happen of itself to bring them about. Whether he himself makes the right move at the right moment or whether someone else does it for him, a higher cause will be at work for the man who truly relies on the higher forces of the Spirit.

195

In that wonderful state the feeling of tension, the troubling by fear, and the suffering from insecurity vanish away. Why? Because the particular problems involved have been taken over by the Overself. Also, because no negative thinking is possible in that peaceful atmosphere. From this we may deduce an excellent practical rule for daily living: surrender *all* problems to the Overself by turning them out of your mind and handing them over, but not in the wrong way by refusing to face them. (*The Secret Path* and *The Quest of the Overself* show the right way.) Jesus taught the same method in simpler language: Psalm 55 holds out the promise "Cast thy burden upon the Deity, and he shall sustain thee." And in the *Bhagavad Gita*, among the final words addressed to the troubled Prince Arjuna, there is almost identical counsel.

196

The universal power will sustain him simply because he has surrendered himself to it. Failure in the true sense, which, however, is not always the apparent one, will then be impossible.

5

GRACE

Grace is a cosmic fact. If it were not, then the spiritual outlook for the human race, dependent entirely on its own efforts for the possibility of spiritual progress, would be poor and disheartening.

2

Grace is the indrawing power, or inward pull, of Overself, which, being itself ever-present, guarantees the ever-presence of Grace.

3

There is either great ignorance or grave confusion as regards grace, some serious errors and many smaller ambiguities. There is need to understand exactly what it is, the principal forms it takes, how to recognize its presence, and how its workings show themselves.

4

Grace is the benign effluence of the Overself, the kindly radiation from it, ever-present in us. The theological use of this term to mean particular help given by God to man to enable him to endure temptation and act rightly is a serious and arbitrary narrowing down of its original meaning. It may mean this sometimes, but it also means the loving mercy God shows to man, which appears variously as enlightenment of the mind or relief of the heart, as change of outward physical conditions or a dynamic revolution-working energy acting on the aspirant or on his life.

5

Out of the grand mystery of the Overself, the first communication we receive telling us of and making us feel its existence is Grace.

6

The rejection of the idea of Grace is based on a misconception of what it is, and especially on the belief that it is an arbitrary capricious gift derived from favouritism. It is, of course, nothing of the kind, but rather the coming into play of a higher law. Grace is simply the transforming power of the Overself which is ever-present but which is ordinarily and lawfully unable to act in a man until he clears away the obstacles to this activity. If its appearance is considered unpredictable, that is because the karmic evil tendencies which hinder this appearance vary considerably from one person to another in strength, volume, and length of life. When the karma which generated them becomes weak enough, they can no longer impede its action.(P)

7

By grace I mean the manifestation of God's friendliness.(P)

8

The Overself extends its grace to all men, but not all men are able to get it. This may be due to different reasons, some physical and others, the most numerous, emotional or mental.

9

There have been many objections to the introduction of the idea of Grace in these writings. It is too closely associated with theology for these objectors' liking, too much connected with a God who favours some but neglects others. Grace was never taught by Buddha, they point out. And to those who have plodded wearily year after year along what seems an unrewarding spiritual quest, the idea either mocks their plight or is simply a remnant of theological imagination—unfactual and untrue. These critics are right in part, wrong in part. If Saint Paul used this term and concept "Grace" several times but may be thought too religious to be considered authoritative by modern seekers of a scientific bent, let them remember that Ramana Maharshi of India also used it several times and yet his bent was quite mystical and philosophic.

10

What I mean by Grace may easily be misunderstood, or only half-understood. Its full meaning is only partly suggested by the Tamil word *arul*—divine blessing—and the Greek word *charis*—free and beautiful gift.

11

Grace is either a gift from above or a state within, a help of some kind or an experience reverently felt.

12

It is a whisper which comes out of the utter silence, a light which glimmers where all was sable night. It is the mysterious herald of the Overself.

13

There are little graces, such as those which produce the glimpse; but there is only one great Grace: this produces a lasting transformation, a deep radical healing and permanent enlightenment.

14

Indian critics who reject my statements about Grace are requested to consider the meaning of *prasada*—so often associated with the greatest holy men. If it does not mean Grace of God or guru, what does it mean? I refer them also to their own scriptural *Svetasvatara Upanishad* which especially states that *prasada* is needed for salvation.

15

To deny the reality of grace is to call into question the presence, in nearly all religions, of an intercessory element—Allah's mercy, God's pardon, Rama's help, or Buddha's compassion. This element has been greatly exaggerated perhaps, or grossly materialized, but it is still there under the superstition.

16

The wicked cannot always be judged by appearances. Some illumination may suddenly be granted because of past good deeds or intensity of suffering. The Higher Self is infinitely accommodating to human weakness and, also, infinitely patient; compassion is its first attribute.

17

Grace is here for all. It cannot be here for one special person and not for another. Only we do not know how to open our tensioned hands and receive it, how to open our ego-tight hearts and let it gently enter.

18

There is a power which inspires the heart, enlightens the mind, and sanctifies the character of man. It is the power of Grace.

19

The grace of an infinite being is itself infinite.

20

The doctrine of grace may easily lead to a supine fatalism if unclearly understood, but it will lead to intense self-humbling prayer if clearly understood.

21

The sceptical view that Grace is a superstition prompted by our human self-regarding and self-favouring nature, that it could have no place on the high altitude of truly divine attributes, is understandable but erroneous.

22

"My Grace is sufficient for thee." What does this sentence mean? For an answer we must enquire first, who pronounced it and second, in what context it was spoken.

23

Those who reject the concept of grace will have to explain why the *Bhagavad Gita* declares, "This Spiritual Self reveals itself to whom it chooses," and why the New Testament asserts, "Neither doth anyone know the Father but . . . he to whom it shall please the Son to reveal him."

24

Those Indian critics who have rejected my inclusion of Grace and stamped it as an alien Christian idea do not belong, and could not have belonged, to the great Southern region of their country, with its far purer Brahmin knowledge (because less subject to admixture by repeated Northern invasion). The mystical literature of that region is quite familiar with *arul*, a Tamil word which has no other and no better equivalent than "Grace."

25

The Grace is always present since the Infinite Power, from which it originally comes, is always present.

26

Grace does not depend on God's intervention in any favouritistic or arbitrary manner. It is not an effect of God's whim or caprice. It falls like sunlight on all, the good and evil alike. Each individual can receive it, according to the quantity of obstacles he removes from its path.

27

Grace comes from outside a man's own self although it seems to manifest entirely within himself.

28

So hidden is the manifestation of Grace and so mysterious is its operation, that we need not wonder why men often deny its very existence.

29

R.W. Emerson put it pithily: "Into grace all our goodness is resolved." These were his words, as far as I can remember them.

30

That is the real Grace which depends neither upon any other person nor upon himself.

31

In the religious symbolism of the Islamic faith, the crescent figure stands for the reception of Grace, as well as for the man who is perpetually receiving grace—that is, the mystic who has perfected himself.

32

I know that many dispute the existence of Grace, especially those who are Buddhistically minded, strictly rational, and they have much ground for their stand. My own knowledge may be illusory, but my experience is not; from both knowledge and experience I must assert that through one channel or another Grace may come: dutiful, compassionate, and magnanimous.

33

If he offers himself to the divine, the divine will take him at his word, provided his word is sincerely meant. The response to this offer when it comes is what we call Grace.

34

There has been some questioning about the idea of Grace. It is accepted by the Christians and Hindus and denied by the Buddhists and Jains. However, even those who accept it have confused and contradictory ideas concerning it. In a broad general sense it could be defined as a benevolent change brought about without the person's own willpower, but rather by some power not commonly or normally his own. But because we have with us residues of former reincarnations in the form of karma, it is impossible for most persons to distinguish whether any happening is the result of karma or of Grace. But sometimes they can, for instance, if they wake up in the morning or even in the middle of the night remembering some difficulty, some situation or problem, but along with it feeling a Higher Presence and then with this feeling beginning to see light upon the difficulty or the problem and especially beginning to lose whatever distress, inquietude, fear, or uncertainty may have been caused by it. If they feel that the negative reactions vanish and a certain peace of mind replaces them, and especially if the way to act rightly in the situation becomes clear, then they are experiencing a Grace.

35

People have curious ideas about what grace really is. So few, for instance, seem to see that in opening themselves up to the beauties of nature or of music and art they would be inviting the attention of grace too. Grace is not just an arbitrary religious factor.

36

It is grace which inspires our best moves, and which enables us to make them.

37

If Grace does not exist, why does the *Bhagavad Gita* contain the statement: "To him whom the Overself chooses, to him does It reveal Itself"? And why did the early Christian Father Clement, whose writings are considered authoritative, state: "It is said the Son will reveal Himself to whom He wishes"? (The Homilies, Vol. xvii, p. 278, Ante-Nicene lib.)

38

Grace may be defined as the Overself's response to the personal self's aspiration, sincerity, and faith, lifting up the man to a level beyond his ordinary one. This working in us (as contrasted with the working *by* us) begins in deep passive stillness and ends in mental, emotional, and even physical activity.

It is true that grace is given, but we ourselves help to make its blessing possible by the opening of self to receive it, the silencing of self to feel it, and the purifying of self to be fit for it.

An unknown mysterious thing inside the self is drawing him to it. He is groping his way, but it constantly eludes him. There must be something very beautiful there, which the subconscious recognizes, for the feeling of being attracted will not leave him and only grows stronger if by remaining passive, meditative, he will let it.

Its transmission

39

If the existence of grace is granted, the question of its means of transmission arises. Since it is a radiation issuing from the Overself, it can be directly bestowed. But if there are internal blockages, as in most cases there are, and insufficient force on the man's part to break through them, then it cannot be directly received. Some thing or person outside him will have then to be used as a means of indirect transmission.(P)

40

When a person is crushed by events and falls to his knees in prayer, his ego is temporarily crushed at the same time. After the prayer has been formulated, whether aloud or mentally, there are a few moments of complete exhaustion, of complete rest, which follow it. There is then temporary stillness and it is in this stillness that the Grace which is always emanating from the inner Being is able to do its healing and helping work. At the same time there may also be a corresponding external activity of a beneficial character.

Ascending to a higher level and studying the case of the aspirant on the Quest who by the practice of meditation deliberately brings about such moments of stillness, we see that he too opens a door to Grace. At this point it is necessary to clear away some confusion which often makes its appearance in spiritual literature and most especially in Indian literature. There we find an insistent and reiterated declaration of the absolute necessity of finding a guru so that by his Grace the aspirant may be helped towards enlightenment. When I say Indian literature I mean of course Indian Hindu literature, because in the Buddhist literature this insistence is generally absent and the aspirant is told to do the necessary work and he will get the natural result. The aspirant who has silently called for help may find that his call is answered by the appearance of a book or a person or a circumstance from whom he receives the help needed at the time. In the case of the appearance of a person, this may or may not be his destined guru, but it will be someone sufficient for the moment. The point is that what is called the guru helps prepare the right conditions which allow the inner Presence to make itself felt or which let it do its gracious work. The real help comes from this Grace—from the aspirant's own spiritual being, from himself. Saswitha, the Dutch healer, once said that he used his patients' own healing energy in order to treat them. Where did this healing energy come from? It came from their own subtler bodies, that is, from themselves; but Saswitha created the necessary conditions which enabled it to be released—when he was successful.

41

Grace is not necessarily bestowed deliberately or conferred personally. It may be received from someone who does not even know that he is its source. It may manifest through nothing more than the physical meeting between these two, or through a letter from one to the other, or even through the mere thinking about one of them by the other person. But, however obtained, Grace has its ultimate source in the mysterious Overself. This is why no man, however saintly, exalted, or advanced, can really give it to anyone: he can only be used by the higher power for this purpose, whether aware or unaware in the surface part of his mind of what is happening.

42

Ask for your share of the divine nectar and it shall not be withheld from you. Indeed, those who have turned from the peaceful hearth that is their due, to move through the gloomy houses of men to dispense it, have done so because of the dark flood of secret tears that break daily through the banks of human life.

43

Grace flows in wavelengths from the mind of an illuminated man to sensitive human receivers as if he were a transmitting station. It is by their feeling of affinity with him and faith in him that they are able to tune in to this grace.

44

No one but a man's own Being gives him grace. From the moment when he lays his head prostrate before It, and returns again and again to that posture, mentally always and physically if urged, grace is invoked.(P)

45

He may receive grace directly from its source in the infinite love, power, and wisdom of the Overself, or indirectly through personal contact with some inspired man, or still more indirectly through such a man's intellectual or artistic productions.

46

The philosophic concept of Grace is different from, and not to be confounded with, the popular religio-theologic one. The latter carries arbitrariness, caprice, and favouritism within it. The former has nothing of the kind. Despite its mysteriousness, it often follows the fulfilment of certain conditions by the seeker; but even when it does not appear to do so, it is a legacy from causes set going in earlier lives on this earth. The notion that it is dispensed in an arbitrary manner by the Higher Power is to anthropomorphize that Power, to regard it as a glorified man. This is nonsense to anyone who can reflect correctly and think deeply on the Power's real nature. The notion of caprice is to make the manifestation of Grace an affair of mere whimsy, an emotion of the moment, a passing mood. This simply could not be, for grace descends from a plane which transcends such things. Lastly, the notion of favouritism is usually applied in connection with a guru, a holy man, or a godlike man. If such a man is really, fully, and profoundly illumined, he has goodwill to all other people, wishes that all shall come to the Light, not just those he favours or who favour him. His grace is always there, but men must be able to recognize him and accept it. He is *always* ready to share his experience of the divine ever-presence with everyone, but not everyone is ready to receive it. In short, grace is what comes to you from an inspired book, or a blessed letter, or a few moments of relaxation.

47

To expect help to come to us through God when it should and could come to us only through man, is one fallacy. To expect it to come through some "master" when it should and could come only from oneself, is another.

48

It is possible for someone to make Grace a living presence either through divine utterance or through extraordinary quietness.

49

Grace is not imparted by any sacrament of any church, although sometimes the state of mind engendered by intense faith in such a sacrament may open the believer to such impartation. The Quakers have several instances in their history of having received grace, yet they have no sacraments.

50

Whether he be a recipient of the Overself's healing grace, or its teaching grace, or its protective grace, the source remains one and the same.

51

Whatever and whoever an adept brings into the Overself's light will eventually be conquered by that light.

52

Grace may be willed and yet not manifest; may not even be thought of, and yet manifest. Someone hears the sound of a sage's voice, and lo! he begins to feel an inner glow without the sage seeking to do anything or knowing what is occurring.

53

No man has the right or capacity to dispense grace, but some men may sometimes be used by the higher power in effecting its own dispensations.

54

I do not use the term *grace* in the narrow sense given it by one of the world religions, that it flows to recipients only through the outward sacraments and ritualized communions of that Church, but in the wide sense that philosophy gives it.

55

It was not Christ's death that brought his grace into the human world, but his life.

56

It is not the teacher's business to impose his own will on the other, but to help the introduction and working of Grace in the other.

57

No words can re-create these moments of grace so well as music. Think of the blessed gift which mankind has received through such works as Handel's *Messiah* and Bach's *Christmas Oratorio*.

58

There has been too much abuse of the idea of special channels of grace and too many claimants have made unwarranted declarations.

59

Each time he deliberately holds loving thought towards anyone—whether disciple or not—he extends grace to that person.

60

Although the glimpse is the chief form taken by Grace, it would be a mistake to believe that it is the only form. There are other and different ones.

61

The man who fervently believes that Christ has the power to forgive his sins is not wrong. But his interpretation of his forgiver is wrong. The Christ who can do this for him must be a living power, not a dead historical personage. And that power is his own Christ-self, that is, Overself.

62

We do not mean by grace that lasting union with the Overself can be given from without by the favour of another man.

63

A master must use words to impart his teaching but he need not use them to impart his Grace.

64

The translator into German of *The Wisdom of the Overself* went to Egypt for a three-week rest to avoid nervous collapse after the death of a most beloved person, who she believed was her twin soul. While she was staying at a hotel in Luxor, various shoeshine men came there and sat outside, offering their services to guests. One day an elderly Arab appeared among them, with a striking face and an even more striking radiation of tranquillity. She was so drawn to him that she let him polish her shoes in preference to the one who usually did them. When he finished she paid him four piasters (which was double the normal payment), because she felt so comforted by his presence. He immediately returned half the money to her, saying, "The Lord will look after the needs of tomorrow. Two piasters are enough for today." He never came again to the hotel, but she constantly thought of him and his peace, to have something to save her from utter despair. After she had returned to Europe still grieving and depressed, he appeared to her in a dream surrounded by light and blessed her. When she awoke, his mental image still seemed there, but it said, "This is the last time I shall come to you. From now on you must take care of yourself." He never reappeared, but she slowly recovered thereafter.

65

That grace can come only through the benison of a minister appointed by some church, and no other channel, is mere superstition. It can come through any man who is inspired, or any book written by such a man, even if he dwells outside all churches. If a parson or a priest has himself entered into the source of Light, he can become a channel for it, but not otherwise.

66

This belief in a master's grace appears in Moorish countries of North Africa, where it is said in spiritual circles that the more time spent in the company of one who is blessed with spiritual power, the more do we absorb some of his power in the reflected form of "baraka."

67

Another channel for grace's manifestation is through circumstances. These may provide the right surroundings, the right persons, and the right happenings for it.

68

It is not for him to know in advance in what form the revelation will come, whether it will be an intuition, a strong pressure, a dream, or a particular happening, words read in a book, a phrase dropped from some-one's lips, a mood engendered by music, art, Nature.

69

No Maharishee, no Aurobindo, no Saint Francis can save you. It is the Holy Spirit which saves man by its Grace. The ministrations of these men may kindle faith and quiet the mind, may help you to prepare the right conditions and offer a focus for your concentration, but they offer no guarantee of salvation. It is highly important not to forget this, not to deify man and neglect the true God who must come to you directly and act upon you directly.(P)

Karma and forgiveness

70

Some have difficulty in understanding the exact place in the scheme of things of Grace. If they believe in the law of recompense, there seems to be no room left for the law of Grace. It is true that man must amend his conduct and correct his faults; that no escape from these necessary duties can be found. But they can be done alone or they can be done with the thought, remembrance, and help of the Overself. This second course in-troduces the possibility of Grace. It can enter only if the first has been followed and only if the aspiration has succeeded in lifting the conscious-ness to the Overself. A moment's contact will suffice for this purpose. What happens then is that the inner change is then completed and the remaining, unfulfilled karmic consequence is then annulled. There is no giving of "something for nothing" here, no breakdown of the law of recompense. The ego must use its will to repent and amend itself, in any case.

71

The forgiveness of sin is no myth, but it can become a fact only after the sinner has done penance and sought purification.

72

He who has himself sinned and suffered for his sin, who has attained inner understanding of it and made repentant atonement for it, who has then felt in his heart the benign grace of being forgiven—such a person can easily extend pardon to those who wrong him and compassion to those who wrong themselves by wronging others.

73

There are three types of Grace: firstly, that which has the appearance of Grace but which actually descends out of past good karma and is entirely self-earned; secondly, that which a Master gives to disciples or aspirants

when the proper external and internal circumstances exist—this is in the
nature of a temporary glimpse only but is useful because it gives a glimpse
of the goal, a sense of the right direction, and inspiring encouragement to
continue on the Quest; thirdly, when a man attains the fullest degree of
realization, he is enabled in some cases to modify overhanging negative
karma or in others to negate it because he has mastered the particular
lessons that needed to be learned. This is particularly evident when the
Hand of God removes obstructions in the path of his work. The philosophic conception of Grace shows it to be just and reasonable. It is indeed
quite different from the orthodox religious belief about it, a belief which
regards it as an arbitrary intervention by the Higher Power for the benefit
of its human favourites.(P)

74

By this grace the past's errors may be forgotten so that the present's
healing may be accepted. In the joy of this grace, the misery of old mistakes may be banished forever. Do not return to the past—live only in the
eternal Now—in its peace, love, wisdom, and strength.

75

We have the authority of Lao Tzu that there is such a thing as pardon.
He says: "For what did the ancients so much prize this Tao? Was it not
because by it those who had sinned might escape?"

76

Would forgiveness be an impossible nullification of the law of karma? Is
there no way out of one karmic consequence leading to and creating a
further one in an endless and hopeless series? I believe an answer to the
first question has been given by Jesus, and to the second by Aeschylus.
Matt. 12:31: "Therefore I tell you, every sin and blasphemy will be forgiven men," was Jesus' clear statement. As for the difficult problem pro-
pounded by the second question, consider the solution suggested by
Aeschylus: "Only in the thought of Zeus, whatever Zeus may be." Karma
must operate automatically, but the Power behind karma knows all things,
controls all things, controls even karma itself, *knows and understands when
forgiveness is desirable.* No human mind can fathom that Power; hence
Aeschylus adds the qualifying phrase, "whatever Zeus may be." Forgiveness does not destroy the law of karma; it complements the work of that
law. "All of us mortals need forgiveness. We live not as we would but as
we can," wrote Menander nearly four hundred years before Jesus' time.

77

The notion of grace as given out in popular religion was helpful perhaps
to the masses but needs a large revision for the philosophic seekers. It is
not granted at the whim of a Personal God nor solely after deserving

labours for it. It is rather more like a steady permanent emanation from a man's own Overself, always available, but of which he must partake by himself. If at times it seems to intervene specially on his behalf, that is an appearance due to the immense wisdom in timing the release of a particular good karma.

78

Just as this generation has lived to see the experience of gravity upset by the weightlessness experiences of spacemen, so in all the generations there have been those who have found the experience of karma upset by grace and its forgiveness.

79

When the ego's total submission is rewarded by the Overself's holy Grace, he is granted pardon for the blackest past and his sins are truly forgiven him.

80

Grace will shatter the power of an evil past.

81

To make the result dependent on Grace alone would be to deny the existence and power of the universal law of recompense. The need of effort can only be ignored by those who fail to see that it plays an indispensable part in all evolution, from the lowly physical to the lofty spiritual.

82

Who can tell the miraculous power of the Overself? Its Grace may lift the most degraded of men into the most exalted.

83

A man who has sinned, erred, or been mistaken much and wakened up at last to what he has been doing, will instinctively seek first for affectionate understanding and sympathetic forgiveness. The more he has strayed, the more he needs them.

84

It is not possible to have the punishment of past errors remitted until we ourselves let them go by taking their lessons fully and fairly to heart.

85

Buddha found himself in a land where degenerate priestcraft had cunningly persuaded the masses to believe that every sin could be expiated, and its present or future effects in destiny circumvented, by some paid-for ritual, sacrifice, or magic. He tried to raise the moral level of his people by denying the pardon of sin and affirming the rigorous governance of karmic law, the strict unalterability of unseen justice. Jesus, on the contrary, found himself in a land where religion proclaimed harshly, "An eye for an eye, a tooth for a tooth." He too tried to raise the moral level of his people. But a wisdom not less than Buddha's made him meet the situation by stressing forgiveness of sins and the mercy of God. "The law of recompense brings every man his due and no external religious form can change its working" is, in effect, the gist of much Buddhist teaching. "True," Jesus might have said, "but there is also the law of love, God's love, for those who have the faith to invoke it and the will to obey it." Let us grant that both the prophets were right if we consider the different groups they were addressing, and that both gave the kind of help that was most needed by each group. Let no one deny to divinity a virtue which is possessed by humanity. The higher self's response to the ego's penitence is certain. And such response may stretch all the way to complete forgiveness of sins.

86

The failure to appreciate the role of grace because of faith in the law of karma is as deplorable as the tendency to exaggerate it because of faith in a personal deity.

87

Such is the wonder of grace that the worst sinner who falls to the lowest depths may thereafter rise to the loftiest heights. Jesus, Buddha, and Krishna have plainly said so.

88

Those who believe that the universe is governed by law and that human life, as a part of it, must also be governed by law, find it hard to believe in the forgiveness of sins, and the doctrine of Grace of which it is a part. But let them consider this: that if the man fails to appropriate the lesson and to amend his conduct, if he lapses back into the old sins again, then their forgiveness automatically lapses too. The law of recompense is not negated by his forgiveness but its own working is modified by the parallel working of a higher law.

89

The Overself acts through inexorable law, yes, but love is part of the law. Grace violates no principle but rather fulfils the highest principle.

90

Grace can be a ripening of karma, or a response to a direct appeal to a higher power, or can come through a saint's appeals. Faith in the Power is rewarded by grace. If the appeal fails, adverse karma must be too strong. Materialists do not make such appeals, so they receive no Grace unless the accumulation of good deeds brings good karma.

91

Lift up your eyes from the ground to the sun of a justified hope. We have it on the authority of Jesus that there is mercy or forgiveness for the worst sinners if they set about obtaining it in the right way. And as you do not come anywhere near that category, surely there is some hope and some help for you too.

92

The notion that we must qualify for Grace before we can receive it may not, apparently, hold true in some cases. But even there the laws of reincarnation and recompense will supply the missing connections.

93

There is hope for all because there is Grace for all. No man is so sinful that he cannot find forgiveness, cleansing, and renewal.

The power of the Other

94

Where is the hope for mankind if there is no Grace, only karma? If it took so many ages to collect the karmic burden we now carry, then it will take a similar period to disengage from it—the forbidding task will continue throughout every reincarnation until the man dies again and again—unless the individual collector, the ego, is no longer here to claim it. But to cancel its own existence is impossible by its own efforts, yet possible by its non-effort, its surrender, its letting in the Higher Power, by no longer claiming its personal identity. The coming in, when actualized, *is* Grace for it is not his doing.

95

The aspirant who depends solely on his own unaided efforts at self-improvement will nevertheless one day feel the need of an outside power to bestow what he cannot get by himself. The task he has undertaken cannot be perfectly done or completely done by himself alone. He will eventually have to go down on his knees and beg for Grace. The ego cannot save itself. Why? Because secretly it does not want to do so, for that would mean its own extinction. So unless he forces it to seek for Grace, all his endeavours will bring him only a partial result, never a fully satisfactory one. Those who say that the idea of Grace violates the concept of universal law do not look into it deeply enough. For then they would see that, on the contrary, it fulfils the law of the individual mind's effort, which they believe in, by complementing it with the law of the Universal Mind's activity inside the individual, which they ought also to believe in. God cannot be separated from man. The latter does not live in a vacuum.

96

The destiny of the ego is to be lifted up into the Overself, and there end itself or, more correctly, transcend itself. But because it will not willingly bring its own life to a cessation, some power from outside must intervene to effect the lifting up. That power is Grace and this is the reason why the appearance of Grace is imperative. Despite all its aspirations and prayers, its protestations and self-accusations, the ego does not want the final ascension.

97

The case for Grace is that only the Overself can tell us what the Overself is, can teach us about itself. The ego-intellect cannot do so; the senses certainly cannot; and ordinary experience seems far from it.

98

No man can render himself so independent of bodily appetites and human desires that they cannot sway his judgements or decisions, unless he is inwardly supported and strengthened by grace.

99

The "me" is in us, and attempts to destroy it and to remove its existence from consciousness yield here and there only to reappear later. Only grace can effectively overcome its tyranny. Surrender to the Overself by constantly turning toward it ends the struggle and brings peace. The ego then lies, obeisant, the victim and no longer the victor.

100

It does not lie within man's power to gain more than a glimpse of this diviner life. If he is to be established firmly and lastingly in it, then a descent of grace is absolutely necessary. Artificial methods will never bring this about. Rites and sacrifices and magical performances, puzzling over Zen koans or poring over the newest books, will never bring it.

101

The closer he comes to the Overself, the more actively is the Grace able to operate on him. The reason for this lies in the very nature of Grace, since it is nothing other than a benign force emanating from the Overself. It is always there but is prevented by the dominance of the animal nature and the ego from entering his awareness. When this dominance is sufficiently broken down, the Grace comes into play more and more frequently, both through Glimpses and otherwise.(P)

102

The Holy Spirit's light alone can open his understanding and that of those around him.

103

Grace acts as a catalytic agent. Where a man is unable to liberate himself from the animal and the ego, it assists him to do so. Where rule of the mechanical responses of his senses, his glands, and his unconscious complexes holds him captive to an established pattern, it sets him free.

104

Nothing that you do can bring about this wonderful transformation, for it is not the result of effort. It does not depend on the power of your will or the strength of your desire. It is something which can only be done to you, not by you. It is the result of your absorption by another and higher Force. It depends on Grace. It is more elusive yet more satisfying than anything else in life.

105

Most things may be acquired by violent effort, but not Grace.

106

It is the power of the Other which pulls him upward out of his attachments to body and earth, cajoling him to do what he cannot do of himself—let go. This power, when so felt, we call grace.

107

Let him leave some room in his calculations for grace. The conquest of self, and certainly the negation of self, must in the end be a gift of the Lord.

108

When the ego knows that it is beaten, when it gives up its strivings, efforts, and goals, when it lies prostrate and calls out to the higher Power in despair or surrender, there is then a chance that the Grace will appear. However, lest there be any misunderstanding on this point, it must be said that this is only one way for Grace to appear, and there are other ways not so unhappy and much more joyous.

109

Where man fails, Grace succeeds. Where his ego laughs at all his efforts to dislodge it, he has to surrender it in humility before the guru or God, whose grace alone can do what his own act cannot do.

110

It is not within the power of man to finish either the purificatory work or its illumination-sequel: his Overself, by its action within his psyche, must bring that about. This activating power is grace.

111

Grace is not a fruit which can be artificially forced. It must be left to ripen of itself.

112

What he is unable to attain by all his efforts will, if he is blessed by Grace, be given him unexpectedly and suddenly when all desire for it has lulled.

113

Grace is a necessity before the ego can go up in the blaze of divine energy.

114
What Grace does is to draw the man's attention away from himself, from his ego, to the Overself.

115
Since grace does not depend immediately and directly on the man himself, on what he thinks and does, he cannot *make* a glimpse happen by any act of will. At best he can draw nearer the source of this experience.

116
Many have failed to disidentify themselves from their thoughts, despite all attempts. This shows its difficulty, not its impossibility. In such cases, grace alone will liberate them from their thought-chains.

117
When the ego is sufficiently crushed by its frustrations or failures—and sooner or later this may happen to most of us—it will turn, either openly or secretly, to the admission that it needs outside help. And what other help can it then find than Grace, whether mediated directly from the Overself or indirectly through a master?

118
The ego, the personal limited self, cannot lift itself into the Higher Self, and if the student at times has felt dismally powerless to make progress by self-effort, he will have learned the priceless lesson of the need of Grace.

119
He cannot take any virtue to himself because he did not make the change by himself. It was a gift—the gift of Grace.

120
The supreme effect of Grace, its most valuable benefit, is when its touch causes the man to forfeit his ego-dominance, when it takes away the personal obstruction to the Overself.

121
Only when the ego, thwarted and disappointed, hurt and suffering, finds that it cannot sufficiently change its own character, is it ready to beg, out of its helplessness, for Grace. So long as it believed that by its own power it could do so, it failed. And the way to ask for Grace is to sit perfectly still, to do nothing at all, since all previous doing failed.

122
Since the very "I" which seeks the truth and practises the meditation is itself so illusory, it cannot attain what it seeks or even practise with success, unless it also receives help from a higher source. Only two such sources are possible. The first and best is the Overself's direct grace. This must be asked for, begged for, and wept for. The next best is the grace of a master who has himself entered into truth-consciousness.

123

He may come at length to the disconcerting conclusion that his spiritual hopes would never be fulfilled. But in doing this he is not allowing for the unknown X-factor, the higher and mysterious Overself.

124

The revelation which brings one's own consciousness into coincidence with the Overself comes only by Grace.

125

When a man's strivings mature, the insight dawns of itself. Yet he cannot tell which day this is to be, cannot precipitate the wondrous event by his own will. For this depends on grace.

126

We need the power it gives, the understanding it bestows, and the solace it brings.

127

If he insists on clinging to the ego, he makes it impossible to know truth, approach God, or experience the timelessness of reality. Only an outer intervention can then help him, only the Grace coming direct or through some human channel.

128

"By him is He realized to whom He is full of grace," says the *Katha Upanishad*.

The significance of self-effort

129

Just as we have to look at the world in the twofold way of its immediate and ultimate understanding, so we have to find enlightenment in a two-fold way through our own self-creative efforts and through the reception of Grace.

130

Grace is the hidden power at work along with his spirit's aspiration and his efforts at discipline. This does not mean that it will continue to work if he drops both aspiration and effort. It may, but more often it will not.

131

It seems a tiring and endless task, this, of tracking down the ego and struggling with it in its own lair. No sooner have we given ourselves the satisfaction of believing that we have reached its last lair and fought the last struggle than it reappears once again, and we have to begin once more. Can we never hope to finish this task? Is the satisfaction of victory always to be a premature one? When such a mood of powerlessness overwhelms us utterly, we begin at last to cast all further hope for victory upon Grace alone. We know that we cannot save ourselves and we look to the higher power. We realize that self-effort is absolutely necessary to our salvation, but we discover later that it is not enough for our salvation. We have to be humbled to the ground in humility and helplessness before Grace will appear and itself finish the work which we have started.

132

It is important to note that in the *Bhagavad Gita* the introduction of the subject of Grace and its actual descent upon the disciple Arjuna come only at the very end of the book—after Arjuna, by patient discipleship, has really earned it. Without Grace there is no entry. We may strive and weep, but unless the Grace falls on us we cannot enter into the kingdom of Heaven. How and when it should come depends partly upon our karma, partly upon our yearning, and partly upon the channel which God uses.

133

The passing over into higher consciousness cannot be attained by the will of any man, yet it cannot be attained without the will of man. Both grace and effort are needed.

134

If all his efforts are concentrated on self-improvement, then the circle of his thinking will be a small and limited one. The petty will become over-important in his own eyes and the insignificant will become full of meaning. It is needful to balance the one attitude with another—surrender to and faith in the power of Grace.

135

Constant self-effort can thin down the egoism but not eliminate it. That final act is impossible because the ego will not willingly slay itself. What self-effort does is to prepare the way for the further force which can slay it and thus makes the operation timely and its success possible. What it further does is to improve intelligence and intuition and to ameliorate the character, which also prepares the individual and attracts those forces. They are nothing else than the pardoning, healing, and, especially, the transforming powers of Grace.

136

To make any spiritual venture explicitly efficacious and to bring it to complete success, certain conditions must first be fulfilled. Most of them can be provided by the venturer himself but a few of them must come from outside himself. These are grace and favourable destiny.

137

However much he exerts his intellect he cannot reach the final revelation, the clearest enlightenment, for this is a gift of grace.

138

While he patiently waits with surrendered will for the oncoming of divine Grace, he directs conscious effort to improve himself and thus, incidentally, deserves it.

139

It is not by special intervention that the divine grace appears in his life. For it was there all the time, and behind all his struggles, as a constant unbroken radiation from the Overself. But those struggles were like the hoisting of sails on a ship. Once up, they are able to catch the wind and propulsion begins automatically.

140

Only the double viewpoint does justice to the double truth that both personal effort and bestowed grace are needed, or that both ego and Overself are present.

141

When your efforts have brought you to a certain point, then only do they get pushed aside or slowly drawn away by another power—your higher Self. What really happens is that the energy or power which you are using spontaneously ignites. It is that which enables you to do, to get done, to achieve. The all-important point is that the active power is not your own will, but is really a direct visitation of what we must call Grace. It is strongly felt, this experience of the higher power or higher Self.

142

A man can look to his own knowledge and his own actions to carry him a long distance on this path, but in the end he must look to grace for final results.

143

He cannot bring this enlightenment into being—much less into permanent being—by his own willpower. It can only come to him. But although striving for it may probably end in failure, the masses' indifference to it is worse. For whereas he will at least be open to recognize and accept it when it does happen to come, their doors of perception will be shut to it, or, bewildered and frightened, they will run away from it.

144

Man has no power of his own to command Grace but he does have the power to turn away from smug satisfaction with his own ego and throw himself at the feet of the Overself—the source of Grace.

145

He who told us to note the lilies of the field also told us the parable of the talents. Whatever the divine Grace brings us, it brings it *through* our personal effort.

146

When he becomes acutely aware both of the sacred duty of self-improvement and of the pitiful weakness which he brings to it, the need of getting the redeeming and transforming power of Grace follows logically. He is then psychologically ready to receive it. He cannot draw Grace to himself but can only invoke and await it.

147

In the end, and after we have tried sufficiently long and hard, we find that the knot of self cannot be untied. It is then that we have to call on grace and let it work on us, doing nothing more than to give our consent and to accept its methods.

148

It is a simple error to attribute to grace what properly belongs to his own nature, but it is spiritual arrogance to attribute to his own power what properly belongs to Grace.

149

If he fails but persists despite the failures, one day he will find himself suddenly possessed of the power to win, the power to achieve what had hitherto seemed impossible for his limited ability. This gift—for it is nothing else—is Grace.

150

If grace had to depend solely on human merit, if it had to be fully worked for and earned, it would no longer be grace. It really depends on the mysterious will of the higher power. But this is not to say that it comes by the caprice of the higher power. If a man puts himself into a sufficiently receptive attitude, and if he applies the admonition "Be still and know that I am God," he is doing something to attract grace.

151

When he has worked and worked upon himself as well as he is able, but comes in the end to acknowledge that success in getting rid of his weaknesses is beyond his power, he is ready to realize the need of Grace. And if it comes—for which such realization is essential—he will discover that final success is easy and, sometimes, even instantaneous with Grace.

152

If he thinks that the result depends wholly upon his personal endeavours after holiness, he is wrong. But if he does little or nothing to control himself because he waits for the Grace of God or the help of a master to come into his life, he is also wrong.

153

The idea of conquering his own lower nature solely by his own efforts does not allow any room for Grace. It would be better to find a more balanced approach. He needs to learn in his efforts that they cannot of themselves bring all he seeks. The first step to attract Grace is to humble himself in prayer and to confess his weakness.

154

When he has passed successfully through the last trial, overcome the last temptation, and made the last sacrifice of his ego, the reward will be near at hand. The Overself's Grace will become plain, tangible, and wholly embracing.

155

Belief in the reality of Grace and hope of its coming are excellent. But they are not to be turned into alibis for spiritual sloth and moral sin.

156

The strength needed for sustained mystical contemplation must come at first from his own ego's persistence but will come in the end from the Overself's Grace.

157

Although personal effort and the will toward self-mastery do much to advance him on this quest, it is grace, and grace alone, which can advance him to the goal in the last stages or assist him out of an impasse in the earlier ones.

158

First, he must attempt to lift himself upwards, taking the needed time and making the needed effort. Then he will feel that some other force is lifting him gratuitously—this is the reaction, Grace.

159

To come into the consciousness of the Overself is an event which can happen only by grace. Yet there is a relation between it and the effort which preceded it, even though it is not an exact, definite, and universally valid relation.

160

We must exert our own will and strength to prepare the way for, and make us receptive to, the divine grace. Thus the one complements the other; both are necessary parts of the World-Idea.

161

Jesus has said that it is Grace which starts and keeps a man on the way to God, even though his heart and will have to make their effort also. Ramana Maharshi confirmed this statement.

162

How can the ego's self-effort bring about the grand illumination? It can only clear the way for it, cleanse the vehicle of it, and remove the weaknesses that shut it out. But the light of wisdom is a property of the innermost being—the Soul—and therefore this alone can bring it to a man. How can the ego give or attain something which belongs to the Overself? It cannot. Only the divine can give the divine. That is to say, only by grace can illumination be attained, no matter how ardently he labours for it.

163

No man is excluded from that first touch of Grace which puts him upon the Quest. All may receive it and, in the end, all do. But we see everywhere around us the abundant evidence that he will not be ready for it until he has had enough experience of the world, enough frustration and disappointment to make him pause and to make him humbler.

164

The aspirant who cries out in despair that he is unable either to make progress or to get a mystical experience and that Grace seems absent or indifferent does not understand that he has within himself, as every man has, a place which is the abode of Grace. When I say every man, I mean every human being—which includes the vast multitudes of non-aspirants too. Just as the exhausted athlete may with some patience find what he calls his second wind, so the man whose thought, feeling, will, and aspiration are exhausted may find his interior deeper resource; but this requires patience and passivity. The need to hope, to wait, and to be passive is the most important of all.

165

Some Questers become depressed and discouraged when they learn that grace is the final essential ingredient for success on the Quest. This seems to put the issue out of their hands and to make it a matter of luck. They are taking too negative an attitude. It is true that grace is not subject to their command, but the atmosphere which attracts it, the conditions in which it can most easily enter, are subject to him.

166

God's Grace is the spark which must fall into human effort to make it finally effective.

167

We may wander about and wait for Grace to come or we may follow a disciplined way of working for it.

168

If the Overself's Grace does not come to the help of a man, all his exertions will be fruitless. But, on the other hand, if he does not exert himself, it is unlikely that the Grace will come at all.

169

His part is to open a way, remove obstructions, gain concentration, so that the Overself's grace can reach him. The union of both activities produces the result.

170

He is not asked to free himself from all feeling, nor to throw out all desire, but to attain a measure of calm. This can come through a twofold source. First, he must learn and cultivate self-control. Second, his aspiration and purification must succeed in attracting grace.

Preparing for grace

171

The fact of Grace being an unpredictable descent from above does not mean that we are entirely helpless in the matter, that there is nothing we can do about it. We can at least prepare ourselves both to attract Grace and to respond aright when it does come. We can cleanse our hearts, train our minds, discipline our bodies, and foster altruistic service even now. And then every cry we send out to invoke grace will be supported and emphasized by these preparations.

172

When his strongest passion is to make real the presence of the Soul and when he demonstrates this by the strivings and sacrifices of his whole life, he is not far from the visitation of Grace.

173

Let him feel even in the very heat of this world's activity that his Guardian Angel is ever with him, that it is not farther away than his own inmost heart. Let him nurture this unshakeable faith, for it is true. Let him make it the basis of all his conduct, try to ennoble and purify his character incessantly, and turn every failing into a stepping-stone for a further rise. The quest winds through ups and downs, so he must make despair a short-lived thing and hope an unkillable one. Success will not depend on his own personal endeavours alone, although they are indispensable; it is also a matter of Grace and this he can get by unremitting prayer, addressed to whatever higher power he believes in most, and by the compassion of his guide.

174

If he wants the grace he must do something to earn it, such as attend to the wastage of time on trivial or even harmful (because negative) gossip and activities; purify his character; study the revelations of sages; reflect on the course of his life; practise mind-stilling and emotional discipline.

175

When the Quest becomes the most important activity in a man's life, even more important than his worldly welfare, then is Grace likely to become a reality rather than a theory in his life too.(P)

176

The commonest way, the most usual way, of attracting grace was indicated by the Carthusian monk Guiges, more than eight hundred years ago: "It would be a rare exception to gain [the degree of] contemplation without prayer. . . . Prayer gains the grace of God."

177

Swami Ramdas gives the advice that the way to get Grace is to pray for it. The philosophical point of view is that one must *both* pray and pay for it.

178

It is said that grace is given only to a few chosen persons and that no matter how hard a man works on himself, unless he is fortunate enough to receive it, the illumination he wants will evade him. This teaching sounds depressing because it seems to put us at the mercy of caprice, favouritism, or arbitrariness. But the mystery of grace is not so mysterious as that. We are *all* children of God: there are no special favourites. Grace can come to all who seek it, but they must first make themselves ready to receive it. If they thirst, hunger, and seek with their whole heart and body, and if in addition they make the gestures of penance, self-denial, and purification both to prove their sincerity and to help achieve this readiness, it is inconceivable that the grace will not come to them in the end.

179

It is deeply sacred, yet could only have been brought forth through the ardent seekings and intense sufferings of a very human being.

180

A man must first recognize his weaknesses, admit his deficiencies, and deplore his shortcomings if Grace is to come to him. By that act and attitude of self-abasement he takes the first step to opening the door of his inner being to its presence. This is a necessary procedure but it is still only a first step. The second is to call out for help—whether to God or man— and to keep on calling. The third step is to get to work upon himself unremittingly and amend or elevate his character.

181

By forgiving those who have harmed us, we put ourselves in the position of earning forgiveness for the harm we ourselves have done.

182

The need for this purification arises from the need to remove obstruc-

tions to the inflow of the blessed feeling of Grace, the light of new understanding, and the current of higher will.

183

Those who are asking the Overself to give them its greatest blessing, its
grace, should ask themselves what *they* have been willing to give the
Overself—how much time, love, self-sacrifice, and self-discipline.

184

These repeated prayers and constant aspirations, these daily meditations
and frequent studies, will in time generate a mental atmosphere of receptivity to the light which is being shed upon him by the Grace. The light
may come from outside through a man or a book, or it may come from
inside through an intuition or an experience.

185

It is true that Grace is something which must be given to a man from a
source higher and other than himself. But it is also true that certain efforts
made by him may attract this gift sooner than it would otherwise have
come. Those efforts are: constant prayer, periodical fasting.

186

The man who has the courage to be his own bitterest critic, who has the
balance to be so without falling into paralysing depression as a result, who
uses his self-analysis so constructively that every shortcoming is the object
of constant remedial attention—he is the man who is preparing a way for
the advent of Grace.

187

Grace is always being offered, in a general way, but we do not see the
offer; we are blind and so pass it by. How can we reverse this condition
and acquire sight? By preparing proper conditions. First, mark off a period
of each day—a short period to begin with—for retreat from the ordinary
out-going way of living. Give up this period to in-going, to meditation.
Come out of the world for a few minutes.

188

The pursuit of virtue and the practice of self-control, the acceptance of
responsibility for one's inner life—these things are as necessary as grace,
and help to attract it.

189

Whoever invokes the Overself's Grace ought to be informed that he is
also invoking a long period of self-improving toil and self-purifying affliction necessary to fit him to receive that Grace.

190

He may fall into dismay at times but should never let it become despair.
This helps grace to come.

191

The fact is that the higher power dispenses grace to all, but not all are able, willing, or ready to receive it, not all can recognize it and so many pass it by. This is why men must first work upon themselves as a preparation.

192

What can anyone do to get Grace? He can do three things: first, want it ardently; second, prepare within himself the conditions which invite and do not obstruct it; third, meet a Master.

193

The conditions which help to make Grace possible include first, a simpler life than that of modern thing-ridden civilization; second, communion with, and veneration of, Nature.

194

The ultimate secret of Grace has never been solved by those who do not know that previous reincarnations contribute to it. Some men receive it only after years of burning aspiration and toil but others, like Francis of Assisi, receive it while unprepared and unaspiring. The ordinary candidate cannot afford to take any chance in this matter, cannot risk wasting a lifetime waiting for the unlikely visitation of Grace. He had better offer his all, dedicate his life, and surrender his loves to one all-consuming passion for the Overself, if he wants the power of Grace to flow into him. If he is unable to give himself so totally, let him do the next best thing, which is to find someone who has himself been granted the divine Grace and who has become inwardly transformed by it. Let him become such a man's disciple, and he will then have a better chance of Grace descending on him than he would have had if he walked alone.

195

The gift of grace is ever available—but on terms—yet few care to benefit by it. This is for different reasons with each person. However, it may be summarized by saying that the effort to lift self out of self is too hard and so is not only not made, but also not desired.

196

The aspiration which mounts upward from his heart is answered by the grace which descends downward into it.

197

If he makes himself worthy of grace, he need not worry about whether he will ever receive it. His earnest strivings will sooner or later merit it. And this is the best way to render its bestowal a likely happening.

198

Grace needs a prepared mind to receive it, a self-controlled life to accept it, an aspiring heart to attract it.

199

If he tries to fulfil these conditions of sincere self-preparation, and if he tries to practise service, compassion, and kindliness, Grace will come and its meaning will be found. For Grace holds a significance that is very close to love, to unselfish love. What he has given to others will be returned to him by the law of recompense.

200

Those who seek grace should do something to deserve it. Let them practise forgiveness of others who have injured them; let them extend mercy to anyone in their power or needing help from them; let them stop slaughtering innocent animals. This will really be as if they were granting grace themselves. What they give to others, they may expect to receive themselves.

201

It has been said that the Short Path is absolutely necessary because the ego on the Long Path cannot by all its own efforts attain enlightenment. The higher individuality must come into play, and that entry onto the scene is called grace. This does not mean an arbitrary intervention, favouring one person and repulsing another. It comes by itself when the proper conditions have been prepared for it, by the opening or surrender of the self, by the turning of the whole being to its source. This openness, surrender, or passivity to the Other is not to be attained by quietening the thoughts alone. The mind is open then but it has to be opened to the highest, directed to the highest, aspiring to the highest. Otherwise, there is the mere passivity of the medium, or of the thought-reader, without the divine presence.

202

If grace is tardy in coming, look to the ego's willingness to follow the path chalked out for it, whether by outer guide or inner voice. Has he been unwilling to obey the higher will when it conflicted with his own?

203

The Grace comes into his mind when thoughts are still and quiet, and into his life when ego is stilled and relinquished.

204

If he cannot compel or command grace, he can at least ask, work, and prepare for it. For if he is not prepared properly by understanding he may not be willing to submit when it *does* come, if the form it takes is not to his liking.

205

Grace, from a source above and beyond himself, is the last answer to all his questions, the last solvent of all his problems, when his own intellect fails with the one and his own management cannot cope with the other. And the first prayerful call for the gift must go forth by way of silencing the confusion within himself and stilling the tumult within his mind. The ego must recognize its own natural untrustworthiness and must pause, stop its persistent activity, in passive meditation.

206

Two things are required of a man before Grace will manifest itself in him. One is the capacity to receive it. The other is the co-operation with it. For the first, he must humble the ego; for the second, he must purify it.(P)

207

When a man feels the authentic urge to walk a certain way, but cannot see how it will be possible either because of outer circumstances or of inner emotions, let him trust and obey it. For if he does so, the Grace of the Overself will manipulate these circumstances or alter his feelings accordingly. But it will do this so as to lead to his further growth and real need, not for satisfaction of his personal desires or his supposed wants. Let him accept its leading, not the ego's blindness.(P)

208

The real bar to the entry of grace is simply the preoccupation of his thoughts with himself. For then the Overself must leave him to his cares.(P)

209

If there is any law connected with grace, it is that as we give love to the Overself so do we get grace from it. But that love must be so intense, so great, that we willingly sacrifice time and thought to it in a measure which shows how much it means to us. In short, we must give more in order to receive more. And love is the best thing we can give.(P)

210

The student may throw himself with full assurance on the mercy of the Higher Power, ask for forgiveness of past error, and pray for the descent of Grace. He will be knocking very loudly at the door of the Overself, and gradually he will find that his own weakness was but the shadow of coming strength, his own helplessness but the precursor of coming Grace.

211

In all spiritual situations where some help, light, or protection is sought, allow for the X-factor—grace. Try to invoke it by entering the silence, keeping the entire self bodily and inwardly still.

212

Confession is a good practice when it is a sincere honest recognition that certain actions of the past were wrong actions, whether they were merely imprudent or wholly evil; that they ought never to have been committed; and that if faced by similar situations again he will try his utmost not to commit them. Remorse, penitence, and a desire to make amends are the emotional feelings which ought to accompany the intellectual recognition if it is to have effective value in the future. According to custom, there are three ways in which confession can be made. There is the way of certain religions, which enjoin the presence of an ordained priest. This is useful mainly to adherents of these religions who can bring themselves to have faith in both the dogmas and the priests. But whether done in a religious atmosphere or not, confession to another person possesses worth only if that other is really of a spiritual status superior to the sinner's own and not merely claiming or pretending it. If this safeguard is present, then confession releases the tension of secretly held sins. Secondly, there is the way of some sects and cults, which enjoin the presence of a group. This too is useful only to fellow believers, and useful in a very limited way. It offers emotional relief. But it degenerates all too easily into egoistic exhibitionism. It is certainly much less desirable than the first way. Private confession done in solitude and directed toward one's own higher Self is the third way. If the sinner experiences a feeling of being inwardly cleansed, and subsequently shows no tendency to repeat the sin, he may know that his confession has been effective and that the Overself's Grace has come to him in response to the act. It is a mistake to believe, however, that a single act of confession is all that is needed. It may be, but most often such response comes only as the climax of a series of such acts. It is also a mistake to believe that any confession has any value if the sinner's ego is not abjectly humiliated and made to feel not only its foolishness and unworthiness but also its dependence on the higher power for help in attaining wisdom and self-mastery.

213

He needs the humility to admit that it is only as the Overself permits itself to be known that it is known at all. That is to say, it is only by grace that this blessed event ever happens.

214

When Christ called his hearers to repentance, he did not mean that they should leave their present state of "sin" and return to a previous state supposedly virtuous. He meant that they should leave the old altogether and go forward into something entirely new.

215

Few men find their way to the real prayer for Grace before they find their hearts broken, their minds contrite.

216

In his reception of grace, whether during the temporary mystic state or during an entire life period, he needs to be perfectly passive, unresistant, if he is to absorb all the benefit. Nevertheless, a certain kind of activity must be apparent in the early stage when he must take part in the operation by putting down the ego and its desires, attitudes, or clingings.

217

When a man begins to see the error of his ways, to repent greatly and lament deeply about them, it is a sign that Grace is beginning to work within him. But how far the Grace will go and whether it will carry him into a religious conversion or still farther, into a mystical experience, no one can predict.

218

Endorsement of the moral value of confession should not be mistaken as an endorsement of the institutional value of absolution. There are churches which require confession from their believers and which give absolution in return. The kind of confession philosophy advocates is secret, private, individual, and made in the depth of one's own heart, quite silently. The kind of absolution philosophy recognizes is grace given by the individual's own higher Self, just as silently and as secretly as the confession itself should be made. No church and no man has the power to absolve him from his sins, but only his higher self.

219

When the ego is willing to let its own tyranny be cancelled—and it never does so unless it has been crushed to the ground by the fates or by philosophy—when it comes to the end of its tether and gives up, the grace of the Overself is the response.

220

We should not egotistically interfere with the working of grace when it comes but should let ourselves be borne unresistingly and, as it were, helplessly upon its gentle current.

221

Some Oriental mystics of the Near Eastern Islamic faith often used a phrase in their talks with me that captured my attention but evaded their definition. It is easy to see why this was so. The phrase was "the opening of the heart." What this means can only be known by a personal experience. The intellect may talk and write about it but the end product will be hollow words unless the feelings talk or write about it themselves. For the experience of opening a door to the entry of grace and love must be felt personally.

222

Having done all he could do by his own strivings, being aware that he has travelled so far by the power of self-dependence, he now realizes that he can do no more except throw himself humbly on the Grace. He must wait patiently for its coming to complete, by its power transcending his own, what has thus been started.

223

Sorrow for a wrong course of life, the resolve to abandon it, and the readiness to make definite amendments are prerequisites to secure Grace.

224

As the desires depart, they leave the heart vacant for tenancy by the Overself.

225

We must make way for the Overself if we desire its presence. But we can do so only by pushing aside the objects, the conditions, and the beings who block the path into our consciousness, through our attachment to them. Removing them will not fulfil this purpose but severing the attachments will fulfil it.

226

It is not the lack of grace that really accounts for our situation, but the lack of our co-operation with the ever-existing grace.

227

In the end Nature will respond to his aspiration. Patience must be cultivated.

228

When he can come to this point and say, "Without this inner life and light, I am nothing," when he reverses the world's values and seeks the Value-less, he is ready for the initiation by Grace.

229

The internal work of Grace is only possible if the aspirant assents to the direction it is taking and supports the transformation it is effecting. If it is severing him from an attachment which he is unwilling to abandon and if he withholds his consent, the Grace itself may be forced to withdraw. The same may happen if he clings to a desire from which it seeks to free him.

230

If no one in this world can achieve perfection but only approach it, the personal realization of this fact at the proper time and after many efforts will lead to a deep humility and surrender. This may open the door of one's being to Grace, and thence to the beatific experience of the Overself, the Ever-Perfect.

231

Let Grace in by responding positively to the Teaching and by letting go of the ego.

232

Grace is not a one-way operation. It is not, as a few erroneously believe, getting something free. There is nothing free anywhere. For when the Grace starts to operate it will also start to dispel those negative qualities which obstruct it. They will resist, but if you adopt the correct attitude of self-surrender and are willing to let them go, they will not be able to resist long. But if you hold on to them because they seem a part of yourself, or because they seem "natural," then either the Grace will withdraw or it will lead you into circumstances and situations that remove the obstructions forcibly, and consequently painfully.

233

There is a point where self-effort must cease and self-abasement must begin. Not to recognize it is to show conceit and hinder Grace.

234

The highest object of worship, devotion, reverence—what the Hindus name *Bhakti*—is that which is given to the World-Mind—what Hindus call *Ishvara*. But remember always that you are present within It and It is ever present within you. So the source of grace is in you too. Silence the ego, be still, and glimpse the fact that grace is the response to devotion that goes deep enough to approach the stillness, is sincere enough to put ego aside. Help is no farther off than your own heart. Hope on!

The mysterious Presence

235

The divine grace brings a man not what he asks but what he needs. The two are sometimes the same but sometimes not. It is only with the wise that they always coincide; with others they may stand in sharp conflict.

236

Even if a man does not respond to it, the divine presence in the world is itself a grace. Even if he is quite unaware of its being in his heart, his centre, its guidance and the intuitive thoughts which may arise are manifestations of grace.

237

There is a difference of opinion about the alleged inaccessibility of the Overself. Among those who call themselves mystics in the West and yogis in the East, some claim that every man may justifiably hold the hope of penetrating to the transcendental realm of Overself, provided he will give the necessary time and effort. But others claim that the certainty which attends scientific processes is not found here, that a man may spend a lifetime in searching after God and fail in the end. This uncertainty of result is absent from standardized laboratory processes and present only in experimental ones. There is a mystery here, both in the object and the operation of the search. It cannot be solved by the intellect, for it is the mystery of Grace.

238

In the early stages of spiritual progress, Grace may show itself in the bestowal of ecstatic emotions. This encourages him to pursue the Quest and to know that he is so far pursuing it rightly. But the purpose gained, the blissful states will eventually pass away, as they must. He will then falsely imagine that he has lost Grace, that he has left undone something he should have done or done something he should not have done. The true fact is that it is Grace itself which has brought this loss about, as constituting his next stage of progress, even though it affords no pleasure to his conscious mind, but only pain. His belief that he has lost the direct contact with the higher power which he formerly enjoyed is wrong: his actual contact was only an indirect one, for his emotions were then occupied with themselves and with their pleasure in the experience. He is being separated from them so that he may be emptied of every desire and utterly humbled in his ego, and thus made ready for the time when joy, once regained, will never leave him again. For he is now on the threshold of the soul's dark night. In that state there is also a work being done for him by Grace, but it is deep in the subconscious mind far beyond his sight and beyond his control.(P)

239

Indeed, the hour may come when, purified from the ego's partiality, he will kiss the cross that brought him such agony and when, healed of his blindness, he will see that it was a gift from loving hands, not a curse from evil lips. He will see too that in his former insistence on clinging to a lower standpoint, there was no other way of arousing him to the need and value of a higher one than the way of unloosed suffering. But at last the wound has healed perfectly leaving him, as a scar of remembrance, greatly increased wisdom.

240

There is an incalculable factor in this game of self with Overself, an unpredictable element in this quest—the Grace!

241

As he pores reminiscently over the book of his past history, he will come to see how Grace entered into it by denying him some thing that he then ardently desired but whose acquisition would later have been a calamity or an affliction.

242

If outer events bring him to a position where he can bear them no longer and force him to cry out to the higher power in helplessness for relief, or if inner feelings bring humiliation and recognition of his dependence on that power, this crushing of the ego may open the door to grace.

243

The Overself's grace meets us just at the point where our need is greatest, but not necessarily the one we acknowledge as such. We must learn to let it do what it wants to do, not necessarily what we want it to do.

244

When the Overself's Grace is the real activating agent that is stirring up his petition, the coming event has cast its shadow before. When this is the case, the meaning of Emerson's cryptic sentence, "What we pray to ourselves for is always granted," becomes luminously revealed.

245

If he could penetrate into the so-called unconscious levels of his mind, he might find, to his utter amazement, that his enemies, critics, or domestic thorns-in-the-flesh are the very answer to his prayer for Grace. They fully become so, however, only when he recognizes them as such, when he perceives what duty or what self-discipline they give him the chance to practise.

246

The grace is bestowed in spite of his negative qualities, in spite of his ego's assertiveness: no one knows why or when it first reaches him.

247

Rufus Jones, eminent Quaker, made such a study and had to conclude, "There is a mystery about spiritual awakenings which will always remain unexplained." Nevertheless those who have studied the working of Grace with the added equipment of the philosophic and esoteric knowledge which he lacked find it more explicable, although still somewhat unpredictable.

248

The connection between the manifestation of grace and the kind of person to whom it comes is sometimes inexplicable. It comes not at all, or it comes sporadically, or it comes so completely that he is changed forever.

249

We dare not leave Grace out of our reckonings. Yet, because it is such an incalculable factor, we cannot put it in!

250

The passage from an earthly attitude to a spiritual one is accompanied either by intense suffering or by intense joy but always by intense feeling.

251

The longer grace is withheld, the more is it appreciated when finally vouchsafed.

252

It is not often easy to discern the why and wherefore of its operations and manifestations. Grace does not conform to human expectations, human reasonings, or human modes. It would not be divine if it always did that.

253

The course of each individual quest, its ecstasies and sufferings, is not easily predictable. The factors of karma and Grace are always present and their operation in different life situations may always be different and cannot be foreseen.

254

Grace may be granted at any unexpected time. We supply the channel but do not determine the means.

255

Although all this working of Grace takes place outside the level of ordinary consciousness—whether above or beneath it is a matter of the point of view—nevertheless it influences that consciousness far more than most people suspect.

256

The advent of Grace is so unpredictable that we dare not even say that Grace will come into action only after a man consciously and deliberately seeks God and practises self-purification. We may only say that it is more likely to come to him then.

257

In our own time the case of Aldous Huxley shows how a scientific agnostic is moved unwillingly toward the intellectual acceptance of truth. The case of Simone Weil shows how a Marxist materialist is moved just as unwillingly to an even farther distance—the direct experience of what she had to call God and the utter submission of the ego which permanently followed that experience. Both cases illustrate the mysterious and unpredictable character of Grace.

258

It is a mystery of Grace that it will come looking for one who is not pursuing truth, not looking for holiness, not even stumbling towards any interest in spirituality. And it will capture that person so completely that the character will totally change, as in Francis of Assisi's case, or the world view will totally change, as in Simone Weil's case.

259

The Overself can work in him—without his knowledge or help—to unfold, balance, or integrate him.

260

Grace happens. But to whom, when, and where, cannot be said with certainty, at best only with probability.

261

It is possible to chart out a course for man whereby he may move step by step towards the discovery of his own divine Overself, and with it the beauty and dignity in life. But it is not possible to say at what point in his movement the working of Grace will manifest itself.

262

Many who ask for Grace would be shocked to hear that the troubles which may have followed their request were actually the very form in which the higher power granted the Grace to them.

263

The influx comes at its own sweet will: he cannot grasp at it. It has to happen of itself. This enforces a full measure of humbleness and a wide stretch of patience on his part.

264

In a dozen different places Jacob Boehme declares that his wonderful illumination was a gift of Grace and that he had done nothing to deserve it. Although in a few other places he balanced this declaration with the idea that he was being used as a serving vessel from which others could draw the teaching given him, the fact remains that he did not aspire to be the recipient of a revelation and was astounded when it came.

265

The Grace works from his centre outward, transforming him from within, and therefore its earliest operation is unknown to his everyday mind.

266

The workings of Grace cannot always be judged by their temporary emotional effects. It depends on the particular circumstances, special needs, and evolutionary stage of a man as to whether these effects will be joyous or melancholy. But in the end, and when he enters into the actual consciousness of the sacred Overself, he will feel intense happiness.

267

Sometimes we are pushed to perform deeds which turn out to be our finest ones, or our most fortunate ones, although at the time we did not know this. Who is the pusher? In those cases it is either karma or grace.

268

Sometimes the Overself does its recondite work in the arid desolation of "the soul's dark night" but sometimes in the rapturous awakening to the new life of spring.

269

The psychological laws governing the inner development of spiritual seekers often seem to operate in most mysterious ways. The very power whose presence he may think has been denied him—Grace—is taking care of him even when he is not conscious of this fact. The more the anguish, at such a time, the more the Higher Self is squeezing the ego. The more he seems to be alone and forsaken, the closer the Higher Self may be drawing him to Itself.

270

Grace breathes where it will. It does not necessarily follow the lines set by man's expectation, prayer, or desire.

271

The Overself's grace will be secretly active within and without him long before it shows itself openly to him.

272

The grace may be barely felt, may come on slowly for many months, so that when he does become aware of its activity, the final stage is all he sees and knows.

273

Those who will not pause to philosophize about life are sometimes forced to do so by illness or distress. Although this brings suffering to the ego, to the aspirant it brings grace, latent in him.

274

The effect may not show itself immediately; in most cases it cannot, for most people are insensitive. But in such cases it will show itself eventually.

275

Grace has no favourites. Its working is characterized by its own mysterious laws. Do not expect it in return for faith alone, nor for just effort alone. Try both.

276

Because grace is an element in this enterprise, the question where will he stand in ten years' time is not answerable.

277

He may be disappointed because he is not more consciously aware of being helped. The forms which spiritual help takes may not always be easily recognizable because they may not conform to his wishes and expectations. Moreover, the kind of help given in this manner may require a period of time to elapse between its entry on the subconscious level and its manifestation on the conscious level. This period varies in actual experience with different individuals, from a few days to a number of years. Its exact duration is unpredictable because it is individual in each case. God alone knows what it is, but its final eruption is sure.

278

He may know that the work of Grace has begun when he feels an active drawing from within which wakes him from sleep and which recurs in the day, urging him to practise his devotions, his recollections, his prayers, or his meditations. It leads him from his surface consciousness to his inner being, a movement which slowly goes back in ever-deepening exploration and discovery of himself.(P)

279

A certain momentum will be imparted to his aspirations. During all this time the spiritual forces have been slowly maturing in mental regions below consciousness. Their eruption will be sudden and violent.

280

The weeping, begging, and worshipping through which the seeker passes is a result of Grace which occurred when, deciding to give up the ego, he felt a great peace. It is an emotional upheaval of an agonizing kind but it soon passes. He will then feel much calmer, more aspiring, and less worldly in character. This permanent change is a reorientation of the love forces; the Sufis call it "the overturning of the cup of the heart." In view of its being both auspicious and beneficial, he should not worry about it, but be patient and have hope.

281

The force which becomes active in his meditation—and which is associated with Grace—will also become active in waking him up from sleep in the morning, or even earlier. It will lead him immediately into the thought and practice of loving devotion to the higher self. He may even dream of doing his practice during the night. This will fill him with great joy. The force itself is a transforming one.

282

All he can do is to accept the inner gift when it is offered, which is not so easy or simple a feat as it sounds. Too many people brush it off because its beginnings are so delicate, so faint, as not to point at all plainly to their glorious consequences.

283

A shadow cast by the light of oncoming Grace sometimes appears as a fit of weeping. Without outer cause, the tears stream without stop or else sadness wells up without mitigation. But most often the cause does exist.

284

If a man misses the chance when grace is offered him internally by impersonal leadings or externally by a personal master, he will have to wait several years before the possibility of its recurrence can arise, if it does arise at all. In the same form, unobstructed by the disadvantages accumulated during the years, it can never arise again. Therefore it behooves him to be heedful that spiritual opportunity does not pass him by unrecognized or unseized. In this affair, the heart is often a better guide than the head, for the intellect doubts and wavers where intuition inclines and impels.

285

If this happens, if he surrenders himself unreservedly to the first faint growth of Grace within his innermost heart, then its blessing will eventually fructify gloriously.

286

The sudden, unexpected, and violent agitation of the diaphragm for a few moments may be a favourable phenomenon. It signifies a visitation of Grace from the Overself, a visitation which is the precursor of coming intellectual change and spiritual redirection.

287

It is one sign of coming Grace when he begins to despise himself for his weaknesses, when he begins to criticize his lower nature to the point of hating it.

288

When the Grace at last overcomes the inner resistance of the ego, the latter breaks down and the eyes often break into tears.

289

The simple working of inward Grace is the essential mystical experience; the extraordinary clairvoyant accompaniments are not.

290

Saint Thomas Aquinas: "Whoever receives Grace knows by experiencing a certain sweetness, which is not experienced by one who does not receive it."

291

It is most important to recognize what is happening—a visitation of Grace—and to respond to it at once. This means that everything else must be dropped without delay.

292

True sacredness is not something which anyone can pick up in his hands, examine, and identify at once. It is impalpable, as subtle and as delicate as perfume.

293

When Grace takes the form of spiritual enlightenment, it may catch him unawares, enter his consciousness unexpectedly, and release him abruptly from the protracted tensions of the quest.

294

The awakening to spiritual need, although often productive of longing and sadness, is also often a sign of the preliminary working of Grace.

295

Sometimes the Grace is felt psychically as a spiritual current actually pouring in through the head, although its posture may be inwardly shaped to the upturned tilt at one time or the bowed depression at another time.

296

When his aspiration rises to an overpowering intensity, it is a sign that Grace is not so far off.

297

Let us look for those wonderful moments when grace has been bestowed and peace has been felt. Let us stop all this busy business awhile, and stand still. Let us listen for awhile for then we may hear the Word which God is forever speaking to man.

298

In its presence it is easier to cast off some of the cares of life and, for the more practised, even feel some inner calm. Such moods are spiritual in the finer meanings of the word.

299

The wonderful effect of profound sleep is not only the recovery of the physical body's energy but much more the man's return to himself, his spiritual self, the pure universal consciousness. Note that all this happens without any effort on his part, without any use of the personal will. It is all done *to* him. Grace acts in the same way.

300

When the grace descends, whether from some action or attitude of one's self, or apparently without cause from outside one's self, if it is authentic, it will seem for the brief while that it lasts as if one has touched eternity, as if life and consciousness are without beginning and without end. It is a state of absolute contentment, complete fulfilment.

301

I dislike the word "bliss"—so often used in translating *ananda*. Surely "beatitude" is the word measuring more clearly the experienced feeling.

302

He may be one of the fortunate ones who can call down upon themselves the workings of Grace. When he feels the urge to weep for no apparent reason he should not resist, as it is a sign of the working of Grace upon him. The more he yields to this urge the more quickly will he progress. This is an important manifestation although its inner significance will not be understood by the materialistic world.

303

The seeker need not be worried about frequent weeping spells, but must be patient and have hope. Such actions assist him in bringing about permanent changes for the better in his character.

304

He is aware that a new force, more powerful than his own normally is, has risen up and taken command of his whole being.

305

When he reaches this stage, he will cease to waver, either in allegiance to the doctrine or in practice of the discipline. He will be steadfast.

306

The need to be alert against negative suggestions, to guard himself mentally against divergent or degrading ideas, exists for a time but not for all time. When Grace begins its operation, the danger from these sources vanishes, for the possibility of his being attracted by or open to them itself vanishes. The Grace enfolds him like a mantle.

307

As the light of Grace begins to fall upon him, he becomes aware of the tendencies and propensities, the motives and desires which obstruct or oppose the awakening into awareness of the Overself.

308

If it is individual effort which has to make the long journey from ignorance to illumination, it is divine Grace which has secretly and silently to lead the way for it.

309

Grace settles the intellect on a higher level and stabilizes the emotions with a worthier ideal.

310

If his mastery of self is established on well-earned and well-worked-for inward grace more than on outward will, then it is well sealed and cannot break down, cannot be wrecked by the lusts and hates, the greeds and passions which agitate ordinary humanity.

311

Grace works magically on the man who opens himself humbly and sensitively to receive it. His personal feelings undergo a transformation into their higher impersonal octaves. His very weaknesses provoke occasions for gaining effortlessly their opposite virtues. His selfish desires are turned by Grace's alchemy into spiritual aspirations.

312

The man's effort must be met by the Overself's Grace. What he does attracts what the Overself gives. This he can understand. But what he seldom knows, and finds hard to understand, is that in certain cases the aspiration which impels such effort is itself impelled by Grace.

313

Wherever you read in history of a religious martyr who was filled with supernatural serenity in the midst of terrible torture, be sure that he was supported by the Overself. The consciousness of his divine soul had, by its grace, become stronger than the consciousness of his earthly body. If you wish, you may call it a kind of mesmerism, but it is a divine and not a human mesmerism.

314

There will be moments when a tendency to sin will suddenly be checked by an invading power which will work against the lower will.

315

When the power of Grace descends into his heart, no evil passion or lower emotion can resist it. They, and their accompanying desires, fade and then fall away of themselves.

316

From that time he will feel increasingly yet intermittently that a force other than his own is working within him, enlightening his mind and ennobling his character. The Overself's Grace has descended on him.

317

His innate tendencies may still be there for a time—they constitute his karma—but the grace keeps them in check.

318

With the coming of Grace, his development takes on a life of its own and is no longer to be measured in direct ratio to his effort.

319

After the descent of grace, he feels lifted by a power stronger than his own above the stormy passions and unpleasant greeds, the petty egotisms and ugly hatreds which agitate the mass of mankind.

320

He experiences a veritable rebirth, an inspiring renewal of all his being, a feeling of liberation from darkness, weakness, and moral blindness.

321

He may watch the working of Grace in its varied manifestations both within himself and in his personal relationships.

322

Grace is a powerful stimulus. It descends from a higher source, urges us to perfect our nature, equips us to complete it. Thus we are lifted up to its own higher level.

323

That enlightenment is a transfiguring event which not only revolutionizes general outlook but also changes moral character, there is testimony enough for anyone in the archives of mystical biography. The old self is laid aside as too imperfect, the old weaknesses are drowned in the overwhelming tide of Grace which pours through the man and his life.

324

The truth is that the Overself's power has worked upon him in advance of his own endeavours. The urge to seek a close and conscious relationship with it, the decision to enter upon the quest—these very thoughts stemmed from its hidden and active influence.

325

The emptied and stilled mind opens the way for the grasp of divine grace. The latter may then gather us up into its fold, leaving behind the ego's conceit and the body's passion. But when it is time for us to return to the world's nervous restlessness, to its tumult and jarring noise, we find how far humanity has fallen.

326

The ineffable peace and exquisite harmony which take hold of his heart are the first results of grace.

327

In the end all this aspiration supported by practical effort attracts Grace. He finds that he is not alone, that in becoming its recipient not only is a glimpse vouchsafed him but also some part of him has now an unassailable faith no matter what vacillations, questionings, or lapses the strains of life, the moods of ill health, or the changes of fortune may do to his thoughts for a time.

328

A new understanding has been gained. It is a possession that may be kept, with care, as long as he lives. Of how many other possessions may this be said?

Index for Part 1

Entries are listed by chapter number followed by "para" number. For example, 1.192 means chapter 1, para 192, and 5.33, 35 means chapter 5, paras 33 and 35. Chapter listings are separated by a semicolon. Please note also that, for the reader's convenience, the first number in the right-hand running heads throughout the text indicates chapter number.

W

Y

Z

Index for Part 2

Entries are listed by chapter number followed by "para" number. For example, 5.218 means chapter 5, para 218, and 2.9, 37 means chapter 2, paras 9 and 37. Chapter listings are separated by a semicolon. Please note also that, for the reader's convenience, the first number in the right-hand running heads throughout the text indicates chapter number.

The 28 Categories from the Notebooks

This outline of categories in *The Notebooks* is the most recent one Paul Brunton developed for sorting, ordering, and filing his written work. The listings he put after each title were not meant to be all-inclusive. They merely suggest something of the range of topics included in each category.

1 THE QUEST
> *Its choice —Independent path —Organized groups — Self-development —Student/teacher*

2 PRACTICES FOR THE QUEST
> *Ant's long path —Work on oneself*

3 RELAX AND RETREAT
> *Intermittent pauses —Tension and pressures —Relax body, breath, and mind —Retreat centres —Solitude — Nature appreciation —Sunset contemplation*

4 ELEMENTARY MEDITATION
> *Place and conditions —Wandering thoughts —Practise concentrated attention —Meditative thinking — Visualized images —Mantrams —Symbols —Affirmations and suggestions*

5 THE BODY
> *Hygiene and cleansings —Food —Exercises and postures —Breathings —Sex: importance, influence, effects*

6 EMOTIONS AND ETHICS
> *Uplift character —Re-educate feelings —Discipline emotions — Purify passions —Refinement and courtesy —Avoid fanaticism*

7 THE INTELLECT
> *Nature —Services —Development —Semantic training — Science —Metaphysics —Abstract thinking*

8 THE EGO
> *What am I? —The I-thought —The psyche*